SURVIVORS

by Zalin Grant

NEW INTRODUCTION BY THE AUTHOR

D0068311

DA CAPO PRESS

. . . to Claude

Library of Congress Cataloging in Publication Data

Grant, Zalin.
  Survivors / by Zalin Grant.
    p.   cm.
  Originally published: New York: Norton, 1975.
  ISBN-10: 0-306-80561-8 ISBN-13: 978-0-306-80561-5
  1. Vietnamese Conflict, 1961-1975—Prisoners and prisons, North Vietnamese. 2. Vietnamese Conflict, 1961-1975—Personal narratives, American. 3. Prisoners of war—United States—Biography. 4. Prisoners of war—Vietnam—Biography. I. Title.
DS559.4.G74 1994   93-33615
959.704′38—dc20   CIP

First Da Capo Press edition 1994

This Da Capo Press paperback edition of *Survivors* is an unabridged republication of the edition originally published in New York in 1975. It is reprinted by arrangement with W.W. Norton & Company.

Copyright © 1975 by Claude Renee Boutillon

New introduction copyright © 1985, 1994 by Zalin Grant

Published by Da Capo Press, Inc.
A member of the Perseus Books Group
All Rights Reserved

Manufactured in the United States of America

INTRODUCTION

IT WAS THE WORST PRISON CAMP OF THE VIETNAM WAR. Lodged deep in the jungle west of Da Nang, South Vietnam's second largest city, the prison camp—or camps, for it was a moveable horror—was not easily imagined by a generation that had grown up watching World War II movies. There were no guard towers, no searchlights, no barbed wire. Instead, the camp consisted of a muddy clearing hacked out of the jungle where sunlight barely penetrated the interlocking layers of branches and vines. A thatched hut served as the prisoner's shelter, a bamboo platform as their communal bed. The young Americans, barefoot, in tatters, and on the verge of starvation, were forced to gather their food, sometimes poisoned by U.S. spray planes, from distant mountainsides. They lived under the constant threat of being bombed by their own forces. A turncoat who carried a rifle, an American Viet Cong, helped their captors keep them in line. Twelve of the thirty-two prisoners of war who entered the camp died—almost 40 per cent. Five were freed for propaganda purposes. One defected. The remaining twelve American survivors, plus two German nurses, were probably saved only by the North Vietnamese decision to send them on a forced march up the Ho Chi Minh Trail to Hanoi.

This is the story of that camp. I have tried, as much as possible, under the constraints imposed by the narrative, to tell it in the words of the survivors. It begins in January 1968 on a killing ground that American soldiers had named, with inverse humor, Happy Valley. There, on successive rainy days, U.S. infantry companies belonging to the American Division were ambushed and outfought by North Vietnamese/Viet Cong regulars who were preparing for the Tet Offensive which took place several weeks later.

Frank Anton and his helicopter crew were shot down while going to the aid of a beleaguered infantry company. Anton, tall and slender, the son of an air force colonel, was to have trouble after his capture because of his eating habits: he hated rice. David Harker, a college dropout from Virginia, passed by Anton's downed helicopter with his company before he was captured three days later. Anton's and Harker's groups were merged and marched to the prison camp.

Willie Watkins and James Daly, two blacks, joined them there. Watkins, soft-spoken and wiry, proved to be the strongest POW. In a jungle world where rank meant nothing and strength everything, he became the camp leader. Daly was the opposite. Big, clumsy, an aspiring Jehovah's Witness, Daly called himself a conscientious objector and claimed—with justification, thought other POWs—that he should have never been inducted into the army.

Watkins and Daly were escorted to the prison camp by Viet Cong soldiers led by an armed white man whom they initially thought to be a Russian. He was Robert Garwood, a young U.S. Marine private from Indiana, one of the first to be captured and held in the camp, who had crossed over to the Viet Cong side. Garwood eventually returned to America in 1979, six years after U.S. POWs were repatriated from North Vietnam, and underwent a court-martial, during which Watkins and survivors of the jungle prison camp testified against him.

Two more blacks, Tom Davis and Ike McMillan, later arrived at the camp. Tom Davis, a serious-minded Alabaman, had been appalled by American acts of brutality he had seen before his capture. He was a hard worker at the prison camp and the best-liked survivor. Ike McMillan puzzled his captors. They wondered why he was so happy and cheerful. McMillan distinguished himself as a talented chicken thief, snatching the Viet Cong's chickens to provide food for the malnourished American POWs.

Why was this prison camp such a horror?

The American POWs point out that their Viet Cong captors were impoverished and poorly supplied. They are as hard on themselves as they are on the Viet Cong. They tell of the errors they made while trying to survive in the jungle, of the disputes and fights among them that may have contributed to the deaths of some of their comrades.

But what emerges, too, from this story are the more subtle forms of brutality as practiced by the Vietnamese communists—of medicine denied, and the Viet Cong's studied indifference to the condition of the starving POWs. Here one finds an explanation for the re-education camps that existed in Vietnam long after the fall of Saigon.

In 1971, when the twelve survivors of the jungle camp walked up the Ho Chi Minh Trail to North Vietnam and Hanoi, they encountered two other American POWs who were to play a role in their lives—Ted Guy and John Young. Ted Guy was an air force colonel who had been shot down on a bombing mission over Laos. Stern and unyielding, Colonel Guy became the secret American commander of the Hanoi prison where the survivors of the jungle camp were held. He ordered them not to cooperate with their North Vietnamese jailers.

John Young, an enlisted man in the U.S. Special Forces, found his position on the war changing after his capture. He began to sympathize with the North Vietnamese and to consider himself a Marxist. With several other enlisted POWs, Young helped form a Peace Committee at his Hanoi prison. The Peace Committee was given special privileges by the North Vietnamese. Two survivors from the jungle camp—one of them, James Daly, the conscientious objector—joined John Young and the committee. After American POWs were repatriated in 1973, Colonel Guy brought charges of collaborating with the enemy against Young, Daly, and the rest of the Peace Committee. The Pentagon dropped the charges after one of the accused committed suicide.

This book ends with the return of the survivors to the United States during Operation Homecoming in 1973. Some of them chose to remain in the military service—Davis, Watkins, Anton, McMillan among them. David Harker finished college and became a probation officer in Virginia. They had, as one of them said, known each other better than their wives ever would, but after the war was over they drifted apart, staying in occasional contact.

They were reunited by the return of Robert Garwood from Hanoi to the United States. At the legal proceedings which began at Camp Lejeune, N.C., in 1979, they testified that Garwood was a turncoat who had lived with their Viet Cong guards, that he carried a rifle and had free run of the camp, that he sometimes left and returned alone. A key charge was that he had punched David Harker in the ribs.

The attitude of the survivors toward Garwood was complicated. They believed he was an opportunist who had crossed over to the Viet Cong side to save his skin. But they acknowledged that on a few occasions he had secretly helped them obtain additional food, although not through unselfish motives, they added. David Harker's quiet testimony sounded as though it was given not in a spirit of revenge, but out of respect for the Americans who had died in the prison camp.

From my early days in Vietnam I had heard about Garwood. I was in Da Nang when he was captured in 1965, and I recalled the details of his case quite clearly. In 1968, Susan Harrigan, later a *Newsday* reporter, and I interviewed a U.S. Marine reconnaissance team who had encountered an armed white man leading a Viet Cong patrol. Four of the recon team members, under a controlled procedure, identified the white man from a photo file of missing Americans as Robert Garwood. They thought they had killed him during the firefight described in this book. Garwood returned home with gunshot scars on his left arm, shrapnel in his upper back, and other scars that could be interpreted as battle wounds. He said he got them when he was captured. But he disappeared in a densely populated area on the outskirts of Da Nang, and there were, I remembered, no reports of a shootout.

I went to Camp Lejeune, the sprawling marine base, to cover Garwood's trial, and wrote an article for *The New Republic*. He was tall, a little over six feet, and well built. He spoke English with a Vietnamese accent. His dark hair was thinning, making him appear older than thirty-three, but his shoes were spit-shined, his uniform neatly pressed, and he looked more like a marine than anyone else in the courtroom.

The Marine Corps seemed embarrassed by the whole affair, by the fact that one of their own had defected, and I got the impression the marines wished he had never come back from North Vietnam. The case was complex, filled with what many considered moral ambiguities, and a lot of people seemed to think a former POW was being punished unfairly. The investigation and court-martial dragged on for months. Garwood's lawyers, having not much to work with, fell back on a psychiatric defense and tried to pick apart the testimony against him with legalities.

Robert Garwood was found guilty of five specifications under two charges. He had, the jury determined, served as a guard, interpreter, informer, and indoctrinator at the jungle prison camp. He was also found guilty of simple assault, of hitting David Harker. Before the sentencing, Garwood's lawyer raised the question of why none of the U.S. POWs repatriated in 1973 had been prosecuted when, in fact, some of them had violated the Code of Conduct. Why Garwood? he asked.

The jury took note and gave him a light sentence. Garwood was reduced to the lowest rank and dishonorably discharged from the marines, with a small forfeiture of pay. Years later, Garwood had become something of a cult figure among MIA activists, who believed he knew of the existence of American POWs still being held in Vietnam. In 1993, he was accompanied to Hanoi by a U.S. senator and met at the airport by his old communist mentor, Ho Van Dich. When Mr. Ho tried to greet Garwood as a friend, the former defector snatched his hand away and snarled, "I was never a friend of yours."

No book, whatever the format, is entirely free of the prejudices of its author, and the reader is entitled to know a little about him. Though I have spent my recent years abroad, I'm from Cheraw, South Carolina, and a graduate of Clemson University. While in college I worked for the Associated Press as a stringer, which may partly explain why I was selected for the U.S. Army Intelligence when I did my military service. Trained as a Vietnamese linguist, I was sent to Saigon and then to Da Nang as an intelligence officer. After completing my military service in 1965, I went to work for *Time* magazine as a reporter and returned to Vietnam. In early 1968, I became the S.E. Asia correspondent of *The New Republic,* a journal whose views on the war coincided with my own. Later, after twenty newsmen were captured in Cambodia in 1970, I served as the staff investigator for a committee of journalists headed by Walter Cronkite who tried, without success it turned out, to bring about their release. All told, I spent nearly five years in Indochina, visited every South Vietnam province, went on military operations with every major U.S. unit, and, counting the interviews I did for the Cronkite committee, probably talked face to face with more Viet Cong than any other American during the war.

I would like to thank the following persons, who, in one way or other, helped make this edition of *Survivors* possible. First, the survivors themselves, who took time out shortly after their return to the United States to submit to my extended interviews—often a painful process. Also, Starling Lawrence, my editor at Norton, Peter Shepherd of Harold Ober Associates, and the editors at Da Capo Press. Annie and Jacques Belaiche of Paris were there, as was Sally Palmer of Greenwich, Connecticut. I'd also like to thank Frank McCulloch, one of the great journalists of our time, and Gilbert A. Harrison, the author and former editor in chief of *The New Republic*. Janice and Wallace Terry of Washington, D.C., were friends from the beginning. And, of course, there's Claude, a Parisian to her last *zut!*, my perpetual springtime.

Zalin Grant
Washington, D.C.
November 1993

FRANK ANTON, 24, *Philadelphia, Pennsylvania. Pilot.*
Captured January 5, 1968, near Happy Valley.

DAVID HARKER, 22, *Lynchburg, Virginia. Rifleman.*
Captured January 8, 1968, Happy Valley.

JIM STRICTLAND, 20, *Dunn, North Carolina. Rifleman.*
Captured January 8, 1968, Happy Valley.

WILLIE WATKINS, 20, *Sumter, South Carolina. Grenadier.*
Captured January 9, 1968, Happy Valley.

JAMES DALY, 20, *Brooklyn, New York. Rifleman.*
Captured January 9, 1968, Happy Valley.

ISAIAH (IKE) MCMILLAN, 20, *Gretna, Florida. Mortarman.*
Captured March 12, 1968, Happy Valley.

TOM DAVIS, 20, *Eufaula, Alabama. Mortarman.*
Captured March 12, 1968, Happy Valley.

JOHN YOUNG, 22, *Chicago, Illinois. Special Forces.*
Captured January 30, 1968, near Khe Sanh.

TED GUY, 38, *Elmhurst, Illinois. Pilot.*
Captured March 11, 1968, in Laos.

1

Frank Anton

The radio message came at 7:01 Friday evening as I was writing a school classmate to tell her I would be home in two months. A battalion commander asked brigade to send a couple of gunships to assist a rifle company under small-arms and mortar attack southwest of Happy Valley. There was nothing unusual about the request. I'd answered dozens of a similar urgency during my tour. This time, though, I felt a little uneasy when the word first came down from the tactical-operations center. I thought maybe it was because I'd just gotten back two days earlier from a Bangkok R 'n' R. I knew of cases where pilots took a week off, dulled their reflexes, and made mistakes when they returned. My co-pilot, who was new in-country, had done the flying all day. To become an aircraft commander it was necessary to be checked out by the old hands in the platoon; and I was the only one he hadn't flown with. I dreaded night flying, especially on a rainy night. But I decided I had better take over. When we reached the helicopter, I slid into the right-hand seat.

On the way to the valley we were shot at by a 50 caliber. The tracers looked like reddish-yellow baseballs coming up at us. The North Vietnamese had green tracers which I don't think they liked to use because we immediately knew it was them. The

1

reddish-yellows we might confuse for friendly ricochets. I turned off my running lights and asked Lead if he wanted me to try to get the gun. "Negative," he radioed. "Let's see what C Company's got out there."

Charlie Company's commander had been killed. The artillery forward observer, a lieutenant, was on the radio. "My unit has been overrun," he said as we made contact. I could tell from the pitch of his voice that he was very scared. They were being hit by mortars—we could see the muzzle flashes. Friendly 105-mm howitzers were firing close-in support from a nearby hill. Lead radioed the lieutenant to shut off the howitzers so we could get the enemy mortars. We didn't want to get knocked out of the air by our own artillery.

"Firebird, this is Goblin," the lieutenant replied. "Negative. Repeat, negative. We may be attacked again. I'll keep it going a few more minutes. Then I'll turn it off and you can come down and get them."

We pulled off to the south and orbited over the river. We drew small-arms fire and climbed higher. Forty minutes passed. It was getting darker. We were running low on fuel. Loaded with ammo we were good for about an hour and three quarters. It was fifteen minutes out and fifteen minutes back to brigade headquarters. That meant we had committed all but thirty-five minutes of our flying time. The battalion commander was on a hill several miles from Charlie Company. The radio frequency was busy with requests for flare ships, more artillery, and ground reinforcements.

Finally Lead called the lieutenant. "Goblin, Goblin, this is Firebird. Look, we're running low on fuel. If you want to use us you'll have to do it fast."

"Firebird, this is Goblin. Roger that. Wait one."

The artillery stopped abruptly. The lieutenant called us down. Two red flares were to mark the edges of the company's perimeter and we were to hit outside the lights. We rolled in. Lead saw both flares but I could get a fix on only one. I ordered my crew not to fire. No help to blast our own troops. Lead made his pass through the area and broke right. As I followed I received quite a bit of ground fire, judging from the flashes. Just as I turned I heard a loud *"Wham!"* and the ship lurched to the left.

I glanced at the Christmas tree, the console between the co-pilot and me. If anything goes wrong, the bank of lights flash on. I thought we had taken a bad hit, but no indicators were showing. I radioed Lead that I had to return to the base. He said, "I want to get those bastards," and wheeled to make another pass. A wingman's job is to follow his team leader. I followed but I didn't intend to go low enough to use my rockets. He rolled in, worked his machine guns and rockets, and broke right again. As I turned out behind him, my hydraulic warning lights flickered on. I smelled the heavy odor of leaking fluid. Without hydraulics a helicopter maneuvers like a ten-ton truck.

My controls were freezing, and as I began a slow turn to the right the whole world opened up. I would say two hundred soldiers with AKs and three machine guns were working us over. In thirty seconds we took thirty hits. I made a mistake by trying to turn left to get out of the fire. This took me west toward Laos, and the sky was filled with tracers. We were not returning the fire. My door gunners' weapons had jammed. In our unit some door gunners' guns never jammed and some's always jammed. Lewis, my crew chief, had the reputation of a jammer. Pfister, the other door gunner, was flying with me for the first time.

A helicopter with a crippled hydraulic system has a tendency to pull to the left, then tuck and roll. Three times it started this nasty maneuver and my co-pilot helped me pull it back. The controls were functioning at about 20 per cent. The helicopter lost altitude—we were holding it at barely four hundred feet. I tried to find my way out of the valley. I came up to the mountains and couldn't get over. I knew I would have to set it down.

I radioed Goblin to give me a light to guide me to his position. The lieutenant answered, "Firebird, this is Goblin. Wait one. Wait one." I began a slow orbit. A C-47 flare ship flying above was dumping out parachute flares, inadvertently illuminating me for the enemy gunners on the ground. I was functioning pretty coolly. But I sympathized with my co-pilot. He had nothing to do but sit there, and he was in sheer terror.

I called the lieutenant again. I reminded him his position already had been given away. "They know where you are, so give me a light and I'll come right in on it."

He didn't refuse my request. He kept saying, "Wait one . . . wait one."

I was practically begging him to fire a flare. I got no response. Finally I said, "I can't wait any longer. I'm going to land."

He said, "Don't land there, it's enemy."

I said, "Sorry about that."

When we got down to a hundred feet, I turned on my searchlight. It made no difference—the enemy could see me anyway. My co-pilot was yelling above the din, "We've got to land! We've got to get this thing on the ground!" Pfister and Lewis were quiet. We came down, down, and at twenty feet I suddenly saw nothing but rice paddies filled with mud and water. That was a lucky break —but we were coming in the wrong way against the horizontal run of the dikes. I radioed my team leader that we were landing in a paddy, a big one, hoping he would try to pick us up.

We skimmed a dike, plopped down between two, then bounced. I blacked out for several seconds. When I looked around I saw the chopper was on its side. My co-pilot and crew chief were hanging upside down. The co-pilot began to yell, "Fire! Fire!" It was a false alarm. But when he yelled we started scrambling out, not thinking about our weapons. The crew chief pushed me out the open side door. I fell into the muck of the rice paddy. We were trained to stay close to our ship after a shootdown. That's the best place to get rescued. The co-pilot and I ducked down. Pfister and Lewis went fifty meters ahead. My team leader started a low approach toward the field. A machine gun opened up. It looked like he took a hit. He lurched and broke off.

I checked for my .38 pistol. I had lost it when we hit. We lay for ten minutes unmoving. It was quiet except for the sporadic firing of artillery. A round landed nearby and shrapnel cut into the helicopter. A lamp flamed in the distance. I saw a hootch about thirty meters in front of us, and heard voices. A group of old men and women and kids cautiously made their way out to the ship. They began to remove C rations, our cameras, and personal gear, anything they could find. After twenty minutes they went away.

"What do we do?" my co-pilot asked.

"We've got to get farther away from the hootches," I said.

We started crawling through the paddies. Four Vietnamese headed toward the helicopter. I couldn't tell whether they were Viet Cong or North Vietnamese, but I could see the banana-shaped clips of the AK-47 assault rifles they carried. My co-pilot saw the soldiers and whispered, "They're going to get us!" He took off his wedding ring and watch, pulled his wallet out, and buried them in the mud. Then he stood in a half crouch and ran across the paddies. It was an act of panic. I burrowed deeper into the paddy bank, certain that he would be caught. I never saw him again. He was picked up several days later by an ARVN patrol, and taken back to friendly lines.

More Vietnamese crowded around the helicopter. They seemed to know the rhythm of the artillery fire. Several minutes before rounds began to fall they retreated to safety on the other side of the paddy; when the fire lifted they returned. Flares dropped by the C-47 dimly lit the area and I saw shadowy figures running to my front and rear. I stayed where I was the rest of the night. At 6:25 the sun rose to treetop level. I could see through a thin drizzle of rain that the day was going to be very cloudy. Rescue helicopters would never get through the thick cover.

The Viet Cong soldiers must have realized the same thing. They began to search the area. I spotted three uniformed men, one stood at the edge of the field covering the other two. They found my helmet, saw where I had crawled through the mud, but didn't try to follow the trail. As I wondered why I felt a presence over me. A Vietnamese in black pajamas stood on the dike six feet directly above my head. He walked away, stopped, looked around, came back again. As he started to turn away once more he looked down.

His expression didn't change. He motioned with his AK for me to get up. I thought he was going to shoot. I jumped up and began to run. I had been lying in water for ten hours without moving; my legs buckled on me before I got three feet. The Vietnamese clambered down and grabbed me, saying, "No, no, no." He tied my hands behind my back with rope and led me across the paddy. Helicopters circled above, my own gunships. They had broken through. As we passed into a woodline across the paddy, the choppers rolled in and blasted the area near my downed ship.

I made up my mind that I was going to die. I totally resigned myself to this. The knowledge brought an inner calmness. I was as relaxed as had I been home looking at television. We moved about fifty meters down a trail. My guard whistled. The whistle was returned by a sentry. We moved farther till we came to a house of stucco and brick. A number of Vietnamese were around the house. Artillery shells started falling around us. The Vietnamese jabbered at each other in high-pitched singsong voices. I laughed and said to no one, "Don't worry. It won't hurt you." They jumped into bunkers dug beside the house. I was left standing outside. A Vietnamese popped out of a bunker and pulled me back in with him. An artillery round hit the house with an ear-splitting explosion. As soon as the fire stopped the Vietnamese hurried from their shelters.

I was led down a trail through the woods. After ten minutes we came to a small clearing that was crisscrossed with wires. Two young girls sat in a shallow bunker talking on field telephones. Other girls armed with rifles stood around. I must admit that even in my condition the sight of girls carrying weapons made me a little happier. During my tour I had sometimes thought that what we helicopter pilots were doing was maybe terrible. Were we killing women and children? Who could tell? As far as I was concerned, an armed woman was the same as a man.

A guard handed me a card with one side written in English, the other in Vietnamese. It said: "Do not try to escape. You are a prisoner of the Liberation Armed Forces. We will not harm you." Pfister and Lewis arrived at that moment. The guards kept us seated awhile, not allowing us to talk. Then one of them ordered us to take off our boots and start walking. He spoke broken English.

"I can't walk without my boots," I said.

"You walk fast," he said, "I give you boots back."

"No," I replied. "I cannot walk fast without my boots." He returned the boots to me and I put them on. Lewis took out his Zippo cigarette lighter and flicked it several times. The guard ran over and slapped him in the face.

"You signal planes." ·

Lewis said, "No, I'm trying to see if my goddamn lighter still works." The Vietnamese had yet to search us.

At 7:30 we started walking, moving west up the side of a mountain. After an hour we came to a set of natural caves. The VC put us into separate caves. The questioning began. They took Pfister and Lewis before me. I was astounded when the intelligence officer walked in. He looked like a Frenchman and spoke idiomatic English. He was about five foot eight, much taller than the average Vietnamese, had rounded eyes, a light olive complexion, and a sharp nose. When I looked closer I could see he was a half-breed, but the Caucasian features predominated.

"You speak English very well," I said after his greeting. "You were educated somewhere in an English-speaking country."

"Maybe," he replied, smiling. He ordered me to sit at a small table. "What is your unit?"

"First Cav."

"That's a lie. What unit of the One Hundred Ninety-sixth Brigade do you belong to?"

"I'm not in the One Hundred Ninety-sixth," I said.

"Don't be silly. I have all the answers."

"Then why do you ask me?" He ignored this and asked another question about my unit. I told him I couldn't answer.

"You are in the Seventy-first Assault Helicopter Company," he snapped. "Your radio code name is Firebird." He gave me our radio frequency, the location of my home base, my commanding officer's name, and other details of the unit.

"That's pretty good," I admitted. "One of the other men told you."

"No," he said. "I know everything. I will show you." He pulled a U.S. Army map from a small leather carrying case. On it, marked in red and blue grease pencil, were the company positions, fire support bases, artillery units, and radio frequencies of the 196th Light Infantry Brigade. It was as precise as the map carried by any U.S. battalion commander.

"Last night we used a three-pronged attack to hit this position." Frenchy pointed to where Charlie Company had been wiped out. "Tonight we will hit here."

David Harker

Delta Company was directed to garrison the battalion's fire support base on January 5. We spent most of the day moving through the valley to the hill. It was hot and very sticky, a day when it was difficult to perspire and swallowing salt tablets didn't help. Several guys in my squad fell out with heat exhaustion, and we had to split up their gear among us, which caused a little grumbling.

The hill had been improved since we'd last been on it. Then it had been just a cleared, muddy hilltop spotted by shallow holes with a few crumbling sandbags around them. It was still muddy, but now a neat bunker system encircled the top, surrounded by a triple-strand concertina wire system interlocked with flamable fu-gas explosive, with Claymore mines and trip flares on the perimeter outskirts. Every third bunker had a sensoring device to pick up enemy trying to move up the hill. Besides staying alert, all we had to do was go out each evening and connect the Claymores, then return the next morning to disconnect them so nobody would accidentally get blown away coming back from patrol.

At 7:00 Friday evening the fireworks started. Three of us were in my bunker. We looked out and saw parachute flares swaying in the sky. The 105- and 155-mm howitzers on the other side of the fire support base began booming. Below in the valley we could see a gunship working out, tracers drifting down in a red stream, others arcing up at it. It would have been a lovely sight if you didn't know people were getting killed and it could be you.

Early Saturday morning we got our gear together and started moving off the hill. A change of orders had come down. We weren't going to pull fire-base duty after all. The terrain was rocky. One man broke his leg going down. We made a litter and carried him to level ground; the company commander called a medevac helicopter to pick him up. Word was passed to get ready for a combat assault. We assembled in groups of six in an open paddy. We waited for two hours before the choppers arrived. The ship I drew was weak, it could only take four of us, and almost didn't get up at that.

The helicopters took us on a short hop and hovered over a swatch of tall elephant grass on a hillside. We slid out the open door and stood on the chopper's runners and then jumped down. I rolled over as I hit the ground and flipped my M-16 off safety. The combat assault was dry—no enemy fire. We joined another company on the ground and moved along the ridge into the valley. We stumbled on some stragglers from Charlie Company. They looked like sleepwalkers. C Company had gotten resupplied shortly before dusk the night before. The men had received Christmas packages that had been delayed reaching the field. They were opening the gifts when the Viet Cong hit them.

We saw Anton's chopper, its tail boom high in the air like the hulk of a sunken ship. It had been booby-trapped with grenades. Someone had marked the places with pieces of white cloth. Just looking at them made my palms sweat. The Vietnamese were artists at making mines. Women and children buried them along trails leading to villages. A mousetrap, hidden with twigs, rigged so that when pressure is applied by a footstep a .45-caliber bullet fires straight up; a shoe box, staved with wooden pegs, filled with explosives, the tiny electrical detonator, the only metal in the mine, fools our best mine sweepers; dud mortar and howitzer shells, our bombs—all were used against us.

The worst, I guess, was the American-made bouncing betty. If you were lucky, you might see the three tiny steel prongs sticking maybe an eighth of an inch above the ground. If you weren't a shotgun shell kicked the main part of the mine balls high, where it exploded. ARVN troops in Da Nang fought a brief internal war among themselves in April, 1966. An ARVN ranger battalion abandoned 1,400 bouncing betties. We got them back one by one.

A week before Christmas my platoon had been on a nearby hill. That morning we were supposed to get resupplied. We policed up the area of sticks and other debris that might get sucked up in the helicopters' rotor blades. I hadn't bathed for nineteen days and I got myself placed on the water detail so I could wash in the stream below when we took the canteens to fill. The choppers had finished the resupply when I got back. Some of the men were returning to our area with cardboard cases of Cs, and I saw Smitty waving a pair of new boots. I stood there, helmet off, waiting for him. Suddenly I heard a sharp ringing in my ears. Smitty screamed. I blacked out. When I came to I grabbed my back, then touched my head, and saw that my hand was covered with blood.

The medevac arrived in a matter of minutes. The pain started. For the first time I lost that distant idea of death I carried, and I was scared as a pup. We were taken to the battalion aid station. The medics were casual with us. They had seen many people die, and I knew from their attitude that my wound couldn't be serious. The X-ray machine wasn't working properly. They sent me to Chu Lai. The doctors suggested I leave the shrapnel in my head instead of trying an operation to remove it. I get headaches when I sleep on the left side. Smitty was lucky; the booby trap had settled with the rain. Last time I saw him he was on crutches.

We found a flight glove near Anton's helicopter. A tracker team was brought in. The dog sniffed the glove and took off across the paddy with us following but soon lost the trail. A river flowed west to east, bordered by rice paddies which were cut by hedgerows of stunted bamboo and tree lines of slender coconut palms. The rest of the day we checked the hootches in the area, then set up our night logger positions to the east of Anton's chopper. When it was time to pull guard duty, I sat in the drizzling rain, feet over the trench edge, watching the shadows in front of me, trying to keep my imagination under control. Everyone was jumpy. The men assigned to listening posts beyond our perimeter didn't want to go out. Nobody had much respect for our platoon leader. He was fresh out of Benning Officer Candidate School and arrogant. He was not at all like the company commander, whom we called Black Death. Black Death knew many of the men personally.

Next morning we split up in platoons and moved out to search our assigned areas. In a nearby hamlet, a cluster of hootches, we found some women and children huddled in a bomb shelter. It was the same old story. We couldn't communicate with them. I remember writing my family when I arrived, wondering how these people lived, where their children were being educated. I thought of a village as a place with schoolhouses and churches and shops. Here I was seeing gray water buffalo, thatched roofs, dirt floors, rice cooked over wood fires, people who looked malnourished and dirty. The old women in particular looked repulsive. Their teeth were snaggled and black; they spit a red juice wherever they went. As I understood later, the betel nut they chewed was as common in parts of Asia as snuff used to be in America, and it had a numbing effect on teeth that had never been treated by a dentist.

We had worked the villages of the valley many times in the two months I had been in Viet Nam. A North Vietnamese regiment supposedly was operating in the area, trying to set up on the hills surrounding our fire base to get in rocket-firing distance. Our mission was to make contact with the enemy, and to check for any men of military age. It was constant searching. The enemy had the ambush, the element of surprise was theirs. We had massive air and artillery support at our call.

We operated in teams. Some soldiers surrounded and secured the village, others took the villagers to an interrogation point. We had a Vietnamese soldier along with us as the platoon leader's interpreter, although he spoke practically no English. It was his job to decide whether someone was a Viet Cong suspect. We picked up mostly old women and children. Our Vietnamese was limited to three words. One was the translation for I.D. card, which we always demanded of any Vietnamese we saw; the second was *"di-di,"* which meant go or get out of here; and the third was *"dung lai"*—stop! Anyone who ran was considered a Viet Cong.

A sergeant, a short-timer with a few weeks to go on his tour, was assigned to my squad for a while. He was nervous and irritable. When we entered a ville he grabbed the girls holding babies and shouted at them, "Where's papa-san? Where's papa-san?" Papa-san and mama-san were not Vietnamese, but slang imported from Japan and the Korean War. The girls would indicate with terrified eyes they didn't understand him. I complained to the squad leader about the sergeant. It did little good. He was with us once when a group of Vietnamese ran as we approached to check their I.D.s. The whole platoon opened up. The Vietnamese hit the ground and crawled away before we got there. We saw blood trails and later discovered some freshly dug graves. The company commander told us to check them for dead Viet Cong. We found a baby.

My platoon usually set up in a ville in late afternoon. The platoon leader took a hootch in the middle of the ville, the squads slept in hootches on the outskirts. We pulled perimeter guard by having one guy from each squad sit in the front door of his hootch. In one ville my squad set up in a hootch owned by an old man with a wisp of a white beard. As we walked in he was sitting on what looked to be a red casket; it's important to the Buddhists to have a proper burial. Tex said, "Look, he's perched on his coffin, ready to fall in." He started giving the old man a hard time, his idea of fun. He offered him a cigarette and as the old man reached for it Tex jerked it away. He was telling him in English how stupid he looked. The old man kept smiling and nodding. The other guys were laughing. I walked out.

It was in this same village that a GI became overly fond of a thirteen-year-old girl. I don't think he actually put his hands on her; he wanted to badly enough. I never saw anyone molest the women, but there were always comments and leers. I was disgusted. Put a man in an anonymous uniform and give him a weapon, send him to a country he holds in contempt out of ignorance, and he sometimes acts like an animal. There's always that small percentage.

That night I slept on the old man's casket. The rest of the squad rolled out ponchos on the floor. I had pulled my hour of guard duty and was trying to get back to sleep when I heard the thump-thump of M-79 grenade rounds going off. The short-timer sergeant yelled, "Get back! I'll get him!" More firing. Then it grew quiet. The platoon leader called on the horn to the next hootch and asked what was going on. A guard said he thought he had seen a man moving up on us and thought he had got him. At first light we swept the area around the ville and found a dead cow. The villagers were upset about the cow. It was the only one they had.

That's one of the first things you noticed about Viet Nam. There were always big, dumb-looking water buffalo, used to plow the paddies, and chickens and ducks, and even a few thin pigs, which were taken to the market in bamboo baskets tied to the backs of Honda motorbikes; but there were few cows around. And in the country village you saw no bread or other things normally considered part of a healthy diet. They ate mostly rice and fish, if they could get it, and some sort of leafy vegetables.

I didn't understand the Vietnamese. It was hard not to feel superior to them. We had everything, they had nothing. But it hurt me to see them caught in the middle of a war they didn't want. I saw leaflets warning the people to get out of the area because it would soon be bombed. We had no business bombing villages like that. If there was enemy activity in the area, we had grunts who could have gone in. And if we operated the way we had been trained, we would have taken few, if any, casualties. We came to an abandoned ville one day. It had been hit by an air strike. A mama-san and her kids sat on top of a charred bunker. She was picking lice from their heads and cracking them with her teeth. I gave her a can of ham and limas. There was nothing else I could do.

On Sunday we continued to search the valley without making contact. The following morning we crossed to the south side of the river. At half past noon the platoon took a lunch break. I opened a can of peaches. Before I had time to finish eating we were ordered to join another part of the company which was moving back across the river. Someone had heard a weapon fired on the north bank. A hamlet of ten hootches was directly across from us. We got on line, threw two grenades apiece to the other side, and waded across the waist-deep water, with men alternately firing and moving. The ville contained nothing but women and children in bomb shelters.

Black Death joined us and brought with him the artillery forward observer, two radio men, and the company first sergeant. We gathered around the captain for a debriefing. Bravo Company, working a few hundred meters downstream, called and said they were in contact. After Black Death signed off the radio, he laughed and said Bravo's company commander had refused his offer of assistance. As we stood there we heard rifle fire. It sounded like it came from across the river and to the west. No friendlies were operating in that area. The captain said we were going to move up the river and go back across. Some of the men were told to remain in the village. He led twenty of us across. I was in the rear of the group.

I had barely crossed when I heard explosions behind me. Incoming! A creek cut perpendicular to the river a few meters to my left. I ran for it and rolled over the bank. Six men had already taken cover there.

Williams, the company first sergeant, said, "The captain's dead. I saw him get hit when they opened up on us. He tried to make it back across the river to the village. They got him in the back." One of the RTOs also had been killed; Cannon was with us but had lost his radio when the firing broke out.

The artillery forward observer, a ·chubby young lieutenant, crawled across the creek bank to where we were. His eyes were dewy bright; words tumbled out without spaces between. "I'm-gonnagethelp." He was up and over the bank and running across an open paddy before we could say anything. The firing seemed to be coming from all directions. Sergeant Williams said it looked like an L-shaped ambush.

We saw a Viet Cong moving toward the creek. Williams fired a round from his M-79. The VC fell forward in the mud, dead. Coglin carried a new M-16 with a flash suppressor. It had jammed. I tried to kick the operating handle to the rear but couldn't. That left us with three working M-16s and two M-79 grenade launchers. I had dropped my backpack before making a run for the creek bank. I had a bandoleer of ammo, five grenades, a flak jacket, and my weapon. I thought we could hold out till help arrived.

There were voices behind us. Williams told us to throw our grenades. The creek bank was five feet high. We lobbed the grenades over without looking. After the explosions there were no more sounds. Williams suggested we move up the creek to a tree line sixty meters forward and to our right. Maybe there we could link up with the others from the company. The firing had almost stopped. It was 1:15.

As we moved up the creek we came to a bend and saw that the bank leveled out directly ahead. To go farther would leave us exposed. To our left rice paddies sloped up the hill like steps. Williams said we were going to try to get up the rice paddies undetected. One man was to move at a time. Williams and Cannon and Booker went over the bank and continued over a paddy dike. Coglin went up and over. Then the Viet Cong spotted our position and opened up with automatic weapons. Cannon and Williams moved to higher levels on the paddy. Cannon reached a concealed vantage point from where he was able to direct Williams' M-79 fire.

There was a momentary lull. Williams called for Oliver to move up next. He turned to me and said, "I'm going."

As he started up we fired our M-16s to cover him. Oliver screamed, "I'm hit! I'm hit! God, it hurts!"

Williams yelled to him, "Take it easy. I'm hit too. I know it hurts but we've got to keep calm. Don't scream. It will draw attention to us. Just take it easy."

Oliver began hollering for his mother. Then things became

quiet again. Suddenly there was a shriek: "Mother! Mother!" Williams said Oliver was dead.

I was alone in the creek. "Okay, Harker," Williams yelled. "Just be as calm as you can. We're going to make it out. We'll get a gunship in here in a matter of minutes. Don't panic. Take it easy. And don't use up all your ammo. I'll tell you when to fire on automatic. Otherwise keep it on semiautomatic."

I was trembling. My first time under fire. I kept telling myself, "I'm going to die. I'm going to die." A Bible passage came floating back from all the Sunday church meetings I'd attended in Virginia: *"For me to live is Christ, to die is gain."* Yes, I thought, I've lived a pretty good life. I believe in the hereafter. I'm prepared. I felt calmer.

The Viet Cong were working their way to our position. They were well camouflaged and wore small conical rain hats of bamboo covered with oyster-colored plastic. One or two would run toward us and drop down. Cannon was calling out directions to Williams, who was in a more exposed position and had to keep his head down because of the heavy fire. "Coming up thirty meters on your left front!" Cannon yelled. Williams fired. When the round exploded I raised up over the bank and sprayed the area with my M-16.

Cannon saw men moving up from our rear right. "Friendlies!" he said. For a moment I felt a beautiful surge of relief. Then Cannon shouted, "No, it isn't!" A small propeller-driven spotter plane broke through the heavy cloud cover and tried to come lower but was driven away by the ground fire. A medevac helicopter flew overhead and it too was driven away by enemy fire. A jet made a shallow dive. I could see bombs falling end over end. Dirt and leaves covered me as the ground shook with the explosions. After that no more planes arrived.

I saw movement at the bend in the creek. Someone was crawling toward me through the reeds. I aimed my rifle and was about to pull the trigger when I spotted a green American helmet decorated with graffiti. "You're the best thing I've seen all day," I said. He was from another platoon.

"Everybody's dead," he said. "I've been crawling around awhile."

I saw blood in the water. "You're hit."

"Nothing bad," he answered calmly. "I'm just hit in the leg." He refused to let me bandage it, and said, "I'll care of the left front and you take the right."

I heard voices. I looked over the bank and saw Williams standing with his hand up. A uniformed Vietnamese held a rifle on him. I raised up carefully and started to shoot. I began to squeeze the trigger slowly. "If I shoot him," I thought, "his friends will probably drop me. Better wait a minute." I lowered myself back into the creek bed. A VC walked up on my right flank twenty feet away. He began to talk past me to two other Vietnamese on my left. They had slipped up unseen and were practically standing on top of me.

The VC walked slowly toward me, holding their rifles at the ready. I pressed my weapon into the mud and stood with hands up. One of them took my helmet off. The other took a couple of steps backward and turned over the wounded American. I looked at him and thought he was playing dead. Then I noticed his lips were chalk white; he had died from a loss of blood. The two VC with rifles left me guarded by a third while they stripped the dead Americans around us of watches, weapons, and ammunition. The guard was armed with a holstered .45 pistol.

It was 5:30. Darkness was coming on fast because of the heavy cloud cover. The drizzle turned into a hard rain. We left the creek and headed toward a tree line. The guard was leading. I looked at my feet with wonder; they seemed to be moving of their own accord, and my eyes saw with a remote detachment, as if I was looking through the reverse end of a telescope. I saw a dirt road to the left. A jumble of thoughts flooded my head. Taking me away . . . must escape soon after capture . . . road to safety . . . got to kill him.

I grabbed the Vietnamese and put my left hand over his mouth and pinned his arms to his side. He wore a bayonet next to the pistol. I tried but couldn't free the knife from its scabbard. I jerked out the .45.

The Vietnamese grappled loose and started yelling. He unsheathed the bayonet. I held the pistol pointed at his head. We stared at each other for a second. He lunged and stabbed me in the right side. I pulled the trigger.

Nothing happened. There was no round in the chamber.

I looked up and saw four rifles pointed at me. I dropped the pistol. My guard, who was a good foot shorter than I, was screaming and shaking the bayonet in my face. "I'm sorry," I said meekly.

A Vietnamese with a rifle pushed me toward the tree line. I stood there dumbly as artillery rounds fell around us. An unseen Vietnamese pushed me into a bomb shelter. The bunker was damp with the pungent smell of fish sauce. When the artillery fire stopped, I was taken out. Women in black pajamas rolled up to their thighs scurried about carrying mortar tubes. Some were armed with rifles. "What are women doing here?" I thought hazily. A man nudged me down a trail. A bomb crater lay at a bend in the path. I smelled the sickly sweet rot of dead bodies. A mass grave? My back tensed for the bullet I was sure was coming.

We continued up the trail and soon arrived at a gray stucco house with a red-tile roof and a brick patio to one side. It was the kind of house rich villagers occasionally owned. A separate open structure intended for use as a kitchen was behind the house. Uniformed North Vietnamese sat around tables lit by kerosene lamps. Field telephones were ringing and being answered. Behind the kitchen was a walk-in bunker tunneled in the ground. It was crowded with women and soldiers with weapons. I was pushed to the squatting position. A lamp was placed between me and a man who sat on his haunches facing me. "I speak little," he began. "You must answer questions. What is your unit?"

I pretended not to comprehend.

"What—is—your—unit?" he repeated.

I told him I didn't understand. He called for a piece of paper and wrote the question and handed it to me. I made no reply. He wanted to lash out at me in English but couldn't. In frustration he started shouting at me in Vietnamese. The people behind him laughed. I was sure he was telling them how short a future I had before me. "Move, move," the Vietnamese said.

I was taken to a dark room on the side of the kitchen, where I found Williams and Cannon. I exchanged a few words with them before the guards ordered us to keep quiet. Williams had taken a bullet round through his right hand. He had continued to fire the M-79 with his left hand after being hit. He said, "My hand is killing me but they won't give me anything for it because I won't talk. I'm not going to tell those bastards anything."

Cannon was in worse shape. A mortar shell had exploded near him. He thought Coglin and Booker had been killed. He had a large hole on the upper right portion of his back, another smaller hole near his neck. He was in great pain but said nothing. My own stab wound had coagulated. I felt a dull throb in my side. After a while a fourth American was brought into the room. He had been with Delta Company two days. I recognized him as the little guy who was to the right of me on line as we assaulted the village across the river. A left-handed guy. Strictland. He had almost blown off my ear with his M-16.

Jim Strictland

I was at the front of the group when we crossed the river and the VC started dropping mortars behind us. It was so noisy that it was hard to tell where they were coming from. We did exactly what they wanted us to do: we ran from the river across the rice paddy toward the woodline. It was like committing suicide. The VC were dug in and waiting for us with AKs and machine guns. Several guys were wounded immediately. The fire actually wasn't all that heavy. It was more a steady pop-pop-pop. If the VC saw someone they shot at him. We were pinned down behind the paddy dikes. The others were spread out along the river.

A soldier with an M-79 grenade launcher was lying beside me. We knocked off an AK position. He and I yelled for the others to shoot back. No one was firing except us. They were crying and hollering. It was not just the new replacements who had come in several days before with me but guys who had been in Nam a long time. We had plenty of ammo. If everyone had helped out we would have escaped.

I wouldn't want his family to know the story, but my company commander wasn't worth a damn. When the VC started firing he and his radioman took cover behind a dike. I saw him trying to call for help on the radio. Then he started running to get across the river. Several of the guys captured with me later asked the question: Who shot Black Death? As he started running with the radio somebody shot him in the back. If it hadn't been for me maybe getting killed trying to kill him, I may have shot him. I didn't. But I wouldn't say it wasn't another GI who shot him.

The VC started flanking us, moving around to our right. I could hear them yelling at each other. Me and the M-79er were keeping our heads down, shooting back when we could. Suddenly three VC stood over us. They wore black shorts and were camouflaged with little branches—looked like walking bushes. Before we could fire they shot and killed the my buddy—I never knew his name—and one of them jumped down on me.

The firing stopped. I could hear myself breathing hard. They searched me. My wallet was in my top pocket wrapped in plastic. That and my watch were the only things they took. They didn't go through my pants pockets. They tied me with commo wire, my hands bound behind my back to my feet. Then they tied some wire around my neck and started dragging. I said my last prayers. Blood spurted from my mouth; I was strangling to death. When we reached the woods they untied my feet and pushed me into a bunker. Artillery shells began to fall.

After a few minutes three guards led me toward a nearby mountain. We stopped at a house. I saw radios and telephones. They took me to a kitchen outside the house. A Vietnamese asked for my clothes. I said, "They must be going to kill me!" But instead they took my boots and put me in a small building next to the kitchen. I couldn't see anything but I heard someone moaning. The guards told us not to talk. If the VC say don't talk, you don't talk. An hour later they returned and tied two of us together. That's when I learned I was with Harker, Cannon, and Williams.

Ike McMillan

Being in the weapons platoon of Bravo Company, I was usually around the company command post, and I monitored the radio. I was listening on January 8 when our battalion commander, Steel Gimlet, called and said Black Death had been killed. I could feel the hurt in his voice. Captain Death was the Gimlet's favorite company commander. He had been on the battalion staff before Steel Gimlet asked him to take Delta Company.

Each evening about 7:00 Steel Gimlet conducted what we called the "Family Hour." All the company commanders, wherever they were operating, got on their radios to talk to him at the same time. Every radio in the battalion was tuned to that frequency, and all of us listened in. "This is Steel Gimlet. I'm sitting here in the officer's club having a beer with the XO, and I feel good. I want an outstanding report today." I guess he was joking, but he spoke exactly like that. He told us his day's activities, who he had seen, where he had been. He was careful not to reveal any real security information.

Then he'd say, "Annihilator"—that was Alpha Company's code name—"we'll hear from you first. Tell me how your day went."

Annihilator would respond: I got such and such body count; I did this or that. Although Steel Gimlet's tone was not strictly military, the company commanders were careful to give their reports in a respectful manner.

After Annihilator, he called on my CO—Barracuda-Six.

If Alpha and Bravo had dead stories he often skipped Charlie

Company and said, "Wait a minute, Charlie Tiger, I want to hear what my man Black Death has to say. Come in, Black Death." And Black Death would give him a snappy report. He most always had a body count.

That was it. Results. Steel Gimlet was the best officer in the 196th. If something was going on, he was over the area in his personal chopper. If he could get down through the fire, he was on the ground. Many battalion commanders never got any closer to the battlefield than 1,500 feet above in a cushioned helicopter. The Gimlet wanted results and Black Death got them. I remember the first day of Operation Wheeler/Wallowa back in mid-November before Harker and Strictland joined Delta. I heard Black Death call Steel Gimlet on the radio.

"Steel Gimlet, this is Black Death. We swept the valley and found nothing but women and children."

"Black Death, this is Steel Gimlet. Go back through the valley and when you come out you'd better have a body count."

Two hours later. "Steel Gimlet, this is Black Death. We have a body count of twenty-one."

That was the Nam, you know.

I heard that Black Death ran the day he was shot. I figured it like this: he was probably trying to get back into position where he could command the whole company. He had no business leading a few men across the river in the first place. That's what got him killed. He was too goddamn gung ho.

2

Willie Watkins

At two o'clock the afternoon of January 8, the first platoon of Alpha Company was ordered to move down to the valley. We could hear a lot of firing. We were told that Delta Company had been hit hard in the same area where Charlie Company was greased. At five o'clock Delta's artillery forward observer worked his way back to our command post. He had lost his sense of direction and didn't know where the rest of Delta was. A small village lay across the rice paddies from where we had set up our CP. The firing seemed to be coming from there. It was too late to do anything else, so we called in artillery on the ville that night.

Next morning everybody was slow saddling up. There was a hesitation in the air as to whether we should advance farther. We were short of lieutenants and had been without a platoon leader for weeks. Several battalion staff officers choppered to our location before we left and gave my squad leader an on-the-spot battlefield promotion to second lieutenant. They first offered it to the platoon sergeant who was acting platoon leader; but he said he had too much time in the service, that he was too old, and didn't want it.

The new platoon leader was young but knew his stuff because he had been in Nam for seven months. Practically all the old guys had rotated home in November and December. I had been there three months and was considered a veteran. The majority of the platoon joined us around Christmas time. Worst still, we were understrength, down to twenty-five men in the platoon.

We linked up with a rifle company from another battalion. The platoon sergeant said we were going to find what was left of Delta Company and then fall back to be air-lifted to the hill where we were originally. It was nearly noon before we moved out. A misty rain was falling. With the heat it felt like we were walking inside a wet plastic bag. By half past noon we had crossed the river and were moving northwest. Of the five platoons forward, mine was on the right flank. We found a GI from Delta who was barely alive, he had a sucking chest wound. We left a medic with him and called a medevac. The smell of dead bodies was all around us.

The terrain was irregular. Rice paddies were terraced down a sloping hill. I was on a paddy at a higher level than anyone else. Suddenly all hell broke loose. The shit came from every direction. Everybody on the right side got killed in the first burst, three files of them. I jumped in a crater behind a dike. Three dead soldiers from Delta were in the hole. My platoon leader was wounded in the initial burst. He was ten meters away, and he yelled for me and the other M-79 grenadier to get some fire going. From what I could see only three or four of us were trying to fire back. All I could do was keep my head down and adjust my fire to where the shooting seemed to be coming from. I took my helmet off and raised it over the dike with a stick. Bullets tore it off.

The platoon sergeant called in artillery, but it wasn't very accurate—it was mainly falling on top of us. Maybe he asked for it that way, I don't know. I hollered and told him to turn it off before we were all killed. A spotter plane was circling above. The ceiling was low because it was raining. I don't know what he was doing up there, but he should have been able to tell what was happening to us.

The firing stopped. The platoon sergeant yelled for us to pull back to the river. When we made it to the bank we found three guys already there. None of them had weapons. They had lost them in the excitement. One of them said an M-16 lay about thirty meters forward near a hole. I crawled up and brought it back. It was jammed with mud and wouldn't fire. While I was gone the platoon sergeant and his radioman had disappeared.

Two men had smoke grenades. We were without a radio, so we started popping smoke to signal the spotter plane. Each time we popped a smoke, someone in the stand of bamboo to our left also popped one. I said, "Maybe there's friendly forces over there." Sikes said, "No, we're taking fire from there. That's the VC trying to confuse the FAC." I saw a man waving his arms to our right front. He was without a helmet. I thought it was one of our men. We fired over his head to see if he ducked. He kept waving. Sikes said, "We're not falling for that either." Two machine guns suddenly opened up on us from a position near the man. He was trying to lure us into the open rice paddy.

Sikes and I jumped for a hole. He got hit three times, accidentally saving my life with his body. My right leg was hanging out the hole. I was trying to pull it in when the VC tossed a grenade. I felt a sharp, stinging sensation in my leg. Sikes was screaming with pain. "Be quiet," I told him. "Let's play dead."

I wiped his blood on my face and clothes. Two Viet Cong approached, one from the left, one from the right. They were armed with AKs and wore green uniforms with trouser legs rolled up. They had pith helmets and were camouflaged with green leafy branches tied around their waists.

I was on top of Sikes. They turned me over, took my pistol belt off, and stood yelling to another Viet Cong across the river. More Vietnamese arrived carrying ropes. They began to pull at me. I moved and they realized I was alive. One said, *"Chieu hoi! Chieu hoi!"* They motioned for me to get up, jerked my hands behind my back, and tied them with ropes made of vines. I pointed at Sikes and asked what they were going to do with him. They pushed me roughly out of the hole, and said, *"Di!"* As I walked across the paddy I saw Daly. He lay face down. Water ran through his opened mouth. He looked dead.

James Daly

I was near the middle of the platoon when the firing started. I saw Willie Watkins back-flip into a hole like he was going off a diving board. A GI near me stood up and fired his M-16 to cover men retreating from exposed positions on the hill. I could see bullets kicking puffs of dust from his clothes as he was hit. He crumpled slowly to the ground, firing till he died.

A general panic took over. We seemed to be without leadership. Every man was for himself. I didn't know whether to run or stay hidden behind the paddy dike. I didn't fire my weapon. Not because of my beliefs against killing. I wasn't thinking about that then. I simply thought I might attract attention to myself and get killed. Meyers and a few others were in a trench behind me. The VC were trying to get them with grenades. The grenades fell short and landed in front of me. I was covered with dirt from the explosions. I received a minor wound in my arm, maybe from a flying rock. I called Meyers.

"Be quiet," he said. "You gonna give away your position."

"Can I come over there with you?" I asked. I was alone. The man next to me had been killed by a grenade.

"If you move," Meyers said, "you gonna get shot, so stay there."

I called him every few minutes. Finally he said, "We gonna wait till it gets a little dark, then try to get away. We'll call you before we leave."

The firing slacked off. I tried again. "Meyers . . . Meyers." No answer. I cried. I couldn't help it. I knew they had left me.

I could hear Vietnamese walking around stripping bodies. I pushed my weapon away from me over the dike. Then I lay with my face in the water and mud, opened my mouth, and tried to hold my breath. A Vietnamese approached and put his foot under me. "To make it easy for him I'd better roll over as he lifts his foot," I said to myself. When he tried to turn me I flopped over and lay there with one eye closed, the other half opened looking at him. He reached and felt my pulse. He took my watch and pistol belt off, removed the grenades from my harness, and went through my pockets. Then he left.

"He's walking away," I thought. "That fool must really think I'm dead!"

I watched them strip bodies for a few minutes and my mind began to work. It was like two different persons talking to me. One said, "Stay where you are, Bubba. When it gets dark try to make your way back to safety."

The second said, "No, you know how clumsy you are. You don't know where you're going. You'll make so much noise you'll wind up getting killed."

I listened to both sides of the argument and decided that maybe I'd better let them know I was still alive.

I started kicking around in the water to get their attention. Two Vietnamese came toward me. One of them said, *"Chieu hoi!"* I didn't know what that meant, but I nodded my head yes. I used my hands to raise myself to my feet. They got excited and motioned for me to keep my hands in the air. I had never been able to walk on rice paddy dikes without slipping off, they are only a foot or two wide. Now every time I lowered my hands to try to keep my balance the Viet Cong jammed rifles in my back. I walked across the rice field slipping and falling. When we got to the woodline I saw Willie. I felt relieved.

Watkins. They brought Daly over at 4:00 P.M. A medic bandaged Sikes. Several guards moved us up a trail. Soon we came to a house of cement and wood. We were shoved into a two-tiered bunker. Sikes was moaning for water. A Vietnamese who spoke a few words of English told us, "Do not be scared. We no kill. We take you to big house." He gave us some C-ration tins of jelly to eat. I had a package of Salems in my top pocket. Another guerrilla took them from me and replaced them with Chesterfields looted from a dead GI. Artillery rounds began to fall, coming closer and closer. One landed squarely on the top level of our bunker. The explosion shook us up but no one was injured. When the artillery stopped they brought another American to the bunker. Matthew. He had been shot twice in the chest.

At nightfall we moved out. The guards ordered me and Daly to carry Sikes; Matthew was carried in a hammock. I put his left arm around my neck and told Daly to get the other side. Daly could hardly keep his own balance on the rain-slick trail and wasn't much help with Sikes. My boot was soggy with blood from the grenade wound. My leg was numb. The guards yelled at me because I couldn't carry Sikes very well. I was dragging him. He was dying, I could tell, and there was nothing I could do.

We came to another house. The Viet Cong called out the owner and they had a fifteen-minute conference. Judging from their voices they were arguing. A teen-age boy came with a flashlight to look us over. He spotted my graduation ring from Lincoln High School and yanked it off. My Seiko, covered with mud, he didn't see. The VC returned and told us to leave Sikes under a small shed near the house. We never saw him again.

As the moon was rising we reached our destination, a large stucco house with a brick patio. I was startled to hear telephones ringing as we approached. I was tied up on the patio and left for a while in the rain. Then I was led inside to a room lit by a single bare bulb. A large map was pinned to one wall. Nearby were three PRC-25 radios. A stack of military I.D. cards lay on the table; one of them, I saw, belonged to the colored captain of Delta Company.

The interrogator wore a brown short-sleeve shirt. He was fair-skinned, had high nose, and just a suggestion of slanted eyes. I thought he was French. He spoke English with a sort of British accent. He asked for my wallet. I carried a code-of-military-justice card, some personal pictures, a few dollars, and my I.D. He kept only the I.D. and returned the wallet.

"What is your radio frequency?"

"I don't know," I said.

"You do know," he said with irritation.

"No, I don't. I'm not a radioman. I have an M–seventy-nine."

"Oh, you carry a big gun?"

"Yes."

He opened a vinyl-covered U.S. Army map on the table and began to point out the 196th Brigade's positions. I didn't know whether the information plotted was correct or not. It sounded right. Obviously I could tell him nothing he didn't already know.

He looked at me and shrugged, "Don't worry. You won't be killed. You will be well treated and given food. You might stay here till the end of the war, or you might be released earlier. Who knows?" He dismissed me. The interrogation had taken ten minutes.

Daly. I knew I would have trouble with the interrogation. It started with the first question. Frenchy asked me my company commander's name. I told him I didn't know.

"You *will* tell me your company commander's name," he said.

"Sir, you don't understand. When I came to the company my commander was on R 'n' R and I didn't meet him. When he returned I was told his name but I don't remember it."

"You do know!" he exploded.

"No, sir, I don't. It begins with a *Y*, if that will help you."

"What weapons do you have in your company?"

"Well, sir, you're not going to believe this either. I know we have M-sixteens and two machine guns in my platoon. But I don't know of any others. If you showed me a thousand different weapons I couldn't pick out which was which except for the M-sixteen and maybe M–seventy-nine."

"Can you draw a map?"

"Oh, no, sir. I can't draw anything, period."

He pulled out an army map. "This is where you were," he said, running a finger along the map. What he said seemed true. Not being able to read a map I couldn't tell for sure. He thought I was refusing to cooperate. How was I to explain that he was talking to a conscientious objector?

Watkins. After interrogation we were joined by a short Vietnamese wearing black pajamas and a .45 pistol belt. He spoke English and served as our interpreter for the next few days. He told us he had the equivalent rank of major in the North Vietnamese Army. He wore black pajamas as a safeguard, he said, in case American troops entered the village he happened to be visiting. He then took off the pistol and pretended to be a farmer.

We had three guards. Two had rifles and the third carried two rucksacks of supplies and sleeping gear. They wore regulation green uniforms and had red-star buckles on their leather belts. We walked through the night and came to a village surrounded by bamboo, where we rested all day. Late that afternoon farmers began to return to the village from outlying fields. An old man spotted us and started running for us waving a machete. A guard yelled for him to stop. He kept coming. I thought he was going to cut our heads off. The guard jumped up and took the knife away from him. The old man stood there, shaking his fists at us, spitting out Vietnamese.

I better understood his anger that evening when we moved down the trail. Every house we passed was burned down, every field bombed out. We saw two dud bombs with fuses removed laying beside a rice paddy. They were saving them, I guess, for booby traps. We stopped for a rest break because Matthew had got worse. He was gasping for breath. He said he could feel the bullet working up from his lungs. He was tied to Daly. He tried to speak: "I want you to tell my wife——" The guards ordered him to stop talking. They untied him and motioned us to continue without him. The interpreter told us the following day that he had passed away that night.

We stopped at a small hamlet. The guards took us inside a hootch and told us to remove our boots. Villagers gathered around, looking at us wide-eyed, giggling, pointing, nudging each other. I struggled off my boots. My feet were two raw hunks of meat. The smell drove them scrambling out the hootch. Next morning we reached a North Vietnamese Army camp. It was in a cleared patch of jungle hidden by overhanging trees and foliage. Five troop hootches elevated on poles stood side by side. The sleeping hootches were unfurnished; the NVA hung their green canvas hammocks from the walls. Soldiers gathered round us, laughing and feeling our hair. The interpreter said we should not get angry. The soldiers weren't making fun of us, he said; it was just that they had never seen Negroes before.

We were locked in a supply shed filled with corn and rice, and given propaganda leaflets to read. The leaflets told about the corrupt Saigon government, said the Vietnamese didn't want Americans in Viet Nam. We were happy to get them. We used them as rolling paper to smoke our cigarette butts. That night I was awakened by Daly's screams.

Daly. I felt something underneath me. I reached down and touched a warm fur. I thought I was dreaming. Then the fur moved and I realized what it was. A guard came with a light and opened the door. When he found it was rat I was screaming about he laughed and went away. I didn't sleep the rest of the night.

Watkins. The North Vietnamese told us to write our autobiographies. We wrote that we were farmers, that we came from small towns, and worked the fields. The interpreter seemed satisfied. Daly was from New York and there weren't too many farms in Brooklyn. What I wrote, though, was basically true. I was born and raised in a rural area of South Carolina. Hard scrabble land. I worked in a drive-in restaurant during high school. My mother and father were separated, and I tried to help make ends meet at home. Several months after I was graduated I received my preinduction notice. I phoned the Selective Service Board and asked if there was a chance I might be drafted. "More than a chance," they told me. I figured there was no way I could plan anything with that hanging over my head. So in October, 1966, I enlisted.

I was assigned to the support unit for the ranger school at Fort Benning till I got orders for Viet Nam. I arrived in-country at the Cam Ranh Bay replacement center. I was kept busy filling sandbags for several days until I received orders from Saigon for the 196th Brigade. Early one morning we were herded onto trucks and taken to the airport, where we were manifested for a flight to Chu Lai. I had never heard of Chu Lai. I asked everybody I saw where Chu Lai was. Nobody in my group of replacements had ever heard of it. Nobody had ever heard of the 196th Brigade either, and that began to worry me.

When I got to Chu Lai my replacement group was sent through

the brigade's school on ambushes and booby traps. The instructors said a month before we arrived, Charlie had pinned down a class right there. I asked myself, "If Charlie can pin us down in an area supposedly secure, what's going to happen when we get to the field?" After we finished booby-trap school a truck came by and a sergeant called out our names, assigned us to different companies, and ordered us to load up. We were taken to the helicopter pad and told to get on the afternoon supply chopper and find our companies. I got to the company area about dark and met the first sergeant. He put me in the first platoon. The platoon sergeant gave me my squad assignment. We were working in platoon and squad-size units, running search-and-destroy operations near the battalion base camp.

We were like any other unit new to Viet Nam, didn't really know what was going on. Brigade headquarters radioed us one night that a platoon of VC had been spotted. We were ordered to set up a blocking force to trap them. What actually happened was that the brigade had sent a platoon out on ambush earlier that evening. They were the ones who had been spotted. And we were about to open up on our own men! We spent a lot of time looking for weapons caches and the enemy's rice supplies. Once we found the rice it was hard to get it out of the area, and a lot of guys just urinated on it.

The platoon's point man got blown away by a command-detonated mine my third time out. We called in tracker dogs and found one VC; another got away. It was my first action where someone got killed. A couple of days later I was pulling guard duty on a bridge. We started taking sniper rounds from a ville across the river. The veterans said it was the Vietnamese Popular Forces, the local militia, shooting at us. That night one of our guys got shot through the rectum. He was shot with a carbine. It must have been the local militia.

I didn't have much contact with the Vietnamese people. During an S 'n' D we ran across a VC mama-san who had "wanted" posters on her wall for two U.S. Marines, members of a pacification team. Charlie had put a lot of money on their heads. We tore the posters up but didn't burn the house, maybe because two elderly couples were living with her. A government compound wasn't a mile down the road. About the only Vietnamese I met were the Coke girls who hung around trying to sell us overpriced soda stolen from the PX. I talked and messed around with them. But when it came to trusting them, I never did.

Daly. I thought there was no use trying to write a true autobiography. It probably would have caused confusion and, therefore, trouble, and I'd already had enough of that. How could they understand? I didn't understand myself.

It began after I was graduated from high school in June, 1966. I was an average student with an interest in clerical courses. Sports didn't appeal to me—I was too uncoordinated anyway. I tried out for the bowling team but didn't even make that. I intended to become a chef. I began cooking as a hobby when I was eight years old. My father was still with us then and my mother was a housewife.

I enrolled at community college in hotel technology after graduation from high school. I had three sisters and three brothers, and we had financial troubles. At times we were a welfare family. I soon realized I would have to postpone my plan of becoming a chef till I earned some money. I dropped out of community college almost before I'd begun and started looking for a job. Everywhere I went employers asked one question: "What is your draft status?" I was 1-A. Nobody wanted to hire someone who might be drafted the next day.

I was raised as a devout Baptist, but I became interested in the Jehovah's Witnesses in 1959, and had attended their services off and on since that time. I completely agreed with their beliefs against violence and killing. I wasn't a turn-the-other-cheek kind of person. I was taught to defend myself. But I believed that should I take another human life, I would lose forever my chances of a resurrection. In December I went to the Selective Service office in Brooklyn and told the lady in charge that I was a conscientious objector on religious grounds. I had finally found a job working in the credit bureau of a department store. She asked my denomination.

"Baptist. But I'm studying with the Jehovah's Witnesses. According to my beliefs I just don't think I can enter military service."

"Well, young man," she said, "I'm sorry. Under our regulations we cannot exempt you unless you have proof that you're not only a Jehovah's Witness, but that you are qualified as a minister."

That meant I would have to work full time as a preacher. Just out of high school, I knew I couldn't make enough money to survive that way. My mother was working to support the family. I was the second oldest. She needed me at least to take care of myself if I couldn't help out at home. I went to see the army recruiting officer. I figured he would know more than the draft-board lady. I told him I was a conscientious objector and asked how I could claim my exemption. He questioned me about my beliefs. I explained that I couldn't belong to two opposing armies at the same time. I was already a soldier of God, committed to saving lives, not to taking them. The recruiting officer, a colored sergeant, seemed understanding. He told me the army had a special noncombat work program for conscientious objectors. I told him I wasn't against the armed forces if I didn't have to be involved in killing. The sergeant said if I voluntarily enlisted I could have my choice of noncombat jobs. But if I waited until I was drafted, he warned, I would almost automatically become an infantry soldier.

"If that's the case," I said, "maybe I should join the air force or the navy."

"Look," he said, "I'm not saying this because I'm in the army. But if you want to travel and to see the world, there's no safer way to do it than by land. Why sign up for a long enlistment in the air force? By 'pushing' the draft, you can come into the regular army for two years. Otherwise you will have to join the air force or navy for three or four years at a minimum. And with us you still get your choice of noncombat assignments."

He was scheduled to go to New York's Fort Hamilton the next day, and he said he would check to see if my name was coming out on the New Year's draft list. He gave me a pamphlet to read on the New Action Army. I went home to talk it over with my family.

When the sergeant returned from Fort Hamilton, he said, "You're on the list to be drafted starting in January." He prepared my enlistment forms. My first choice of assignments was cook's school, my second was clerical training.

"Sometimes they don't give you your first choice," he said, "but you'll definitely get your second."

I signed my name in all the blocks he marked with Xs. I had no reason to read the long forms. I trusted him.

My mother gave me some advice the night before I left for Fort Jackson, South Carolina. "Son, don't tell anyone you are a conscientious objector," she said. "Don't tell anyone except those you have to tell. It will only cause trouble for you."

I followed her advice and tried to get through basic training as quietly as possible. "What's the spirit of the bayonet?" the instructors yelled.

"To kill! To kill! To kill!" the recruits were supposed to answer. It was stupid, childish stuff, but I went through the motions. I barely passed the physical-training test. I was shocked, I must say, by my drill instructors' language. I was brought up to believe that in order to get respect you had to earn it. How could a soldier respect someone who called him dirty names? The average GI, I saw, showed respect only out of fear—and that wasn't a good basis for an army or anything else. Once they got to Viet Nam and their fear was transferred to the VC, the GIs stopped showing much respect for their officers.

My new orders were posted the day before we were to graduate from basic training. I was assigned to advanced infantry training at Fort Polk, Louisiana. I went to my training-company commander and said, "This can't be right, sir. I had my choice of cook's school or clerical training. I'm a conscientious objector." My company commander was polite but said he was positive I'd come into the army unassigned.

"No, sir. I was guaranteed by the recruiting officer that I would have a noncombat assignment."

"Did you get the guarantee in black and white?" he asked.

I caught my breath. "I don't know," I admitted.

He pulled my records from a filing case. "See, here's where you signed your name agreeing to come into the army for two years unassigned." He was right. "I'm sorry it happened this way, Daly," he said. "I wish I'd known earlier. But there's nothing I can do now. You'll have to wait till you get to Polk. Tell your new company commander about this as soon as you check in."

When I arrived at Fort Polk my platoon sergeant refused to give me permission to see my new company commander. I went to a telephone and asked the operator to connect me with the general who commanded Fort Polk. Whoever I spoke with in the general's office agreed that I should be able to see someone about a personal problem. The company commander sent for me shortly after I returned to the company area. I entered his office and saluted.

"Have you ever heard of the chain of command?" he asked.

"Yes, sir. But for four days I've been asking the platoon sergeant if I could see you, and he said no."

"What's your problem?"

I told him. He said he would get me an application for discharge from the army as a conscientious objector. I received the application and went about getting the required endorsements from various military officials. Meanwhile, I took the post chaplain's advice and continued my infantry training, which at first I'd refused to do. Fort Polk was a way station for Viet Nam. War slogans were written on banners hung around the post. The PX sold T-shirts decorated with a picture of a Vietnamese in a coolie hat. Stamped across the shirt in big black letters was "Kill a Cong."

I graduated from the infantry course as a rifleman in May, 1967. I was held over at Polk while my application for discharge was considered by the Pentagon; and I volunteered to become a cook while I waited. In early September I was told to report to the first sergeant's office. As I walked in he said, "I want you processed out of here this afternoon. You're on orders for Viet Nam."

"How can I be on orders for Viet Nam?" I said. "I haven't heard anything about my application for discharge."

"You haven't?" he asked. "Where have you been? That's been back for weeks. It was disapproved by Department of Army."

I was stunned. The sergeant told me that maybe I should try to see the training-brigade commander. I went to his office. He listened for a few minutes till I came to the part about being a conscientious objector. Then he threw me out. "I wouldn't lift a finger to help a conscientious objector," he said.

My application for discharge, I learned, had been disapproved by almost everyone concerned. The chaplain, whom I'd thought to be so understanding, was one of them. In his statement he said he believed I was claiming to be a conscientious objector because I didn't want to be assigned to Viet Nam. Of the various officials required to endorse my application on its way to the Pentagon, only the post psychiatrist was of the opinion that my request should be granted.

I got an appointment with the post inspector general, whose job it was to deal with the unusual complaints of GIs. He listened as I gave him the details. Then he said, "There's nothing I can see that can be done right now. The only thing you might do— and I'm not telling you to do this, mind you—is go home on official leave and stay there and not report to Oakland for shipment to Viet Nam. When the military police come to pick you up, tell them why you are AWOL. Maybe that way you can get a court to rule on your case."

I telephoned my minister in New York. He was also a lawyer. I told him what the inspector general had said. "First of all," my minister told me, "if you do what he suggested you're going to be charged with being absent without leave. And nobody is going to listen to your plea of being a conscientious objector if you go AWOL. You'll be treated like a common delinquent. If you want to fight it, you'd better fight in a legal manner, step by step." He told me to see him when I got home.

I processed out of Fort Polk on September 6, and went home

to Brooklyn. My orders said I had to be in Oakland, California, outside of San Francisco, on September 29 for shipment to Viet Nam. My minister counseled with me and repeated what he'd said before. "If you intend to stick to your refusal to go as a conscientious objector," he said, "you'd better be prepared to go to jail."

The prospect of my going to jail upset my family. None of my immediate relatives had completed high school. They thought my job opportunities, which seemed to be so much brighter than theirs, would be ruined by a prison sentence. As my grandmother said, "Everybody does their time in the service. Why do you have to be different?" My minister gave me a letter to take to Fort Hamilton explaining what had happened to me. The recruiting officer by this time had been transferred to another post. Officials at Fort Hamilton told me they could do nothing. They advised me to report to Oakland two days early and resubmit my application for discharge. In Oakland I was told I would have to get to my permanent-duty station in Viet Nam before anything could be done about the application; Oakland was simply a transit shipping point.

As the plane took off that night I saw why San Francisco's Golden Gate Bridge had been given its name. It was truly beautiful. But even such beauty could not lift me from my depression. I was convinced Viet Nam was wrong and I would be severely punished for going. I prayed that my life might be spared so I could return to my family.

The inspector general was the first person I talked to when I got to Chu Lai. I can't remember his rank, even to this day I don't understand the system of rank very well. He asked what type of application I had filled out. For a separation from service, I said. That was a mistake, he told me. Such applications were routinely turned down 98 per cent of the time. He said I would have a better chance by applying for a conscientious-objector change of status—that is, an application for a noncombat job. He said he would radio the chaplain who would handle it once I got to my company assignment in the field.

I went out on a supply convoy with a group of replacements.

When I arrived my platoon leader, Lieutenant Kitney, was wait-ing for me. "Who's Daly?" he asked as we climbed off the trucks. "Who's the conscientious objector?"

The heads of the other men whipped around to look at me.

"I'm Daly," I said.

"Come with me," he said. "The chaplain wants to see you."

The chaplain was a pleasant fellow. *All* chaplains seemed to be pleasant. I was learning that didn't count for much. He told me it would be best to do as the inspector general at Chu Lai had suggested and said he would help me with the application. Lieu-tenant Kitney said meanwhile I would have to remain with the platoon in the field. I asked why I could not have a temporary noncombat assignment.

"The matter will be decided by Department of Army," the lieutenant said. "Until then you'll do your duties like every other soldier."

"The Bible says 'Thou shalt not kill,' " I said. "It doesn't say 'Thou shalt not kill over five or ten.' If I stay in the field a month until the Pentagon recognizes I'm a conscientious objector, why don't I stay and kill for a year?"

"Sorry but that's the way it's gotta be," he said.

"If that's the case I'd prefer to go on to Fort Leavenworth right now."

"You just can't request to go to prison," he laughed. "I'll do whatever I can to get your application through. That's all I can say." He turned and left.

On my first operation I was walking through the paddies when another member of the squad sidled up to me. It was Shriner. "Ain't you gonna lock and load?" he said with a deep southern accent.

"Okay, okay," I said. I pulled an ammo magazine from my bandoleer and snapped it into the M-16 and slapped back the operating handle.

"Let's see that magazine you put in there," said Shriner.

"Why?"

"Just let me see it."

I removed the magazine and handed it to him.

"You motherfucker," he said.

Shriner showed the empty magazine to Sergeant Lashore, my squad leader, and Lashore showed it to the platoon sergeant. That afternoon when we returned to the base camp the platoon sergeant called for me. "I don't ever want to hear of this again," he said. "Let somebody get hurt because of you and I'll guarantee you one thing. If nobody gets you before I do, I'll personally take care of you."

That evening Lieutenant Kitney ordered me to report to the mess hall for KP duty. The platoon sergeant came by four days later. "Ready to do your job?" he asked.

"What you're really asking is have I given up my beliefs," I said. "The answer is no. A few days on KP can't change me." I washed pots and pans for two weeks. Then I was sent back to the platoon.

I was against all wars. I knew little about Viet Nam when I arrived. Now I was learning. I saw Vietnamese men and women going through the mess-hall garbage cans as though they were sitting down to Thanksgiving. The whole of the country looked ragged and poorly fed. I couldn't believe the way they lived. I thought they were at least five hundred years behind us. I felt deeply sorry for them, especially the children. I wrote home and asked my mother to collect old clothes in the neighborhood and send them to me along with a few bags of candy, so I could make the Vietnamese presents at Christmas.

I was also learning on the battlefield. One day we were moving through a ville checking I.D. cards. It was cloudy and overcast. Everyone was nervous. An old man got shot. He was seriously wounded. I didn't see it happen. His wife ran out of a hootch waving his I.D. card and screaming, "Okay! Okay! No VC! No VC!"

The medic asked Lieutenant Kitney if he was going to call for a medevac chopper. The lieutenant said no. He ordered several guys to pick up the man and carry him away from the ville. The wife tried to follow and the lieutenant told her to *di-di*. They threw the old man in some bushes outside the village. Guys in my squad complained. The medic asked the lieutenant why he had done that.

"Because he's a gook," Kitney said. "Besides the weather is too bad. They won't send a medevac out now."

"What if one of us gets shot?" someone asked.

"That's different," he said.

Another day we were approaching a ville when we saw someone running in the distance. Two men in the platoon opened up. The figure fell.

"That's my man, I got him," said one soldier.

"No, I shot first!" said the other.

Anyone who killed a VC got a three-day pass. They continued to argue about who should get credit for the kill. I went to look at the dead enemy. It was a boy of about twelve.

I got along fairly well with the platoon. I learned not to try to debate my beliefs with them. It always started and ended the same way. Why was I a conscientious objector? Why did I feel I shouldn't serve my country? Then on to a more personal level. What would I do if I saw a VC about to shoot another American? From there it was like a truck going downhill. One night I was pulling guard duty on a bridge. Shriner had also drawn the assignment. He began questioning me. I explained. I could see he was getting angry. I suggested we'd better stop.

"No, no, I'm not angry," he said. "I just want to know what you believe."

At the same time he kept pressing closer, pushing me back toward the bridge railing. I was getting scared; I couldn't swim. A third guard, who was off-duty, yelled for us to stop arguing. He went to get Sergeant Lashore. The sergeant came down and told Shriner he should be ashamed of himself. "No matter how much you argue," he said, "you're not gonna get the man to change his beliefs." Sergeant Lashore and I had become friends. He tried as much as he could to watch out for me.

On New Year's Eve Lieutenant Kitney ordered me to go out on a night ambush. Lashore asked if he could go in my place, but

Kitney refused to let him. Lashore told us before we left to sandbag the assignment—pretend to go by calling in a false position report on the radio. The three of us hid in some hootches all night. Next morning I felt that Kitney knew we had not gone on the ambush, but he didn't say anything.

All this time I was waiting for my application to be processed through regular channels. I had run into a snag at first. I was required to attach references to the request from people at home who knew me. To save time I typed out a form letter and sent it to my sister and asked her to get various leaders in the community to sign it. The application was bounced back after I submitted it. My reference letters, I was told, had to be written individually by persons who signed. A form letter wouldn't do. I was waiting for these letters from home when I was captured.

I had not fired my weapon in the three months I was on the front lines.

Watkins. The North Vietnamese soldiers had a celebration at Tet. We heard a lot of singing and clapping. They gave us a pack of Ruby Queen cigarettes, a bag of candy, and some water-buffalo meat, which almost ruined our teeth it was so tough. A guard asked us if we wanted to see a movie. They took us to a nearby jungle camp that had a small market place. I saw sewing machines in hootches, and a gas generator provided electricity. Once again I was surprised. I had been told that the VC were untrained and unequipped.

The movie theater was a long shed with a white sheet at the rear for a screen. The film showed North Vietnamese PT boats wiping out the entire French Navy. The soldiers clapped and shouted. Our guards asked us if we wanted something to drink. We thought it would be beer or whiskey. They brought us glasses of lukewarm amber water. They called it tea.

I had never heard of Tet before and didn't understand exactly what it was. I didn't know a big military offensive was going on all over the country. I did see a lot of wounded soldiers being brought to the camp. The humor of our guards seemed to depend on the number of casualties there at any time.

Daly. Several weeks later some soldiers brought a dog to camp, tied his hind legs, and strung him up to a pole. They took his temperature with a thermometer and then began to beat him with sticks. The poor dog was howling for dear life.

"What are they doing?" I asked the interpreter.

"They're making the meat tender," he said. I skipped dinner.

3

Frank Anton

Frenchy put an interpreter in charge of us, and we began to walk westward. We could see a 196th fire support base to our left on a hill about three miles away. Helicopters zoomed in and out of the base, others flew about the area, dipping low, apparently looking for us. Our guards were rotated and replaced by four teen-age girls with long black hair. Two of them were lovely. Pfister, Lewis, and I looked at each other. If we were to escape this was the time. It would take only a minute to overpower them and take their weapons. A chopper flew overhead and drew my attention to a tree line two hundred meters forward. I saw movement. Three hundred soldiers were resting in the woods. The whole valley was crawling with them. They were preparing for the Tet offensive.

In a few minutes we joined the soldiers and marched with them till our guards were rotated once more and men took over. That night we stopped at a hootch near a river which was occupied by a woman and four children. Practically every house in Viet Nam, grass-woven hootch or whatever, had a mud-packed bomb shelter adjoining it, as this one did. Sometimes bunkers were dug at the end of the bed, so they could jump straight in during a night attack. The dugout we were placed in was so small that we couldn't all sleep at once. Each man was allowed a two-hour shift in a comfortable position at the expense of the other two.

Much of the next day was spent crossing paddies and creeks. In the afternoon we stopped at a hootch owned by a woman who looked to be about sixty but was probably younger. There was no middle age in Viet Nam, just as there was not much of a twilight. Forty-five seemed to be the sharp dividing line. On one side of it people looked ten years younger than their actual ages; on the other side, the same amount older.

I took off my boots. She saw that my feet were wet. She removed my socks and dried my feet with a rag. She left and returned in a moment with a pair of clean white socks belonging to her. She pulled them very gently on my feet and hung mine up to dry. Other villagers had hissed and thrown rocks at us as we passed. But this act of kindness was unexpected, and I was touched.

We continued on to a hilltop base camp. That night two hundred soldiers arrived, preceded by alert signals that sounded like owls hooting in the distance. They handed their weapons and rucksacks to the same number of waiting soldiers who were without gear. The fresh troops moved out quickly and quietly. The men coming off duty made themselves comfortable around lean-tos and slowly, by degrees, shook the tension from the night's operations and began to laugh and joke.

My feet were swollen from the constant walking. I had developed a case of jungle rot. I didn't think I could go further. On the third day in camp the North Vietnamese brought some condensed milk and candy to the hootch. They gave it to Pfister and Lewis, and the interpreter said, "Anton, your milk is outside. You'll have to get it if you want it." They wanted to see if I could walk; and I hobbled out to get it. Shortly afterward an officer arrived. The interpreter said he was a high cadre (he pronounced it "cater") of the Liberation Front. For the first time we were searched. The officer looked through my stuff. He told me I could keep my watch or my ring. The ring was given to me by my father when I was thirteen. There was no question as to which I would keep. As I slipped it on my finger I thought of home and wondered if my family knew.

My father was a waist-gunner in World War II, and worked his way up to the rank of colonel in the peace-time air force. We moved from post to post (I have five brothers and a sister) to more than a dozen states. I went to four different high schools, two in New Jersey, one in New York, and graduated from Labrador, where I lettered in basketball and was an average student.

I tried college several times. I first entered the University of Missouri. Called myself majoring in sociology. My real major was a girl. My interest in sociology and the girl declined after a year, and I dropped out to work at a variety of jobs, as a greensman on a New York golf course, factory hand in New Jersey, and as a fill-in here and there. Then I re-entered a small college in New York for two semesters.

At the end of 1965 I found myself bored with college once again. The education I was receiving seemed remote and useless. This time, though, the situation on the outside had changed. The war had expanded, and I was twenty-two. I would be drafted if I dropped out again. In late November I visited the air force recruiter's office to see what would be available to me if I did quit school. He was out to lunch. On my way out the building the army recruiter asked me to stop and chat with him. During our talk he mentioned the new warrant-officer program the army had set up to train helicopter pilots. Only a high-school degree was needed. You had to pass a tough flight physical and to fall within certain height and weight limits. First step in the program was regular basic training, same as every GI took, then eight months of flight training, at the end of which you received a commission as a warrant officer, a rank somewhere in limbo between sergeant major and second lieutenant. In short, the program was an assembly-line production of helicopter pilots needed for the Viet Nam war.

I had always wanted to fly. The idea of going to Viet Nam, which I knew little about, didn't bother me. I entered the program in January, 1966, and left for eight weeks of basic training at Fort Polk. My attitude and military bearing couldn't exactly be described as gung ho, but I got by; and I looked forward to the flying part. On my first solo flight I was supposed to fly to a field two miles away. We used highways as navigational aids. Every freeway looks about the same, and when I got airborne I picked the wrong one. I flew west instead of east. After looking in a daze at the flat Texas terrain for two hours, I was forced to land to refuel. Wrong-way Anton. My classmates enjoyed a few drinks on that.

A lot of guys went into the program thinking they were going to wash out. Some, in fact, tried to flunk on purpose. Those who didn't make it through had only to serve the remainder of a two-year enlistment and were honorably discharged from service. With luck you could find a cushy stateside assignment for that remaining year. I must admit I thought about it myself. I'd always had a tendency to prepare myself for failure. Anything I didn't like or succeed at right off, I'd usually give it up fast. But I finished the course as an average student, and was commissioned on March 13, 1967. After two weeks' home leave I shipped out for Viet Nam.

The chartered Continental jet landed at Bien Hoa, just northeast of Saigon. Of the one hundred thirty men on the plane, seventy were from my flight class. Most of us were assigned to a helicopter replacement company. In flight school we had talked to returning veterans about the different units in Viet Nam. The First Cav was pictured as the one where the action was. It was an elite helicopter division created for Viet Nam. After I got to Bien Hoa I tried to wangle an assignment to the unit. It wasn't a matter of looking for action. I'd never measured myself in terms of physical courage. I wasn't the sort of kid who tried to prove himself by climbing water towers at night or by racing the family car. I thought I could do as well as the next man. I wanted the Cav because some of my best friends from flight school were assigned there.

As it turned out, I drew an assignment purely by chance to the

Seventy-first Assault Helicopter Company, which was known as the Rattlers. It was an old unit with a high reputation in Viet Nam. The Rattlers had recently returned to Bien Hoa from Operation Junction City, and were on standdown for a month while preparations were made to move north to Chu Lai to support the 196th Brigade and other units of the newly formed Task Force Oregon.

There wasn't much to do the first several weeks. The company was billeted in a large villa in Bien Hoa. We played cards in the afternoon, and at nights went to the bars. I was given a secondary job as the unit's plaque officer. Each officer leaving for home was presented with a metal-and-wood plaque with the company's insignia, in our case a helicopter with a coiled rattlesnake. It was my job to fly to Saigon once a month to pick up the plaques from a small cluttered shop off Tu Do Street near the river front.

Saigon was once a lovely city, or so I was told. There were wide streets lined with tamarind trees in the center of the city, and spacious French-style colonial villas with yards filled with hibiscus and flaming-pink bougainvillea—and usually a sandbagged guard bunker outside the fence denoting that it had been taken over as an office for this or that American organization. But the city was bloated with war refugees, and had incredible traffic jams of military trucks, blue-and-cream Renault taxis, Honda motorbikes, and pedal cyclo taxis. Most of the people were crowded together in firetrap hovels ringing the city's heart.

I usually hit the Tu Do and Princess nightclubs. Both were overcrowded, overly air-conditioned, and overpriced. I preferred the quieter places where you could sit at the scratchy wood bar and drink *ba muoi ba* and play gin rummy or blackjack with long-haired girls not long out of the rice paddies. Some of them were as sharp as Las Vegas hustlers. They lightly massaged your thighs and encouraged you with dark almond-shaped eyes to buy them a shotglass of tea, which went for about a buck and a quarter. They were business girls—you never forget that—short-time or all-night.

They all had sad stories to tell of nonexistent soldier-husbands, officers and heros to a man, who were killed in the war, forcing them to find work in the bars. Still, the less aggressive ones were amusing. I loved to listen to their slangy broken English. *"Hey GI, you buy me Saigon tea . . . I love you too much . . . Me no butterfly."* Or to see the lightninglike change of sentiments if you refused. *"You cheap charlie . . . number ten . . . fuckyou!"* Or if you did buy them a drink, as you usually did, at least one or two, to see them suddenly rise when they thought they'd exhausted your possibilities and float off like the butterflies they had denied to another GI with money. The girls were delicately built, fine-boned, with small breasts and shockingly little pubic hair. Some of them were beautiful. But I didn't think they could compare with American girls.

We reached Chu Lai the latter part of April, settled ourselves into a wooden prefab building (stolen one night from the Seabees) and began to prepare for operations. "You've been to flight school," my commander told us, "and now you're going to learn to fly." It turned out to be true. We had learned to fly by textbook procedures in the States. Now we learned to fly under combat pressure, to get in and out of landing zones with the quickest speed. I was assigned to the slicks, troop-carrying helicopters.

I flew my first mission on May 1 as co-pilot with a captain who had been in-country some months. There were ten ships in our group. We were practicing inserting and extracting ARVN troops. Our training village was supposed to be friendly. Apparently someone had gotten the wrong info. As we came in we started taking ground fire. This caused a bit of confusion. My chopper was left hovering fifty feet off the ground waiting to see whether we were to land.

Suddenly the engines quit. We hit the ground and rolled over. Several Vietnamese soldiers in the rear suffered broken backs and legs. The rest got cuts and bruises, as did the aircraft commander and myself. Our crew chief was uninjured. The other door gunner was a lieutenant flying what he thought was a safe mission to take pictures and to practice-fire the machine gun. He was due to rotate home in several days and wasn't even from our unit. He tried to get out before the helicopter came to a complete stop. The rotar blade got him.

We started taking sniper fire when we crashed. Our gunships

rolled in and pretty well shot up the village. We were on the ground only about ten minutes before we were picked up by another ship. It was exciting and terrifying. For the first time I began to think something could happen to me. It got to me for the next few days. Because the incident had occurred so early in my tour, my commander asked if I would rather have a nonflying job. I declined. I wanted to fly. I soon decided I didn't want to fly slicks, however. I had a run of mechanical trouble, another engine failure, and several minor hydraulic failures. To fly slicks took discipline and courage, you had to stay together and continue the mission even when the ship in front got shot down. But it was the gunships who were really engaged in combat; and I asked for a transfer to the Firebirds.

The gunship platoon commander said the Firebirds would try me for one mission. If they liked me and I liked them I could join the platoon. That day we got a radio call from a long-range patrol shortly after we were airborne. The patrol had spotted forty-eight armed VC walking across a paddy. As we circled the field the Vietnamese waved at us. We saw no weapons. We told the patrol they must be mistaken, all we could see were farmers. The patrol radioed back that the VC had hidden their weapons in the bushes before we arrived. We orbited for five minutes discussing what we should do, then rolled in and hosed down on them. Sure enough, soon as we fired we got return fire. The gunship in front of me was hit and the door gunner wounded. We got twenty-five confirmed enemy by body count.

The incident happened on a peninsula not far from Chu Lai. Just south of there was Lieutenant Calley's hamlet of My Lai. The area was always hot. I considered the Vietnamese friendly until one of them shot at me. This didn't mean we could shoot up a village because of one sniper, we had regulations against that. But eventually we accumulated so much fire from a particular village that the word came down, "Okay, next time you're shot at you can return fire." And we returned it. Very heavily. There were usually two helicopters in a situation like this. One carried forty-eight rockets plus machine guns. As a wingman I carried fourteen rockets and 7,000 machine-gun rounds. In the helicopter's nose were the miniguns, two five-barrel fast-firing machine guns. During a run on a target the aircraft commander fired the rockets, the co-pilot handled the miniguns, and the two door gunners worked out with their swivel-mounted M-60 machine guns. It was quite effective.

We made our runs with the sun to our backs if possible, came down at eighty knots, fired our stuff, and broke off at an altitude of five hundred feet and sometimes lower. Between two and five hundred feet you got hit the easiest. The leader would usually break right; the pilot was in the right-hand seat and he was more comfortable maneuvering in that direction. As the team leader broke, the wingman started firing. It all happened in a flash. White phosphorous rockets were our favorite ammo. With them you could see what you were hitting, and it was no problem to burn an enemy ville.

South of Chu Lai and a few miles west of Highway 1 was considered hostile territory. A few friendly villes were in these areas that we had orders not to shoot up. If we received sniper rounds, grunts were sent in to check it out. Before all major ground operations leaflets were dropped warning villagers to flee the area. We ferried the refugees to safety in our helicopters. I once had more than fifteen women and children in my chopper. They were terrified to fly but amazed to see the South China Sea for the first time in their lives. The sea was five miles from their homes.

I knew a couple of pilots who would have blasted a village without being fired upon first. But I knew of no specific instances when they did. Their attitude was that all Vietnamese should be wiped out. Most of the pilots weren't like that. Sure, we called them slopes, dinks, and gooks. But those were simply slang words. It was strange to think of the Vietnamese as foreigners, because they were in their own country, but to us that's exactly what they were—foreigners.

I saw women cry when children were wounded, when husbands didn't come back from the rice paddy, when buffalo were killed.

At Chu Lai it was standard procedure to shoot any water buffalo seen in enemy territory. You could pump bullets into a buff and he'd stand there, dumb-eyed, for thirty seconds before he fell. It all sounds callous and cold-blooded, I know. I felt sorry for the villagers, I really did, and sorry for the ones in the jungle who had to take sides or be killed. To an extent, however, my attitude was that the misery was the result of war, and war is hell. Right, a cliché. But it's true. More so in this particular war because you couldn't tell the innocent from the enemy. As I rolled in on a target I thought of nothing except how I could stop them from shooting at me. Sometimes we saw people running from a ville. We didn't fire if we could see, without getting too close where it might be fatal to look, that it was old men, women, and children. But often as not it was impossible to tell who was down there.

Operations in the summer of '67 were routine. We flew close support for ground troops, resupply missions, whatever came up. In September and October we had little contact. Then in November the heavy activity started again. We picked up a lot of Viet Cong suspects and took them to headquarters for interrogation. They were always tightly tied. We had the Vietnamese interpreters to tell them that if they made a move they would be beaten or shot. One acted up and started squirming around and got a few bruises on his head. But I never let my door gunners beat up VC suspects just for the hell of it, something I heard went on.

Nor did we use the airborne interrogation method that journalists were always writing about. I didn't see anyone else in my unit use it either. We did scare a couple of VC suspects one time. They were blindfolded when we took them up. After circling around for a while, we slowly descended and hovered about five feet off the ground. We told them, "Okay, we're going to throw you out because you won't answer questions." Then we pushed them out and they fell to the ground. Of course they didn't get hurt, but they were mentally shaken by the whole thing. I don't know whether they talked or not; the military intelligence people took them away and we never heard.

Everybody usually screwed off a couple of days when they

returned from R 'n' R. I had planned to fly to Plei Ku to see my best friend when I got back from Bangkok. But on the day I landed at Da Nang I ran into a pilot from Chu Lai who said my unit was getting into some heavy stuff. So I skipped Plei Ku and hurried back to join the Firebirds.

Harker. That night the four of us were taken from the big house and tied with black commo wire in the most painful way imaginable. My forearms were held parallel to the ground while elbows were pressed to my sides and drawn to the rear. The wire was then wound tightly around biceps and elbows, duck-wing fashion, and continued behind me to tie Williams and, in turn, Cannon and Strictland. Anyone who failed to maintain the pace would torture the others by pulling the wire tighter. Two guards took positions in front of us, two in the rear, and with me leading we began to walk westward toward the mountains.

The trail was muddy and slippery. As we moved I held my face to the sky, gasping for breath, taking what coolness I could from the rain. When we came to streams I fell to my knees and drank. The water momentarily took my mind from the wire cutting into my arms. I was groaning from the most intense pain of my life. I didn't think I could go much farther. I wanted to stop and let them shoot me. I lost all desire to live.

"Harker, you've got to keep going," Williams said. "Cannon and I are hurting, but we move and you've got to move too." I felt ashamed. At the first inclines we reached I lost my footing and pulled the wire deep into Williams' wounded arm as I fell into the mud. He was patient with me. Cannon, who was involuntarily moaning from his wounds, said nothing. At Williams' suggestion we began to walk with better organization. When we came to embankments and inclines we sat and slid down together. Once in a while our guards whistled or hooted like owls. When the signal was returned, they went off into the bushes. I could hear them talking. Often we began backtracking. It seemed they weren't familiar with the route. I thought we would never get there. At daybreak they put us in an underground cave with wooden bars. We were cramped, unable to stretch out, and still tied.

Next morning the guards loosened the wire somewhat. My arms were numb and swollen to twice their normal size. The feeling in them did not return for hours. A girl of seventeen joined us as our guide. We followed a river till late afternoon and then crossed by boat and entered a village. A man approached and told us that the villagers hated Americans but would allow us to stay in their guest house. "This shows," he said, "the generosity of the Front." We were to hear that phrase many times.

The guards took us to a hootch and brought us rice. The villagers' curiosity exceeded their hostility, and they gathered around. As we ate the interpreter pointed to various people and said, "This one lost a son, this one a wife, this woman lost her husband." The village had been bombed. Undoubtedly there had been casualties. Everyone we met in the following days told the same story; and we were skeptical of some of the reports. On the third day we were joined by a friendly young man named Bay, who had learned English in North Viet Nam. He told us we would be allowed to take a bath, eat well, and go fishing in the river. He said a doctor would be by to treat our wounds. It took us a day to realize he was lying. It was our first lesson in the Oriental custom of telling you what is thought you would like to hear.

A medic showed up to look at Williams' and Cannon's wounds. Williams' fingers were intact, but the top of his right hand had been torn away, leaving a bloody thicket of bone splinters. The VC's field medical technique was typical of what we were to see; he turned his head, held his nose, and poured alcohol on their wounds. It wasn't enough. The wounds of both had begun to turn gangrenous. They insisted on eating separate from Strictland and me so as not to spoil our appetites. Blowflies had laid eggs in Cannon's back wound. Maggots fell out as he walked.

Cannon was twenty-one. He topped six feet, had a medium build, deep-set eyes, and even with the full-face beard you could tell he was handsome. He was from Missouri. He had been a drifter before entering the service. He accepted his new condition quietly as he received everything else life tossed his way. Tobacco was his one vice, and he spent his spare time trying to wheedle some out of every Vietnamese he saw. The Vietnamese tried to teach him to say the word in their language. He could never learn to pronounce it properly. "Goddammit, it don't matter," he would say in exasperation. "Just give me some."

Two guards arrived and ordered Williams and me to follow. We thought at first we were heading for the promised bath, but we swerved away from the river toward the jungle. At a fork in the trail a guard took Williams to the right, the other pushed me to the left. Bay was waiting for me at the hootch door. A Vietnamese stood at attention inside with a fixed bayonet on his rifle. Bay told me I was to be interrogated by an important official. "When he comes in you must stand up and bow in salute," Bay said. "You must show respect to a cadre of the Front."

The cadre entered. He looked about fifty and had steel-gray hair. He told me to sit. He took a seat on the other side of the wood table. "How are you?" he said.

"Okay, I guess."

"Have you eaten well?"

Bay shot me a sharp glance. The expected answer was yes.

"You must tell me everything," he said. "You must cooperate."

"All that's required by the Geneva convention is that I give you my name, rank, service number, and date of birth," I said with an assuredness I didn't feel in my stomach.

"If you do not cooperate," he said in a slow monotone, "great harm will come to you." He asked my name, rank, and service number. I told him. Then he asked my unit designation.

"I can't tell you, sir."

"If you do not cooperate great harm will come to you." He glowered. I refused several more times to answer questions on military matters. He then switched his line of questioning to ask about my family. "Your mother and father are very worried about you. You must tell me their address."

"I can't answer that."

"Why not?"

I thought for several minutes before answering. "That's a good question. I don't know why." I tried to recall the exact wording of the Code of Conduct. It had been put into effect after Korea when numerous POWs had collaborated with the enemy. We were required to memorize it during infantry training. Its six paragraphs had seemed simple and concise at Fort Bragg.

I

I am an American fighting man. I serve in the forces which guard my country and our way of life. I am prepared to give my life in their defense.

II

I will never surrender of my own free will. If in command I will never surrender my men while they still have the means to resist.

III

If I am captured I will continue to resist by all means available. I will make every effort to escape and aid others to escape. I will accept neither parole nor special favors from the enemy.

IV

If I become a prisoner of war, I will keep faith with my fellow prisoners. I will give no information or take part in any action which might be harmful to my comrades. If I am senior, I will take command. If not, I will obey the lawful orders of those appointed over me and will back them up in every way.

V

When questioned, should I become a prisoner of war, I am bound to give only name, rank, service number, and date of birth. I will evade answering further questions to the utmost of my ability. I will make no oral or written statements disloyal to my country and its allies or harmful to their cause.

VI

I will never forget that I am an American fighting man, responsible for my actions, and dedicated to the principles which made my country free. I will trust in my God and in the United States of America.

I felt lonely, exhausted, empty. My world, which a week before had seemed so overwhelmingly large, so unconquerable, had

suddenly shrunk and now was inhabited only by two persons—
and I was facing the other one. "I can't violate the Code of
Conduct," I thought. "But if I don't tell him something he's
going to shoot me. Where are Strictland, Cannon, and Williams?
Maybe they've been shot already." The interrogator's eyes told
me he had done much worse in his lifetime. The readiness to die
I'd felt soon after my capture had vanished. I'd made it this far.
I wanted to live.

I was determined not to give him any information that might
endanger the life of another American soldier. What difference
did it make if he knew my parents' names and that my father was
an electrical engineer in Virginia? Or that I'd attended college
several years before I was drafted? *I will evade answering further
questions to the utmost of my ability.* "That's vague," I thought. "How
do you determine ability to evade questions with a fixed bayonet
at your neck? How do you decide whether or not evading will get
you killed?"

I answered questions about my family for an hour. I steered
away from military subjects. I did tell him I had come by jet plane
and that it had taken me about seventeen hours to travel from
America to Viet Nam. Hearing this Bay and the guards said, *"Choi
oi!"* (My God!). Even Stoneface seemed amazed at this remark-
able feat. I was returned to my old hootch. Williams was there.
Strictland and Cannon were having their turns at interrogation.
Williams told me Stoneface has asked him the same questions,
and had finally found out he wasn't with the Cav as he claimed.
We talked briefly about the possibility of escaping. Williams said
it was out of the question because of his and Cannon's wounds.

We resumed our march the next morning. The jungle had the
damp smell of rotting ferns and vines. The rain had slacked to
a drizzle. The terrain was becoming more rocky. We were without
boots, I was walking in my socks, and my feet protested every
step. We pushed deeper into the western highlands. It was land
owned by the Viet Cong and inhabited mostly by ethnic mountain
tribesmen called montagnards. The montagnards were darker
skinned than the Vietnamese, spoke their own dialects, and were

almost a country within a country because of their isolation and separate culture.

They were a primitive folk who believed in spirits and witchcraft, and were skilled in the use of spears, traps, crossbows and arrows. They farmed the mountainsides by slash-and-burn methods, moving from place to place with their bare-breasted women as the soil was exhausted by crops of corn and manioc and rice. They were fierce fighters. The U.S. Special Forces recruited many of them for operations against the enemy. So did the Viet Cong. We were walking up a stream bed when I saw my first montagnard. He stood watching us, holding an ancient musket by his side. He was dressed in a sports jacket and a loincloth.

Anton. The trail meandered through the jungle. Here and there stood clusters of hootches, woven elephant grass and palm fronds sun-dried into colors of mottled gray-brown, each house carrying a suggestion of deprivation larger than the previous one. Civilization seemed to be diminishing by measurable degrees, as if shades were being drawn behind us, each one progressively darker, every few miles of our march. There were the sudden incongruitites—a barber shop by the trail; a shiny bicycle appearing out of nowhere. But this was poor country. The people were lucky to see meat on their plates a dozen times a year.

As a kid I'd hated rice. I had never eaten it in my life, and I refused to eat it after I was captured. A week had passed and I'd had nothing but candy and condensed milk. At first all I could think about was a Coca-Cola. A cool, sparkling Coke. I thought of the hundreds I'd wasted, tried to recall each individual case to determine why I'd been so foolish as to throw one away. Then the Coke dissolved into an obsession for fried chicken. Jungle vines in front of me took the shape of drumsticks.

As we approached a hootch Pfister saw a stalk of bananas. He got a guard's attention, pointed to his stomach, then to the bananas. The officer with us said the bananas belonged to the people. "Well, tell the people we want them," said Pfister.

"If you walk fast I will get you the bananas," he said. We agreed. He returned with twenty.

"You must make them last three days," he said.

We mumbled okay as we wolfed down two apiece. Then we looked at each other and looked at the VC. He said, "No!"

We began walking. An hour later we stopped and ate the rest of them. After that we told him we would have to get more or we couldn't walk fast. He wasn't impressed.

We had established an easy relationship with our guards. They gave us what they had and treated us in a friendly manner. We saw no reason not to reciprocate. Every time we ran into girls on the trail the guards would giggle, point at the girls and then to us, and say, "Okay, okay," and use the graphic international sign-language for sex. We laughed. It was a hollow laugh. Sex had receded so quickly as a point of interest that I could hardly recall how it used to be.

We stopped to rest in a village. After several days Frenchy arrived. I was glad to see him. I told him I had not eaten for about ten days. "You must eat the rice," he said. I told him I couldn't. He went away. In an hour a guard brought me a warm canteen cup of chicken soup. Beak and claws were thrown in but I wasn't particular. I ate about two thirds of it and gave the rest to Pfister and Lewis. I was feeling better when Frenchy returned. We engaged him in a relaxed conversation, and at first opportunity began to question him about our prospects for an early release.

"If you have a good attitude maybe you can go home before the war's over," he said.

"How long?" I asked.

"If you are progressive, maybe two years."

"Two years! I can't wait two months. I can't live two weeks here."

"I don't know. Maybe one year."

"Shoot me! I can't survive in the jungle one year."

"Six months?"

The conversation ended on that note. Frenchy left. We began to talk.

"He said six months. Maybe we can make it that long."

"Yeah, they don't really hold POWs—they release them after a few weeks."

"Sure, we can last six months."

We actually thought Frenchy was bargaining with us.

Harker. On the seventh day Cannon collapsed by the trail. Bay told us to help him because we hadn't much farther to go. We were walking west on a fairly large dirt road which led into a valley. We entered a village and stopped at a hootch surrounded by a bamboo fence. Bay went inside. "I'll allow you to see the other Americans, but you cannot talk to them," he said when he returned.

"What?"

"They are very progressive," he said. "They cooperate. If you cooperate maybe you will be treated as them."

We turned a corner and saw three Americans lying in green hammocks slung in an open hootch without siding. Two white guys and a black. They looked clean and well fed. "Don't say anything to them," said Williams. "They're collaborators."

Anton. A guard told us, "Do not talk to the Americans." We thought he meant not to talk among ourselves. Suddenly round the corner came four men. They were haggard and muddy, hobbling on bare feet. One had graying hair and a scraggly white beard; he looked sixty years old. Another had a thick bushy beard. We thought they must have been captured for months. They walked silently by our hootch, glaring at us as they passed. We badgered the Vietnamese for permission to talk to them but were refused.

Frenchy came by at 11:00 the following morning and said an important officer of the Front had arrived to interrogate us. He advised me to answer all questions fully. I was taken to a hootch which had two sentries at the door. Inside three Vietnamese sat at a table. One of them had gray hair and looked distinguished. He was treated by the others with a respect that suggested high rank. He asked my name. I told him. He asked my unit. I told him. Then he asked what job I held. I shook my head, indicating I would not answer. He motioned a guard behind me. The guard slammed a rifle butt into my back. "You must answer the question," he said.

I made no reply. He took out his .45 and made a show of pulling back the slide to cock the weapon. He placed it on the table in front of him. "If you do not answer the question," he said, "I will shoot you. You may think about it."

The room was silent. All eyes were on me. I tried to read something in their faces. It was like looking a blank yellow wall. A minute passed. He repeated his question.

I answered everything he asked.

Harker. I was grilled once again for forty-five minutes. This time it was Bay, Stoneface, and a hard-looking North Vietnamese I'd never seen before. They began by asking questions about my family. Somewhere along the line they had gotten the impression that my family meant a great deal to me. Then they moved to military matters. I ducked and dodged and gave them little more than I had before. Afterward Bay brought a nurse to our hootch. "The nurse hates you very much," he said. "You have come to bomb her home. But she is a very good friend of mine and is doing me the favor of treating you."

She changed Williams' and Cannon's bandages. Cannon's back had turned into a big abscess. She mashed on it and started the pus running, then rammed a cotton-tipped hemostat under the skin to swab it out. Cannon barely flinched. She wore a surgical mask, but not from fear of infecting her patients. She couldn't stand the stench.

At 6:00 the next morning we started climbing the steep mountains facing us. Montagnards laden with food and military supplies were coming down as we were going up. Bamboo steps were niched into the mountainside and rest benches placed at intervals. The three Americans were behind us. "Phew, what's that evil smell," one of them asked. We explained that Cannon and Williams had maggot-filled wounds. The conversation continued, with an exchange of names and home towns, till a guard ordered us to shut up.

Anton. We were told before we left the village that our permanent prisoner-of-war camp was one day's march away. The Vietnamese described the camp with enthusiasm. All the World War

II movies I'd seen flashed through my mind. I knew just how it was going to be. A large compound surrounded by a high barbed-wire fence with uniformly spaced wood barracks inside. Watch towers. Guard posts. Searchlights.

4

Ike McMillan

Like I say, I'm the sort of dude who can feel when something is going to happen. On January 9 I had that feeling. Oh, man, did I have it. My R 'n' R was supposed to start the thirteenth. This wasn't a Friday, but that didn't matter. I respected the thirteenth whatever day of the week. In midafternoon we got word that Watkins and Daly's company was getting hit hard not far away in the valley. The battalion had lost radio contact with them.

Just as I thought! Something had to come up. With all the action I wouldn't be able to get out of the boonies. I went over and talked to the first sergeant about it. "Mac, I got a chopper coming in a few minutes to pick up a wounded man," he told me. "Put the guy on your back and take off. Watch it though. Charlie's got three machine guns round here."

I saw the helicopter circling lower and lower. I piggybacked the wounded man and got ready. As the chopper made to land in the open paddy—boop! boop! boop! Charlie shot him down. I took cover. A second escort ship swooped down to rescue the crew and took off. A couple of hours passed. At dusk the sergeant told me another chopper was going to try to land. I got ready again. I could see the helicopter on the horizon. I heard the faint whump-whump-whump of blades beating the air. Then I saw tracers streaking up at it. Five minutes later the sergeant said he had gotten a radio call that the chopper had been shot down and its crew killed.

"You gonna have to wait till tomorrow before you get off," he said.

"Top, I'm supposed to leave for Singapore in four days," I said. "I'll never make it."

"You'll make it," he said. "I'll send you to the fire support base in the morning with a note for the battalion sergeant major."

When I got to the fire support base the next day the sergeant major read the note and put me on the first chopper for Chu Lai. At Chu Lai I asked for a booking to Da Nang. The earliest flight I could find space on left the twelfth. Good enough. I went to rack out. I was tired. The past few days had been rough. Several times I had gone without food. We had run out of Cs and couldn't get a resupply in because of bad weather and enemy fire. For the first time I drank water out of the rice paddies without using purification tablets. I was surprised I'd not gotten diarrhea.

I found a bunk in a tent reserved for transients. It was late afternoon. Someone was playing a portable record player at max decibel next door. The bass beat the tent canvas like a sledge hammer. It took a few minutes before I could fall asleep. I woke up about midnight to go to the john. I could still hear the music. Same beat, same record. I thought, "Man, somebody's gotta be partying hard." I stuck my head in the tent. I saw twenty guys, all of them black. The tent was lit by one dim light bulb. It was a thing for the brothers to wear sunglasses in the Nam, you know, and everybody was sitting around in their shades. I put mine on and walked in. I spotted Coles, a dude from Cleveland who used to be in my company.

"What's happen'?"

"Don't know it, man," Coles said.

"How long you been at the rear?"

" 'Bout a month. Know the latest slap?"

"Oh, man, you know I been beating the boonies since November." He hit me on to the newest handshake the brothers had invented.

"You know the mint?" he asked.

"No, man, what's that?"

He brought out a small bottle of oil of wintergreen which the Vietnamese were always dabbing around their noses and foreheads to keep from getting airsick. Then he pulled out a bag of Js. "I haven't had anything to smoke since November," I said.

"Hey, Mac ain't had nothing to smoke since November!" he shouted. Everybody started pulling stuff out of their fatigue jacket pockets and offering it to me.

"Okay, you do like this," Coles said. "Put some mint in your palm and then rub the J with it up and down on both sides. When you hit the J deep, hard, and heavy, you can feel the menthol taste."

This was nice. We were sitting there getting our heads bad. A dude from Jersey started playing disc jockey, calling on certain guys to get up and dance by themselves to the records. "Break down and do the funky," he'd say. "Okay, now give me the boogaloo." The dancers shifted to the new dance. "Now take it back to the jerky." It was a stage show, a trip to the rest of us.

Guys started talking about their dreams of the world. Everybody spoke about what kind of wheels they wanted. Most wanted a pea-green Eldorado Cadillac with a black vinyl top. Coles said he had to have white on white with a black interior. Then separate conversations broke out. You got high and five minutes later you were rapping to a dude like he was your wife or girl friend. Just trying to get over, you know.

"Where you from, Mac?" Coles asked.

"Florida."

"Oh, yeah, that's right. Big place?"

"Naw. Gretna. We have a twenty-acre farm outside town, you know. My grandfather's a preacher."

My mother and father were never married—to each other, I mean. They later married someone else, and I have a lot of brothers and sisters on both sides. We lived with my grandparents; I knew them as mama and daddy. My real mother I called sister till I was of some size. I grew up with my uncles, two of them were about my age. We'd be playing marbles or something and

—boom!—we were in a fight. It was like that every day. I got by because I was my grandmother's pet, even among her own children. She had twelve of her own, counting my mother.

I had my ups and downs in school but I made it through in May, 1966. I had three choices as I saw it. Trade school, college, or the army. My grades weren't good enough for college and I didn't have the dough besides. Trade school meant I would probably go part-time and work on the farm the rest of the time. I was fed up with that.

So it looked like the army. I joined up in June, '66. They put me in mortars. At first I thought the army was the worst mistake I'd ever made. I didn't like it mainly because of the harassment. I understood the reason for the training techniques but I disagreed with them wholeheartedly. You never had time to do things on your own. At night you had to be in bed by a certain time, up in the morning at a certain time, and on the week end only got Sunday off.

I went to town as much as I could, which eventually caused me the only trouble I had during basic. It was with one of my drill instructors. A friend and I were sitting on the mess-hall steps one day talking about a girl we'd met in town. This sergeant walked by and asked who we were talking about. We told him. It seems she was his girl friend. I felt that if she had really loved the dude, she wouldn't have let us go as far as she did. Naturally he didn't see it that way. I had to sand the paint off the barracks when I didn't deserve to; and I got to know KP pretty well.

One day on the rifle range the sergeant called me up, pointed down range, and said, "Go bring me a leaf from that tree in the far corner."

I brought him a leaf.

He pulled a needle and thread from his top pocket. "Now go sew it back on."

When I returned I laughed at him.

"Give me fifty," he ordered. "And after this, mister, you better get down in the thinking position when you see me coming."

Pushups didn't bother me—I was in excellent shape. I did them and laughed again. This really got to him. He ranted and raved and accused me of having a bad attitude. "What's wrong with laughter?" I asked. "Am I supposed to have a low morale?"

My girl friend from home got pregnant when I entered basic training. She telephoned and asked what I was going to do about it. She expected me, I think, to get my hat and beat feet. I wasn't going to do that. I had intentions of marrying her. I'd known her since we were in the ninth grade together. I was deep in love. I just hadn't planned to get married as soon as I did.

I volunteered for jump school after mortar training. That came to a quick end. I hurt myself between the legs the first week. My left scrotum was out of place and the parachute harness almost tore it off as I went out the thirty-four-foot tower. I decided to quit. My wife was worried about me jumping from airplanes anyway.

The instructors said I could return the following week to pick up my training.

I said, "No, I want out."

They called me a quitter.

"If I don't want it," I said, "I don't want it. And you aren't gonna hurt my feelings by telling me all this." This is the way I was about anything. It didn't matter what they called me as long as they didn't hit me.

After that I pulled duty as a cook at Fort Benning. I started off as a KP pusher. Then I began to move up to the salads and finally worked my way up to second cook. I liked cooking in a way because it really wasn't that much to do. The menu book told you what to put in, how to cook it. The army spells things out.

I got my news about Viet Nam mostly from Walter Cronkite. Returning veterans I talked to had two stories. One said, "The Nam is a party, you know."

The other: "Oh, man, the Nam is the land God forgot."

A shell-shocked sergeant told me, "Young Blood," that's what they called me cause of my boyish looks, "you won't be coming back." I didn't know what to make of it. But I knew my time was coming. I got a temporary deferment because my wife was expecting. She had the kid in January. I went on levy in May, came home on leave in June, and reported to Viet Nam in July.

As the plane for California made a last circle, I looked down and saw my wife holding the kid, standing with my grandparents. It was a heartbreaking, tear-jerking thing. It grabbed me heavy, it really did. I reached over my head and got a pillow and cried into it for a while till this little boy tapped me on the shoulder. He had never had a chance to meet a real soldier, he said, and he wanted to talk to me. My homesickness faded till I got to Oakland.

At Oakland I was playing poker with some sergeants, waiting for my plane, when this dude from New York comes up.

"Hey, man, I got a letter from home," he says. "You guys wanna help me read it?"

I said, "How long you been here, man?"

"Got here yesterday."

"And you already got a letter from home?" I didn't believe him.

"Yeah. Wanna help me read it?"

"That's weird," I thought. I didn't want to read his mail. I was puzzled. I left the game after a few minutes and went over to where the dude was. Eight guys were sitting around. I discovered what he was talking about. Everybody was smoking marijuana. They sat there rapping, everybody talking about two different things at once. I was on the outside, you might say, trying to get in. I had always hung around with liquor and had never tried grass. I decided the stuff must be really good.

The dude said, "Come on, man, we'll break you in now before you get to Nam."

"No, I'm not ready for it," I said, and returned to the poker game.

We got to Bien Hoa early in the morning. I thought Viet Nam was the nastiest, filthiest place I'd ever seen. The monsoon season was in full swing. Water was seeping into the hootches the Vietnamese called homes. Molly-faced little kids were running around bare-assed. On the bus ride to the replacement center we passed a lady walking beside the road. Suddenly she squatted down, pulled up her pants leg, and did what she had to do right there. I said, "God Almighty!" Farther down the road we saw another lady taking a bath in a muddy hole of water. I couldn't believe it.

The mess hall at the replacement center was dirty. The mess sergeant was drunk half the time. He couldn't keep his hands off the giggling Vietnamese girls who worked the serving line. I went to the snack bar but even that wasn't much. They had this real thick type of bread—somebody said it was French bread—that crumbled when you tried to make a sandwich. I waited till I got to Chu Lai before I started eating.

After I got to Chu Lai and finished booby-trap school I was assigned to my battalion. At battalion they gave me my company assignment. A jeep was to take me to my company area that afternoon. I was in the battalion mess hall when some veterans started talking to me.

"Hey, man. You in Bravo Company?"

"Yeah."

"Oh, man! You might get killed before you even to get to your area."

"What's going on here?"

"Charlie's always putting mines on the road, man. Probably got some sitting out there now. Waiting for you new guys to come in."

That scared me. It stayed with me on the jeep ride to company headquarters. As we pulled up I saw an artillery battery of 105s. The familiar sight brought a little cheer. I had thought I might be going straight to a line platoon in the bush. But the company was settled into a compound.

The first sergeant assigned me to the weapons platoon. It was so understrength that it was more like a reinforced squad. It consisted of three mortars, a big 50 caliber machine gun, and seventeen men. We were without an officer. Sergeant Smith, the platoon sergeant, was our leader. Several of us replacements checked in with him. "I don't want to talk to any of you individually right now," he said. "Tomorrow we go on S 'n' D. We'll talk when we get back."

This I couldn't understand. I had been through small-unit training in the States. I knew the weapons platoon didn't have any business going on search-and-destroy missions. They were supposed to stay behind to fire support for the rifle platoons.

Next morning we loaded up with all the ammo we could carry and moved out. I was sort of shaken. I didn't know what we were going to get into. We walked all morning. It seemed we were going round in circles. We finally entered an old ville. Suddenly Sergeant Smith shouted, "Get down! Get down!" Everybody fell over each other taking cover. We thought someone was firing on us. I could almost imagine I heard the bullets overhead.

Sergeant Smith got on the radio and called Top. He told him everything was okay and he was bringing us back in. That's when I realized we were on one of those play-play things.

When we returned the veterans yelled at us, "How'd you like your day playing soldiers?"

I said, "We ain't got no business doing that in the Nam." The guys agreed.

"Smitty does that to everybody," someone said. "He's Top's right-hand man. He got short and Top put him in a good position as weapons-platoon commander."

"Good thing I wasn't here sooner," a new guy said. "People get blowed away for pulling tricks like that."

The machine gun was mounted over the gun shed and bunkered with sandbags. It offered a view of the whole area. The following afternoon I was manning the weapon when I heard an explosion. I could see dust and smoke rising on the road leading from battalion headquarters. Charles had laid a command-detonated mine and blown up a truck filled with artillery ammunition. Sergeant Smith ran from his tent and yelled, "Everybody mount up!"

The truck driver reached the company area by foot before we got out the gate. He was shaking uncontrollably. The GIs with him had been killed. As he jumped from the truck he saw the VC who had set off the mine in a hole beside the road. He emptied an M-16 magazine into him. When we arrived the Vietnamese was trying to talk. Maybe he was asking for water. His chest was held together by a few strands of skin. Somebody finished him off.

I saw a blood trail. I followed it and yelled for the rest of the men. Sergeant Smith came over, looked, and told me it was betel-nut juice. He ordered me to guard the area. Everybody else moved out to look for Mr. Charles. I was left holding my weapon on a dead man. Sly Charles had escaped, that was apparent. The men returned. Sergeant Smith said that since the company had been there, Charles had laid two big mines on the road each day. Usually a truck was hit; 50 per cent of the time someone was killed. I decided to take as few trips as necessary.

A white guy in the platoon called me a few nights later. He was a Virginian named Strong. We were to become close buddies. "Hey, Mac," he said. "Come join us. We're gonna show you how to get over in the Nam."

"What do you mean?"

"There's not but one thing to do. That's survive."

Strong and a guy named Calloway led me to a bunker. "We're gonna smoke here," Strong said.

"Jesus, an ammo bunker!" It was filled with explosive mortar shells.

"Yeah, pretty good, huh? Who would think to look for us here?" He pulled out a joint of marijuana and lit it. "You know how to smoke a cigarette?"

"Yeah."

"Okay. Take a draw off this toke. Inhale deep as you can and hold it."

I took a deep draw and started coughing. The smoke felt like sandpaper on my throat.

"It's good! It's good!" Calloway said. "Once you learn to smoke it's good."

I caught on quick. I was hitting it hard. One of them said, "Hey, man, you sure you ain't smoked this stuff before."

"Naw, I ain't. This is my first." We continued to smoke. I was getting good and mellow. "What are we supposed to do during the day?" I asked.

"Mac, you're in the weapons platoon," Strong said. "You ain't got no bush to beat. You might have KP now and then. You fire H-and-I at night and pull guard on the bunker. Most likely you'll be off twice a week——"

"But what do we do during the day?"

"Sit around. One man from each squad has to be on the mortar at all times in case of a fire mission. Another man has to be in the fire-direction center to compute whatever fire mission might come up. Rest of the time you're in the platoon area writing letters, listening to the armed forces radio station, playing records on the portable, or doing what you want to do."

"That's the size of it, huh?"

"Yeah. We got the best fuckin' platoon on the hill. Don't nobody like us cause they say we ain't got enough to do. Mostly we blow grass all day. And if we're off, at night too. But if we have something to do, we don't touch it."

"That's definitely nice." During the day we'd go to the 50-cal bunker and put a Marvin Gaye album on the record player and get really nice. It wasn't long till I got into my first big poker game. Boom! Dropped my whole paycheck. Guys in the Nam, I discovered, played poker like money didn't mean anything.

Strong came by and said, "Hey, man, we got to fire H-and-I tonight."

"What time we go on?" I said.

"We've got the four-to-six shift."

"Good. I'll be sobered up by then."

It started to rain. We had smoked through the afternoon. Smoking made us hungry, we called it the "hungry Js." We opened a case of C rations and chowed down. Strong suggested we go out to the mortar pits and check the guns to see what we had to fire that night. Battalion sent down a daily sheet that told us the range, direction, and amount of ammo we were to expend on H-and-I. The mortar looked like a piece of lead pipe elevated by two legs and positioned on a metal base plate. Strong and I broke out the ammo, set the proper charges, and left the rounds under a poncho. We went to a bunker and tried to get some sleep.

Shortly before four o'clock Strong woke me and asked if I would be able to fire. I felt fine.

"You think you can handle another J?" he said.

"Why not?" I said.

He threw me a bag. We got high all over again.

Then we went out to the guns. The rain had eased off. According to the H-and-I sheet, we were to fire four rounds every ten minutes. This was supposed to be enough to keep the VC off balance in case they were trying to infiltrate our area. Instead, we decided to fire ten rounds every four minutes. Our radio was in the ammo bunker. The all-night rock music of AFRN blasted out at us. We fired and fired. It was a trip for us, you know. We were having such a good time that we didn't even bother to reset the base plate. It sunk deeper and deeper in the mud from the recoil as Strong poured in the rounds.

Next morning the new platoon sergeant came by. He was madder than hell. He asked us what we had done.

We said, "Nothing, just fired our mission like we were supposed to."

He said, "Go take a look at the mortar base plate." It was buried three feet in the mud. I mean *buried.* We had to borrow the company commander's jeep to pull it out. We were told we wouldn't be allowed to fire H-and-I again. Lucky for us there were no radio calls saying a patrol or a night ambush or a ville had been hit by our stray rounds. As punishment we were ordered to pull guard duty in the 50-cal bunker. That was like throwing the rabbit in a briar patch.

We had a Vietnamese kid of about thirteen who hung around the compound. When he tried to say "pot" it came out "Phat." So that's what we called him. I told him before we left for observation-post duty, "Hey, Phat, when the man brings us our hot chow at noon every day, you come with him and bring us some hot smokes."

He said, "Okay, Little Mac." They called me Little Mac because McIntosh was in my squad, and he was Big Mac. I mean, he was big. As wide as a super TV set and about six four. He had a good nine inches on me. The marijuana came ten tailor-made joints to a small plastic bag. If the Vietnamese merchants found you were new in-country they jacked up the price. I was only paying ten cents a stick, getting over like a rat in a cheese.

From time to time I gave Phat fifteen or twenty bucks in military script to change for me into Vietnamese piastres. The legal exchange rate was 118 to a dollar. Phat changed the money at a higher rate on the black market, gave me 118 p, and kept the rest for himself. For this he brought me extra hot smokes.

Once in a while he would say, "Little Mac, I souvenir you beaucoup hot smokes. You never souvenir me."

I'd say, "Yeah, you right man," and give him a ten-dollar bill.

"Oh, number one, number one." Little Phat was shrewd.

Shortly before a friend's tour was up, I spoke to Phat about a going-away gift for him. I said, "Look, my boy is getting ready to go back to the world. He wants to take some hot smokes back."

Phat said, "No, he take hot smokes back he go to jail. Maybe he go back to world you send him hot smokes at post office."

"Don't worry. Just give me some fuckin' hot smokes, man."

"How much?"

"Twenty bags."

"Beaucoup! Beaucoup! Cannot souvenir you twenty bags."

"I'll tell you what I'll do. I'll pay for fifteen and you souvenir me five."

"Okay, okay, deal."

I wound up, though, paying for the whole twenty bags. I knew I had beaucoup time to spend in the Nam and I needed Phat to help me get over. I didn't want to lose his good will. My friend taped some of the bags around his legs and put the rest of the Js in his pocket linings. I said, "Best of luck. If you get caught, that's you." When he got back to the world he wrote me that he had no problem with customs.

I knew a lot of guys were getting on hard stuff. Heroin was

coming up; there was always morphine around, you could get it from the medics. I couldn't dig on that, you know, because if you're hooked you're hooked. I knew I could get away from marijuana. I never even thought about the hard stuff. And even if I had I couldn't take the needle—I was scared of shots.

I smoked with most of the guys in the company. Soon everybody was calling me "Chief of Smoke." When we were on S 'n' D nobody messed with grass. We were business then. Of course, if you bedded down for the night and knew you were going to be there two or three days, that might be a different story. Boom! There was a smoke cloud rising over the company perimeter. But if we knew we were moving out next morning into Charlieland, nobody touched it.

After Strong got hit I practically gave up smoking. This was back in November during an operation in Happy Valley. The first sergeant ordered the weapons platoon to pull rear-guard security behind some armored personnel carriers.

We were on our knees covering the rear when the VC fired a recoilless rifle at a carrier. The round had too much elevation. It went over the carrier and hit in the middle of us. I was on the far end. I blacked out when the shell exploded. When I came to I felt myself all over. I looked around. Everybody was wounded except me and the first sergeant.

Strong was hit from the back. His chest was blown away. "Strong is dead," I said. "Strong is dead." I don't think I really believed it, though, till three days later. I thought about his wife. He had been married shortly before he came to the Nam.

I remembered he always carried a lot of money on him. His wife would probably never see it. This happened a lot in the Nam. A guy got knocked off and the first thing another GI hit was his wallet. Their attitude was, "This guy doesn't feel pain, doesn't know sorrow, and someone has to spend his money."

I started to tell the first sergeant about the money but I said, "No, it ain't time for nothing like that." I just watched as they carried him away.

The most seriously wounded already had been evacuated when

McIntosh came up holding his face. I knew he wasn't hit that bad, but Big Mac wanted to get out of the boonies. I couldn't blame him. That's the time, man, if you've got a little scratch and you know the shit is hot, get out, man, get out! So Mac said, "Top, I'm hit," and the first sergeant sent him back to be evacuated.

That left Calloway and me. He was wounded too, bleeding in the face from a piece of shrapnel. I called him over. I said, "Do me a favor, do yourself a favor, tell Top you are wounded and ask to be evacuated. Then it will be only me left in the weapons platoon. They're not gonna leave me out in the field to fire the mortars by myself. They'll have to evacuate me too."

"No, I can't do that," he said. "I just got a scratch."

"Look, man, they don't need us. When we get in fire fights, what happens? They call in artillery and air strikes, right? But if you stay here, Calloway, Top is gonna take a man from each line platoon and assign them to carry these mortars. Then they're gonna look to me and you to fire support if it's ever necessary."

He didn't seem to be listening. I wondered how I could make him understand. "Look, you've got five months left in Viet Nam. Your tour in the army is finished at the same time. That means you've got five months left in the war, period. You'll never have to come back here. You've beat the bush since you arrived and you'll beat it till you leave. Why risk your life when you've got a chance to get out?

"No, I can take it."

You see, Calloway was in line for promotion to buck sergeant. I could understand his point. But a promotion wasn't worth anybody's life. Just as I'd predicted, Top reassigned the company commander's driver and another guy to the weapons platoon. And—boom!—here we were still stuck with the mortars. Soon more replacements joined us. Davis was among them.

Tom Davis

At Chu Lai I was put on a chopper and sent to Bravo Company. When I jumped out of the helicopter I hit the ground with my weapon at the ready. I didn't know whether we were under fire or not; I wasn't taking any chances. The company was sitting in the elephant grass under lean-tos made from gray ponchos pulled together. At first nobody seemed to notice me. I was still sprawled flat waiting for the enemy when I saw some guys get up, stretch, and scratch. The first sergeant came over and took me to my squad.

Six of us were in the weapons platoon. The line platoons went out on search-and-destroy operations while we sat around guarding the company command post. That changed, however, when we got a new company commander. The new CO was twenty-three, fresh out of OCS, and very gungy—an airborne-ranger type. Nobody seemed to like the way he ran things. I think it had a lot to do with his being so young. He knew his job. It was just that he replaced a company commander whom we all respected and knew to be a cool head.

McMillan. The new company commander started changing things around. First day he arrived word was passed that he had gone out on S 'n' D with a rifle platoon.

We asked Top, "Did the Old Man go out?"

"Yep, sure did."

"Oh, my God!" Everybody caught the ass then, because we knew the weapons platoon would be next.

Sure enough, that evening he called the weapons platoon sergeant and me to a poop session. "From now on," he said, "you will send a sixty-milimeter mortar with a line platoon on S 'n' D."

Next morning we saddled up and moved out. Davis, the new man, was my assistant gunner. We hadn't gone too far when a grunt saw two armed VC running along a paddy dike.

The platoon sergeant yelled to me, "Chief of Smoke, set up

your mortar! That hootch by the coconut palm!" He pointed to a house where the VC had taken cover.

I said, "Give me three rounds to get it." That was normal, to take at least three rounds to adjust your fire.

I aimed the mortar and fired the first one. Boom! The top of the house blew off. Guys went running in three different directions. The line platoon got one VC. We dropped some mortar rounds on another. Judging from the powder burns on his body, we hit him dead center.

When we got back to the company the captain called us up and said, "Good job, weapons platoon."

I said, "Yessir." Secretly I was hoping we wouldn't have to go out again.

Davis. He had a big hole in his chest. He was still jerking—no, quivering—as if someone was jabbing him with needles. A GI pulled his clothes off. I could never understand that. Why bother a dead man? I'd seen others killed, but this was the first I'd helped to kill. I didn't like the feeling. When I went to sleep I saw him in my mind.

It soon wore off. I became harder and harder to the killing. You can't let things like that bother you in a war. You just have to hope it won't be you lying in the mud.

Most villagers seemed friendly. I later found they were simply trying to play the middle against both sides to stay alive. I had sympathy for them. But I had a lot to learn. I saw a little boy begging and gave him my last can of Cs. Right after that we went up in the mountains for three days and I almost starved. Some of the GIs, I thought, were too hostile. Some of them hated the Vietnamese with intense passion. And they'd never seen the people before or known anything about them till they arrived in Viet Nam. We didn't have many like this in our company but a few were bad about yelling and screaming and pushing the Vietnamese away. Sometimes they even pulled weapons on civilians to scare them. I can't explain it.

McMillan. The soldiers' reaction to the villagers depended on each individual and what he thought of the Vietnamese. If the

Vietnamese put on a pretty good show when we came into a ville, nothing was likely to happen. But if they acted hostile the GIs looked at them as VC sympathizers. One time we asked this guy of about thirty-five for an I.D. card. He said he didn't have one. He started rapping about how he took care of his kids and didn't fight. Some of the GIs got pissed and knocked his teeth out, then took him in for interrogation as a VC suspect.

On another occasion we had received sniper fire from a ville about the time we saw an old man running across the paddies. The line grunts hollered, *"Dung lai! Dung lai!"* He didn't stop. A grenade launcher went boom! and blowed both his legs off. I couldn't have any sympathy for the old man. He heard them say *"Dung lai."* How were we supposed to know where he was going? Of course, there were bound to be mistakes if you had a system like ours, where a VC killed won you a pass to a rear-area rest.

We had a brigade saying that "A body a day will get you three." Meaning three days off.

Davis. On Christmas Eve helicopters circled overhead with red, green, and yellow flares attached to skids and tails in colorful designs. Next morning a headquarters sergeant choppered out dressed as Santa Claus. The chaplain was with him. I attended the brief services. I received a small package from home. Everybody got a hot meal of turkey. Christmas night we watched as B-52s lit up a mountain not far away.

5

Frank Anton

We came down a steep mountain, holding on to bushes to keep
our balance, and then headed up a heavily wooded hillside. I
heard a dog barking in the distance and the faint sound of voices.
As we moved closer I saw the outline of several hootches through
the trees.

"We rest here, huh?" I said to the guards. They smiled.

A man came down from the area of the hootches. He was short
and looked stocky for a Vietnamese. His black hair was parted
poorly to the left side and he continually brushed it from his face.
He had buck teeth and penetrating dark eyes, a high forehead,
a mouth frozen into a smirk.

"You are now in a prisoner of war camp," he said.

"You've got to be kidding," I mumbled to myself.

"You! You stand at attention! I did not give you permission to
speak."

We shuffled our feet and he became angrier.

"You will be allowed to meet the other prisoners. But if you
do not obey the rules you will be punished severely."

Harker. His name was Huong, though the best we could ever
manage was Mr. Hom. He was about twenty-three or maybe
older, it was difficult to tell with the Vietnamese. He ordered

Williams to drop his walking stick and stand at attention.

Then the camp commander arrived. He was an older man, gray-haired, soft-spoken, and carried himself in a dignified manner. He spoke only one or two words of English. Mr. Hom acted as his translator. At the end of his welcoming speech he said, "Tomorrow we have a celebration. Two men will be released from this camp. If you show progress maybe in some months you too will be released."

I looked at them blankly. I was still unable to believe I was a prisoner of war. Now he was speaking about a celebration and a release. My mind refused to comprehend. A guard escorted me to the compound, which was surrounded by a crude bamboo fence. As I entered I saw a man—was he American?—looking at us curiously. He was several inches over six feet, had an unkempt Poncho Villa mustache, and his body was covered with a red scaly skin disease. Russell Grissett.

Anton. As we walked up Russ Grissett turned to the hootch and said, "Bob, we've got company."

The thing that struck me about Grissett was his large flattened out feet. They were the feet of a man who never wore shoes or sandals. He had on a pair of black pajamas rolled to the knees and was bare-chested. His hair, which was rather long on top and closely cut on the sides Vietnamese fashion, was a dirty straw color. I had not got over the shock of seeing Grissett's poor condition when Bob Sherman walked out of the hootch. He was small and completely mousy looking except for his eyes, which had the glint of a cornered cat. Grissett introduced himself and told us he had been a prisoner for two years, Sherman for several months. Both were marines.

All of us were in shock and didn't know what to say. I looked around for other prisoners. Grissett said there were only four total, plus the two Puerto Ricans scheduled to be released the next day.

Strictland. Russ Grissett had lost a lot of weight, down from a hundred ninety pounds to one twenty-five, but you could see he was still plenty tough.

Harker. Grissett was excited, practically dancing around. He kept saying, "We're going to have a lot of rice tonight! Maybe they'll kill a pig tomorrow!" He sounded as though he was celebrating his own release.

He told me two other prisoners were washing up at the water hole. I walked down to see them. On the path I met Capt. Floyd Harold Kushner. Kushner was a doctor in the army medical corps. He had been a flight surgeon with the First Cav till his helicopter crashed into a mountain in late November. He had broken a tooth and had a shoulder wound which he thought came from exploding ammo as the chopper burned. He was the only one to escape from the crash. After wandering around for several days he was picked up by the VC. I had always thought of doctors as being older, at least in their mid-thirties, but Kushner looked young, and I discovered he was twenty-six. He had recently served as an intern at Tripler Army Hospital in Honolulu. He was a friendly and voluble small-built guy. He'd attended the Medical College of Virginia; I'd dropped out of Virginia Tech, where I was majoring in accounting. He was from Danville and I from Lynchburg. We were practically kin. Kushner looked at the bayonet wound in my side and said it appeared to be healing nicely.

I continued on to the water hole, which was formed from a stagnant spur of a creek, and saw a stocky, well-muscled man with reddish-blond hair busily washing clothes. He looked like a sunbronzed surfer. He introduced himself as Earl Weatherman, pointed to the sharp punji stakes lining both sides of the path, and warned me to be careful. Then he said, "Don't believe everything you hear about me." He grinned and walked off.

Anton. Grissett said the two Puerto Ricans would be released the next day but the camp authorities had not announced the exact timing. I asked how he knew. He said, "Because yesterday Mr. Hom came down and told them to move up to the Vietnamese compound. They're living there as guests of the Vietnamese. That's how they always do it."

"You mean they've released others?" we asked.

"They freed fifteen ARVN prisoners not long ago."

Kushner walked up. He was in much better shape than Grissett and Sherman, though his soft features were beginning to run hollow. He called me aside and said, "I must tell you something about Grissett." He related how on the second day after he arrived Grissett had gone to the Vietnamese and told them Kushner planned to escape. It was a convoluted and completely false story that had endangered Kushner's life. He still seethed with anger.

That evening Sherman and Grissett prepared our food. As night fell we went inside the hootch. Everyone was too excited to sleep. We were swapping life stories when Grissett interrupted. "Listen, I've been here two years," he said. "I know how things are. You'll learn. I don't want any of you to say anything in front of me I can use against you. Because I will. I'll tell the Vietnamese anything you say. So if you want to try to escape, don't let me know. Understand?"

No one spoke. He said it with such seriousness that we had to believe him.

Strictland. From the first we were a little scared of Grissett. The man was capable of anything.

Harker. Next morning we were taken to a small classroom farther up the hill. It was a three-sided hootch and resembled the crude split-log classrooms of frontier America. Only instead of log benches ours were of split bamboo without backing. A scratchy wood table was at the front. A banner on the wall made of red and white polka-dot *ao dai* dress material read: "Welcome to Lenient and Humane Policy Towards Criminals of War."

Being Americans we naturally rushed to get a seat on the back benches. The camp commander, whom Grissett had named Slime, sat at the table along with several other officials. All looked solemn. Mr. Hom acted as translator. He made a speech about the Puerto Ricans, said they were going home after more than a year's captivity because they were "progressive." "If you study hard and be progressive maybe you will go home in the near future. The Front did not kill you. The Front takes very good care of you. The Vietnamese will surely win, the Americans will surely lose."

The Puerto Ricans rose and read thank-you speeches for the

"lenient and humane" treatment shown them by the National Liberation Front. I was startled to hear them condemn the U.S. as imperialist aggressors. Would American soldiers use such words? The jargon rang strange on our ears. Grissett got up and gave a little pep talk on how we had to be progressive, keep neat, and work hard. He concluded by saying the Front had done a lot for us, we should be appreciative. So obvious it was how desperately he wanted to go home that I was overcome by a feeling of despair for us all.

Anton. Early that morning we heard the Vietnamese killing a pig. A pig's death squeal later would send our blood pressures soaring and we would shout and yell with the excitement of a child's best Christmas. But it meant little to us then. Before we went to eat Grissett gave us instructions. He was the coach, we were the rookies. "Get the lean meat first," he said. "Then the blood. And the fat last." He savored each word.

"Fat!" we said. "You can have the fat and blood, Russ."

"Yeah, they all say that. But later you'll eat it because you'll consider yourself lucky to get it."

Two crude tables sat in the open. The dirt around them had been swept clean with split bamboo brooms. The two Puerto Ricans and the Vietnamese camp officials took seats at one table, we were at the other with a few guards. Three plates of pig fat, three plates of blood, and one of relatively lean meat were placed on our table with bowls of rice and a leafy green vegetable that tasted like a jungle weed. The blood was coagulated and cut into slices, looked somewhat like liver. The meat was thumb-sized chunks of boiled pork. I picked over the meal. I had not yet begun to eat rice. Moreover, we new prisoners were hampered by our awkwardness with chop sticks. While we fumbled Grissett and Sherman ate. They were all arms, reaching from one end of the table to the other. The common Vietnamese ate by holding the small rice bowl to their lips and shoveling in the food with rapid motions of the chop sticks. Grissett had adopted and improved upon the technique. He seemed to inhale his food.

Harker. The release ceremony was a neat gimmick. All of us began to reflect privately and wonder what being "progressive" meant. The Puerto Ricans came to say farewell before they began their walk back to freedom. We found a piece of paper and wrote down our names and service numbers. Kushner palmed the paper and passed it to one of them as they shook hands, managing to convey in Spanish the request that they get the names out so our families would know we were alive. My parents were notified by the Pentagon four months later that I was being held. I don't know what caused the delay; it had taken ten days to get word to them that I was missing in action after my capture.

We waved good-by as they headed down the trail. Shortly afterward the Vietnamese ordered Grissett and Lewis to begin moving our cooking utensils to a new camp. Several medics arrived to work on Williams' and Cannon's wounds. Kushner was not recognized as a doctor by the Viet Cong. They were very emphatic about this. He was forced to sit by helplessly while the Vietnamese worked with clumsy and unskilled hands on the injured and sick. Williams' wound had turned black. The medic said a doctor would have to amputate his arm. Kushner thought they wouldn't try this because they lacked proper anesthesia. We washed their smelly bandages and hung them out to dry.

Grissett and Lewis returned in the afternoon and said the guards were still building the new camp. They estimated it would take us six hours walking time to get there. We tried to get some sleep. At first light the Vietnamese woke us and gave us woven bamboo baskets filled with camp supplies to carry. We left at 7:00. The sun had poked through the clouds and was beginning to burn hot. We walked across several wooded hills. Now and then we passed through a primitive and impoverished montagnard village, where we would wait till the slow ones caught up. Then we followed a rocky creek bed for two hundred meters. The faster prisoners moved ahead with the guards, the stragglers traced our water steps in the shallow creek. There was no fear of anyone trying to escape in that wilderness.

As we pressed up the mountainside I caught sight of a hootch. It sat on the creek bank, which rose to a height of about twenty feet. Steps were cut into the bank. We made our way up and turned to the left. The compound was surrounded by a bamboo fence. The enclosure was surprisingly small, about thirty meters long and ten or fifteen meters wide. It was in the midst of a scraggly stand of bamboo. Many of the trees drooped naturally. Others had been pulled over and tied to break the hootch's outline and thus conceal it from planes flying overhead. The creek bank itself served as a secondary security for the rear of the compound. The lower portions of the bank were lined with poisonous punji stakes. Anyone trying to escape by jumping over the rear fence would be impaled.

Our hootch door obliquely faced the compound gate, which was controlled by a guard shack. The gate in turn pointed up the slope to where the Vietnamese had constructed their own several sleeping hootches, a kitchen, and a supply hut. They were about fifty meters away but with a commanding view of our compound.

The surrounding area was impenetrable forest and jungle—ferns, vines, bamboo thickets, wild banana trees, hardwoods, and other tropical exotica. The jungle floor was covered with thick brush and rising ferns. Above that grew broadleaf trees of middling height, and above that giant hardwoods rose a hundred feet or more and spread their branches to interlock. The effect was that of a triple canopy which closed out the bright tropic sun and left a damp twilight of perpetual gloom.

Our home was the grass hootch. A platform made from split bamboo ran the length of the hootch on one side. The platform was six feet wide and stood three feet off the ground. This was our communal bed. Between the platform and the outer wall was a walking space three feet wide. At the end of the walkway was a dirt hole braced with several rocks: our kitchen. A small hole dug in the ground at the farther end of the compound was our latrine, and dried banana leaves were our paper.

There were ten of us. Already we were somewhat cramped at night. Soon there would be eighteen prisoners sleeping on that hard bed, and it would be impossible to move or turn over without hitting the person on either side. The only possible advantage of such an arrangement was that we could use our huddled body warmth to get comfortable enough to fall asleep. It was cold in the mountains at night, especially during the rainy season. We had one blanket per person, if you could call it that—a burlap bag, split and sewn together, the kind of bag in which the U.S. Agency for International Development shipped free rice and bulgar wheat to Viet Nam. On its side was the two-clasped-hands insignia of international friendship.

Anton. On the walk to the new camp we heard Grissett's and Sherman's stories. Grissett belonged to the marines' elite reconnaissance battalion. A marine officer had disappeared during a large ground operation in early '66. Grissett's patrol was sent out the next morning to look for him. The patrol was ambushed. During the fire fight Grissett was separated from the group. He was trying to rejoin when he saw a helicopter picking up the survivors. The helicopter lifted off and flew over his head at a low altitude. Grissett waved and screamed but the chopper kept going.

He had a map. He stopped to orient himself to the terrain. He realized he was several days' march from a U.S. Special Forces camp. He set out along a river that would lead him there. After a few miles he stopped to eat. A montagnard kid armed with an old French rifle approached from behind. Grissett jumped up and grabbed the rifle and told him to go away. It was a terrible mistake, he said; he should have killed the kid. The boy returned with a squad of VC soldiers.

Grissett was bitter about the helicopter pilot who, he was certain, had intentionally left him behind in the jungle. I considered it extremely unlikely and told him so. As a pilot I knew how difficult it was to see well under such circumstances. Grissett at the time wore camouflaged jungle fatigues that blended in with the foliage around him. My defense of the pilot—and perhaps being one myself—didn't help our relationship. I'd already sensed a kernal of antagonism when he found I was a few months younger and yet outranked him. The last straw, as he saw it, was when I began to give the food I wasn't eating to Sherman. My attitude was that I should be able to give my food to whomever I wanted. I hadn't yet realized that to prisoners on the edge of starvation the question of who got extra food was no small matter.

Harker. Grissett had slapped Sherman around a bit before we arrived. Grissett made light of this and blamed it on Sherman's laziness. Grissett was a Texan. His parents were divorced. He told us he had smacked his high-school teacher, and later had been taken to court because of some subsequent violation. The judge ordered him to get a job. Grissett joined the Marine Corps. I'm sure he'd been an excellent marine; he was a hard worker, but he had something of the bully about him.

The Puerto Ricans told us before they left that one incident between Sherman and Grissett had occurred at the fireplace. The quicker a fire was made the less smoke it created. On clear days smoked drifted up through the camouflage. It might attract the attention of spotter planes, which likely would bring bombs down on us. The guards got upset about a poorly made fire. Sherman was on his knees blowing to make the flames catch up when Grissett grabbed him by the neck and pushed his face down, roaring, "This is how to do it, Sherman! Stick your face in it!" The Puerto Ricans had to pull him off.

The matter wasn't entirely clear-cut. Sherman did seem uninclined to work and we were to discover in later months what that meant. But something about his case aroused our sympathy. He was on his second tour when he was captured. On his first trip over he had served with an infantry line platoon till he was transferred to duty at the Da Nang morgue, where he became, in his words, "a body stuffer." One day his old line platoon got into some heavy action. Bodies were brought to the morgue for processing. As he unzipped the rubber bags one by one he recognized the shot-up remains of his closest buddies. He went berserk, got into a fist fight with his sergeant, and had to be restrained.

He was sent back to the States for psychiatric treatment. The

Marine Corps was small, its strength overtaxed by the war. Every available man was sent to Viet Nam, and somehow Sherman was shipped back and placed in a line unit. One Sunday afternoon he was pulling guard duty at a marine compound. He admitted he had been drinking, which of course was against regulations. A sexy Vietnamese girl walked by and suggested he join her for a surprise in a house up the road. He left his post and followed. As he walked in the door he was greeted by a Viet Cong.

Sherman told his story quietly. He sensed he should've never been returned to Viet Nam. He had read the medical reports placed in his file. Dr. Kushner asked him to try to recall what the reports said. Sherman could remember one word. "Schizophrenic."

Anton. The Vietnamese seemed to be divided into two groups. The first consisted of the camp personnel. The camp was run by a three-man board of directors ("deretters" the Vietnamese pronounced it). Slime was board chairman and thus camp commander. He was a native South Vietnamese, as was a second member whom we named Jolly because he was usually just that. He was the carpenter and chief handy man and scout for new camp locations. The third, who would join us shortly, was a North Vietnamese. We thought he deserved his nickname of Ratface.

The camp personnel also included two cooks, an old mama-san and a younger woman we called Hannah, who was ugly as sin and at least half as smelly. A still younger girl served as our medic. Despite her lack of medical knowledge, some prisoners thought she grew more attractive as time passed. Our main contact was to be with Mr. Hom. It wasn't clear what his rank was beyond that of interpreter. We suspected he had none. But because he was the only one who could communicate with us he assumed a power much greater than that of mere translator. He was for all intents and purposes our camp commander. And he took great pleasure in reminding us of this.

The guards made up the second group. Usually eight to sixteen were around at any given time, and frequently the number was larger. When we first arrived they were armed with an assortment of old Chinese burp guns and carbines. Later they received new AK assault rifles. Although we had no way of knowing, the guards probably belonged to a security company that reported directly to COSVN, the ultimate headquarters for VC and NVA operations in South Viet Nam. This was the usual VC practice. COSVN had a special detachment of soldiers who acted as bodyguards for high officials, secured base areas, and guarded POW camps.

Thus the upward chain of command for the two groups probably was different, with the camp personnel coming under the control of COSVN's political section perhaps through a subregion or provincial setup, and the guards falling under COSVN's security section. The difference between the two groups was to become apparent later. But for the moment they appeared to our eyes as a single unit. Discipline seemed to be maintained through frequent criticism sessions. They would assemble in a circle at night and go to it. Sometimes we could hear them singing. We picked up rumors that the women were the most active participants in the criticism meetings.

A montagnard village was about a quarter of a mile from the camp. Several houses were even closer but out of sight. The relationship between the Viet Cong and the mountain tribesmen was one of friendly liaison. The "yards" were farmers trying to stay alive. The Saigon government had never done anything for them. They associated Americans with bombing and crop defoliation. Their manioc crops were our second most important source of food, paid for by the Viet Cong with barter materials, usually salt. Once the VC traded them a transistor radio and the village chief returned it a few days later, complaining that the "man in the box had died." The Viet Cong normally invited several tribal elders to eat with us on any special occasion.

Our primary food was rice. At first we received it through regular VC supply channels. The guards made a supply run every so often for other necessities such as cooking oil, condensed milk for the sick, and nuoc mam, the watery brown fish sauce made from the brine of fermented fish. The supply runs took about ten days. As best we could gather, the VC probably had covert agents buy the supplies on the regular market in the coastal town of Tam Ky, capital of the province in which Chu Lai was located, and then bring the goods to a pickup point outside town.

Harker. Several ARVN prisoners were kept separate from us in a hootch outside our compound. Weatherman lived with them. He had free run of the area. I began to understand his cryptic comment of the first day. He had passed himself off as a defector.

Anton. To us Weatherman was a mixed-up kid. He'd made a mistake somehow. We thought he realized this. He was a happy-go-lucky guy twenty years old, charming and friendly, always smiling. He apparently was pretty handy with his fists. According to his account he hadn't adapted very well to the regimentation of Marine Corps life. He was tossed into the brig at Da Nang for slugging a superior, whereupon he promptly escaped. He had a Vietnamese wife/mistress at Chu Lai. He jumped on the rear of a Lambretta motor scooter and hired the driver to take him to her. Instead, the Vietnamese took him to the Viet Cong.

This had happened several months earlier. He told the VC that he wanted to cross over to their side. They received him warily. I don't think the guards really trusted him. And they had reason not to. We were there only several days when he stole some condensed milk from the Vietnamese kitchen and brought it to us. Mr. Hom later called us to the classroom for a routine political lecture on the just struggle of the Vietnamese and was making an interminable point when Weatherman interrupted him with, "That's a big crock. I don't believe a word of that shit."

Hom told Weatherman he had a bad attitude, and ordered him to his hootch. Afterward Weatherman asked for permission to live with us, but the Vietnamese refused. He began to talk about escaping. We couldn't tell whether he was serious. The prospects didn't exactly sound encouraging. He told us about the gentle Vietnamese pharmacist from Da Nang who had been brought to a camp with him. The man was guilty of no apparent crime against the Viet Cong and could not understand why they had taken him. He became desperately homesick and tried to escape. He was tracked down and speared by the montagnards. Weatherman buried him.

Harker. The Vietnamese made a water line by running bamboo tubing from the creek at a higher elevation down to their kitchen. We carried water from their kitchen to our compound in a five-gallon can, used a large pot to boil it. No one was particularly interested in making sure we had enough potable supply on hand at all times. Some of us, finding the can empty, occasionally drank unboiled water. Kushner told us we were asking for a case of dysentery. But it depended upon the degree of our thirst whether or not the warning was heeded.

So at first we fell victim to a lack of self-discipline. No, perhaps it was a failure to understand what we were up against. No one knew anything about surviving in the jungle. Although most of us were from rural or semirural areas, our lives had been relatively soft, accustomed to flush toilets, soap, hot showers, soft beds, clean food. I'd never been hungry in my life. Maybe I thought I had, but I was learning that I'd never experienced true hunger. And there was the shock factor. None of us could actually believe we were prisoners of war. Arriving in Viet Nam we had subconsciously anticipated being wounded or killed—but never captured. It wasn't a war in which people were captured in the south. That was for pilots flying over the north.

Anton. It was sort of funny. Right after we got to camp we started saying to each other, "The war can't go on much longer. It will be over in a very short while." We all agreed on this.

Harker. I tried to cook for the first time at Tet. The Vietnamese gave us our first meat since the Puerto Ricans left. It was a small strip of water buffalo. It looked like fatback, and there was just enough to make several tiny chunks for each of us. Three rocks made up our cooking unit. I failed to notice as I began that one of the rocks was loose. The pot suddenly toppled over. The fire went out in a ball of steam.

Grissett ran up screaming, "Goddamnit, Harker, you've ruined the fuckin' meat! We get beef once a year!" He started furiously poking around in the dead fire. Someone pulled me back and led me from the kitchen area.

"Russ is cooking. Let him do it."

The meat was found and put back into the pot. I walked away. I was on the verge of tears.

Another prisoner said, "Hey, it's not the end of the world. Everything's okay. Forget it." Russ apologized after he calmed down. But I continued to feel bad about my carelessness.

Those first days seemed to be an unending lesson on our inadequacies. Small matters became vastly important. We had to gather wood for our cooking fire. Dry bamboo burned about as fast as pine kindling and a lot was needed. A good whack with a sharp knife would split bamboo. Only we didn't have sharp knives, just pieces of dull metal without handles and difficult to hold. Those of us who had cut wood in our lives had done so with an ax. Now with our primitive implements we were as awkward as children.

The Vietnamese guards were improving the camp. We were taken to a nearby hillside to cut elephant grass for roofing. It sounded like an easy proposition till we tried it. We couldn't seem to get the hang of how to cut and tie bundles, let alone carry them. The grass ate into our skins like hydrochloric acid. The guards yelled at us contemptuously. All Vietnamese knew how to cut and tie. Why didn't we?

At three o'clock each morning a guard woke up the cook for that day. At first Russ Grissett was chief cook and we were his assistants. We quickly saw the need to establish cooking teams to rotate the duty. But we sensed he was against this because he didn't want to lose any of his responsibilities and thus authority over us. Once the decision was made, though, no one told the Vietnamese. The guards assumed Grissett was the one to be awakened. He would go into a frenzy of screaming, "Don't wake me! I'm not cooking!" The guards understood no English. The result was that we were all being awakened at 3:00 every morning.

Anton. There's no rain in the world like that of a tropical monsoon. It slants down in sheets, often unending for days, taking a breather now and then as a drizzle, only to hammer down again. If it's not raining there's the fog which advances and retreats over the mountainsides like a ghost. We were under the influence of the northeast monsoon from November to March. The low-level flow originated over Siberia and in its course southward the cold dry air gradually heated and was moistened by contact with the China mainland and the South China Sea. As it touched the slopes of South Viet Nam's highlands, the heavy air was forced to rise and in doing so dumped its load. Most of it fell on our camp. It was like living in a mud bog. We tried to lay down paths of wood but without much success. There was mud on our bed, mud on us. We were barefoot.

Harker. I had thought the tropics were supposed to be sweltering. It was cold at night and seemed to be getting colder. We slept in every piece of clothing we had and pulled ourselves into the fetal position under our thin burlap blankets. We grew weaker.

Anton. We were all in our twenties except for Williams, who was forty-one. A healthy young man can live a surprising number of weeks on little or no food. The body first burns surplus fat for energy, then lacking meat begins to cannibalize its muscles. We could see ourselves slowly shrinking, almost feel the vitamins and minerals seeping away.

With Dr. Kushner's help we recalled the basic health courses we had taken in school. There were three main groups of nutrients: fats, carbohydrates (starch, sugars), and proteins. The first two provided fuel, the latter kept the body and blood in healthy condition. Vitamins came mostly from fruits and vegetables and kept the skin in good condition. Our diet had a big protein deficiency since we received hardly any meat or fish. And our staple of polished rice was almost devoid of the B group of vitamins.

Harker. Besides lacking vitamins and proteins, the amount of rice we received didn't begin to fill our stomachs. Or to give us enough strength to do the smallest tasks. It was clear that to survive we must have something else. The only other available food in the area was manioc. It grew in fields on the farther mountainsides and belonged to the montagnards. The Viet Cong made a deal with the montagnards for the manioc. They said it would be up to us to gather it.

6

Ike McMillan

I didn't buy any grass before I left for Da Nang. I had lost touch with my boy Phat and, besides, guys who knew told me the military police searched you when you got on the plane at Chu Lai. They were having a problem with GIs taking dope on R 'n' R. Officials in Hong Kong and Singapore and those places were bitching. When I got to Da Nang I had to look around for something.

I met a Puerto Rican named Martinez who was going to Singapore too. We walked around Da Nang three hours and found nothing.

We were about to give up when I saw this kid standing by a fence at the airport. He said, "Hey, soul. Me same-same you. I got some marijuana. Buy from me."

The kid was black; black as I am, and had real curly hair. The question went through my head, "Where'd this kid get his color?" He was about twelve. I walked over and rubbed his face and felt his hair.

"You really a soul, huh?" Now I could tell he was Vietnamese but he sure didn't look it.

He said, "You go boom-boom? I can get you a short-time girl for three dollars."

I laughed and said, "Man, you could really get over back in the world, you really could."

He pulled out a couple of dollars and said, "Hey, do me a favor. When you go to PX buy me a disc."

"You gonna have me a hundred Js when I come back?"

"Yeah. Yeah."

When I returned from the post exchange he sold me ten bags. We smoked a few that night but I was set on saving the rest for R 'n' R. We left for Singapore the next day.

I had played a lot of poker before going out on operations in November. I was in a stud game and drew four sevens back to back; walked away with nearly eighteen hundred dollars. I got some guys in the company to each get me a hundred-dollar money order; the amount of your paycheck was the max you could legally send home by money orders. Then I mailed my wife one thousand dollars.

She wrote me, "Where did you get all this money?"

I wrote back, "Woman, take it and put it in the bank. Don't ask questions."

Next letter: "You're gambling, aren't you?"

"Yeah, I'm gambling heavy."

"I thought you were supposed to be fighting a war. You're going to lose your money."

"You don't know. The first month over here I lost my entire paycheck. Now let me tell you something—I just won two grand."

"Well, why did you only send me a thousand?"

I played some quick in-and-out in the boonies and soon dropped all but three hundred dollars. About two weeks before I was to go on R 'n' R we were on S 'n' D and had stopped in a ville for three hours. Four grunts got up a stud game and they were on me to make it a fifth. I jumped in and lost two hundred fifty just like that. I said, "Lawd, have mercy!" I had fifty left. The company commander gave the ten minute warning to move out.

My first four cards were two queens and two kings. The pot was nice and big. I said, "What's the limit since this is our last hand? I'm good for a hundred." I pulled a hundred out of the pot to draw light. I'll be damned if the four guys didn't go along with me. I said, "Watch out. I got a boat. Cowboys over ladies." Nobody believed me. The last card was dealt. I sweated the card without looking, moving it back and forth across my fingers. I felt a king. Hot damn! I said, "I'm in for another hundred." Three people called me. I left that pot with a thousand bucks. I sent five to my wife and took the other five with me to Singapore to buy clothes.

I met this girl in a bar my first night in Singapore. She was a pretty decent girl. I paid for the first drink. And then for the first night. But after that I didn't have to pay. Four nights and five days. Got over like a bandit.

I said, "Tomorrow I go to the hotel tailor shop and buy some clothes. Take back to America with me."

She said, "No, if you buy in hotel you pay very much money."

I said, "Okay, you take me somewhere to buy and then I take you sight-seeing."

She took me to a shop where I got five three-piece suits for about fifty bucks each. She didn't want to go sight-seeing. She had two kids and her husband had divorced her. We went to her house.

She said, "See, I make sure nobody take you money."

I said, "Yeah, and now you want to go back to America with me, huh?"

She said, "No, my home here. I stay here."

I said, "Well, what can I do for you?"

"You fight in war. You come to Singapore to have good time. I give you good time. I think you good man. If you no good man I tell you quick and you pay me much money."

On the last day we were to have a good-by party by the hotel's peanut-shaped pool. I picked up my new suits. That evening I wore a double-breasted gray sharkskin with matching gray suede shoes and had on a pearl tie pin that cost me thirty-six dollars. It was boss. I mean, really tucked down. I got there early and stood by the pool with my sunglasses on, high as a Georgia pine. My broad arrived. Like I say, she was decent. She never wanted me to buy her a thing, asked for nothing. We had a whole chicken that night. Chicken is my favorite food.

When I got back from R 'n' R, the company had moved to a fire support base. Some new replacements had come in while I was gone. I began to break them in. Several guys were really sharp.

Ten of us got high one day and we walked in single file through the artillery section. It was very overcast. We had on our sunglasses. Some officers were standing near a gun. As we passed a major said, "Don't you men know how to salute?"

We came to a halt, each man bumping against the one in front.

A guy said, "Sir, Steel Gimlet told us we didn't have to salute in the boonies."

We marched off.

One of the officers shook his head and said, "Something is wrong."

Another replied, "Yes, but what?"

Everything went well till one day in March when the company was sent again deep into the bush around Happy Valley. We set up on a hill. Two platoons went on S 'n' D at the base of the hill, one to the left, one to the right. Another line platoon and the weapons platoon stayed on the hill in reserve with the company commander. Before lunch a platoon radioed that it had walked into a thirty-man ambush. It was in heavy contact. The platoon leader had been shot in the stomach.

We picked up the binoculars and saw nothing but little moving trees in the valley. It was much more than a thirty-man ambush. The company commander told the two platoons to merge. Then he ordered the reserve line platoon to saddle up. He told us to remain on the hill as a security and fire-support element. He led the line platoon down the hill. All this happened so quickly that no one thought about asking him to leave us a radio. Since we were usually with the command post and were so understrength, we depended on his radio men. The weapons platoon sergeant spread us around the hilltop with our rifles. We left the mortars in the center of the hill. We could see the company moving below and see the location from where enemy fire was coming.

A few guys took out their Instamatics and photographed the jets and choppers working out. I decided to write a letter to my wife. Artillery shells were whishing over our heads and down below we could hear the heavy firing. But we weren't really sweating it too much. We were sort of spectators. A couple of guys were listening to music on our transistor radio. I was trying to think of something to write my wife when I saw a Viet Cong running below through the rice paddies. He took fire from the company and switched directions. I saw where he took cover. I told the platoon sergeant and asked if he didn't think we should drop some rounds out there. He agreed. We fired three shells. The first round fell short. We didn't see or hear the other two because of noise from the air strikes.

Three minutes later we heard a whistle. Boom! It hit at the bottom of the hill directly below us. Then Boom! BOOM! They were walking them in.

I said, "Hey, Sarge, we're coming under a mortar attack. Let's get off the hill."

He said no. We weren't dug in and the hilltop was barren with no place to take cover.

A few guys started scrambling down the side. The mortars were falling right on top of us now. BOOM! BOOM! BOOM! Shrapnel was flying every place.

Davis and Calloway shouted, "Let's get off the hill!"

This time the platoon sergeant agreed. He said, "I'll get the other guys and meet you at the bottom."

I took my rifle and ammo and flew. I mean I practically jumped off that hill. My steel pot came off and I left it hanging in the air. When we got to the bottom there were three of us. We had to decide what to do. I said, "If we try to link up with the company from the rear anything can happen. We don't have a radio to let them we're coming and the guys are sure to be trigger happy with all these gooks in the area."

We hadn't decided what to do when a spotter plane flew over and fired a smoke rocket near where we were. He didn't see us.

He was calling in jets to work over that sector. We started moving fast across the rice paddies. As we got across the paddy a jet rolled in and dropped a bomb on almost the exact spot where we'd been holding our talk. Whew!

Maybe we could make it back to the fire-support base. If not, one thing was for sure. We had to get out of the area. It was crawling with North Vietnamese troops. I outranked Calloway and Davis so I said, "I'll walk point." We started out. We moved a few meters and the North Vietnamese opened up.

Davis. We ran smack into an ambush. It was a machine gun. All I saw were bushes in front of me shaking and rounds spitting out at my head. The three of us hit the grit. I was in the middle because I was one of the new guys in the platoon and McMillan and Calloway were trying to protect me. Calloway was on his next to last month in Viet Nam.

McMillan. I thought we were completely surrounded. To break through we'd have to get together and concentrate our fire.

I yelled, "Calloway, move up to where we are!"

Davis and I began to lay down a base of fire. Calloway was a short-timer and in a complete panic. Instead of low crawling to our position he jumped up and started to run. He took a hit through the upper right thigh.

He said, "I'm hit!"

I said, "Hold tight and stay down." I yelled for Davis to rescue Calloway while I covered.

Davis. Jesus Christ, was I scared! I broke out in a sweat. It took me twenty minutes to crawl back. McMillan and the NVA machine gunner were battling it out. Bullets cut the air overhead. I told Calloway to lie flat. I grabbed his hands and pulled him over my back. He used his unwounded leg to help us move. As I pushed off my left ankle cracked.

It was evident by then that it was only a small ambush, maybe several guys with a machine gun. A hootch was to the left at the edge of the paddies. We slowly worked our way to it. We bandaged Calloway, tried to stanch the bleeding as best we could, and then moved into a small bunker beside the house. I put my fatigue shirt over Calloway to keep him warm. He was in shock. The house belonged to a middle-aged Vietnamese woman. She was calm and ignored the battle going on around her. She was cooking as we arrived. Later she brought us some bowls of rice.

McMillan. From the hootch we saw a Vietnamese who was part of the ambush team. He was prone and had his back to us. We could have blown him away, but decided not to run the risk of calling attention to our position. We would wait till nightfall and try to get away.

Davis. Shortly before dusk we could hear them moving up. I sat in the bunker doorway with my feet cocked up, the M-16 cradled in my arms. I was smoking a Salem. I wasn't afraid anymore. If I was going to die, I would sure as hell take a few of them with me.

McMillan. Someone arrived and started jabbering at mama-san. She led him away for fifteen minutes. The same guy returned. He wasn't satisfied. He argued with her. I think she was trying to protect us. He started looking around.

Davis. I looked up. I was face to face with a man in black pajamas. I opened up with a quick nineteen rounds. He tumbled back out of sight. After our capture I saw the same man again. He was very upset. He told us bullets had cut through his hair. I denied it was I who shot at him. I told him the American must have got away.

McMillan. We crawled deeper into the bunker behind some large earthen rice jars. We were out of ammo. The Vietnamese began tossing in grenades. There was little fragmentation, it was mostly gas grenades. I covered my face with my T-shirt. The gas made me drowsy and stung my eyes.

Davis. They threw in four gas grenades and McMillan said, "We've got to get out of here."

I said, "No we don't. If we move out they'll kill us for sure. Let's play dead."

I was covered with blood from Calloway's wound. I put my T-shirt over my face and sprawled out. Several Vietnamese entered with a lantern. One of them jerked off my dog tags and removed my watch and rings. He felt my pulse, then put his ear to my nose. I held my breath. He couldn't understand. He tried to feel for a heart beat. He looked me over for wounds. Finally he stood and clucked, "Tsk-tsk-tsk."

McMillan was pulled out of the bunker, then me. I lay unmoving. It was black dark and rain had begun to fall. I was cold. Every mosquito in Happy Valley had received word that a fresh supply of O-Positive was to be had. I said, "Aw, shit, I may as well get up 'cause they're not gonna leave without me."

I started to rise. Thirty Vietnamese around me leaped back crying "Uhhh!" as if the dead had begun to walk. I toppled over. My ankle had a bad sprain, it was swollen, and the pain was fierce.

A mix of uniformed North Vietnamese and guerrillas in black pajamas had captured us. They carried an assortment of weapons. McMillan stood smoking a cigarette. Calloway was in a hammock. Someone handed me a smoke.

I asked with gestures if they were going to kill us.

He said, "No, no, no." I didn't know at this time that Ho Chi Minh had recently put out an order to capture all Americans possible for leverage during peace negotiations.

They ordered me to start walking. Artillery shells began falling around us. My ankle was killing me. Two guys on either side dragged me across the paddy. The artillery rounds fell closer.

I said, "Let's get down," and made gestures to indicate the danger.

They replied, "No, no," and we continued to walk through the artillery fire till we reached a village.

McMillan. There they took our boots. A medic gave Davis a shot of novocain for his ankle. Calloway was given a shot of morphine. They brought us tea and some meat left over from Tet. Calloway was too sick to eat. Then we moved out. I walked; Calloway and Davis were carried in hammocks.

Davis. They tried to make me walk. I told them I couldn't. An officer ordered two privates to carry me. The two soldiers were highly pissed off and dropped me every chance they got. There must have been 1,500 North Vietnamese in the area. Some of them were still fighting. Our immediate group consisted of a hundred soldiers. Late that night we stopped. McMillan was tied to a tree. Calloway and I were put into an underground bunker. Calloway was still bleeding. The medic hadn't been able to stop it. He was restless all night.

Next morning Calloway gasped, "Tom, you've got to pull me out and give me artificial respiration. I can't breathe! I can't breathe!"

I couldn't move my left leg the pain was so intense. I tried to drag Calloway out and call for the guards.

One of them at the doorway snarled, "Sit! Sit!"

I said, "You sonofabitch! The man is dying!" He pointed his bayonet at me and tried to push me back.

I managed to get Calloway to the entrance. A green mucus was running from his nose and mouth. Another VC saw what was happening. He helped me get him to a table outside.

Calloway mumbled, "Can't breathe," and made convulsive sounds like a man with dry heaves. A VC rushed up with a bottle of plasma. It was too late.

We passed the day in the hills and returned to the valley that night. The entire area had been bombed and strafed—leveled. In the hills we were interrogated by Frenchy. He wore black pajamas and had a small brown handbaglike satchel across his shoulders. It was the kind of document-carrying case that usually indicated a VC or NVA official. He had keen features marred by a knife scar on his left cheek. He questioned me, and said, "You must tell me the truth or I will punish you." I told him I was a recently arrived Pfc., so what did I know? He showed me maps of the area, said 43 per cent of my company had been wiped out the day before, and generally answered every question he asked.

McMillan. Frenchy called me for a separate interrogation. "Do not lie to me," he said. He unholstered his 9-mm pistol and laid it on the table. He asked some questions. I told him my name but the rest of the stuff I made up or changed around.

He jumped up, drew back his hand, and said, "If you lie I will slap you."

This shook me up. I said, "Are you going to kill me?"

He said, "No, but we will punish you if you lie."

He asked more questions. I think he discovered I knew less than he did. He took out a map and showed me various unit locations, told me we called our battalion commander Steel Gimlet, and gave me details about the aviation units that supported us.

I said, "Why did you ask me?"

He said, "To see if you lied." He told me that if I made progress I might go home soon. I began to wonder what I had to do to get released as soon as possible. Just what did progress mean?

Davis. A buck-toothed girl about seventeen years old was assigned to guard us. I asked her for a cigarette. She screamed, "Sit down!"

A number of female soldiers were in the area. Some were armed and others were humpers carrying oil, ammo, and food to the front. They shouldered U.S. AID burlap bags with straps sewn on them. Big banana leaves were spread on their backs to keep sweat from soaking through the food bags. Black pajamas were rolled up thigh length, their long hair tied high with white kerchiefs.

Villagers from Happy Valley gathered around us. They laughed and pointed and said, *"Meey, meey, meey"* [American].* Some were just curious, some wanted to feel the hair on our arms, but others came up and pinched us.

One kicked me on my sprained ankle and said, *"Do may,"** which I later learned was a favorite Vietnamese expression that meant motherfucker.

McMillan. We marched westward that night with the soldiers. Our column was strung out for two miles. The trail was marked with banana-tree bark. Here and there at intersections was a piece a foot long, an inch or two wide, sharpened at one end like an arrow, pointing in the direction we were supposed to take. We passed through villages I had visited before on S 'n' D. The kids

*Phonetic spelling.

then had said, "Okay, okay, chop-chop." And I had given them cans of Cs, candy, or chewing gum. Now the same kids were spitting on Davis and me.

We reached a base camp. An officer took my belongings and looked through them. "All military papers in wallet we must keep," he said. "Now you have your choice of wallet or watch."

I said, "I'll take my watch then."

He said, "No, cannot give you watch. Maybe you signal plane. We give wallet." The watch was put in a bag along with my military papers and taken to the next camp.

The camp commander came with a translator to talk to me. He said, "I like your watch very well. You sell."

I said nothing.

He said, "You sell or I take." It was a Seiko worth maybe twelve bucks. He gave me two thousand p. Their officers had this thing about saving face. He wasn't worried about what we thought, but what the other officers might think about his taking my watch.

The translator said, "Maybe when you get to your permanent camp you can buy milk and candy." He described the POW camp. He said we would have a big shop with many machines to work on, and ended, "I think if you make progress, maybe in one-two-three months you go home."

From his description I knew we were headed straight for Hanoi.

Davis. One night a guy in black pajamas asked us to come inside a hootch. It was lit by a small candle. Tea arrived. We sat down. Suddenly the man jumped up and shouted, "We don't murder, we don't maim!" Then he told us with a fanatical gleam in his eyes that the Front had killed ten thousand Americans the previous month, shot down six thousand planes, and destroyed two thousand armored carriers.

It was propaganda, of course. But the important thing was that the Vietnamese themselves believed it. The effect of their other propaganda, based on true facts about the war and our involvement in it, was to be lowered by their exaggerated battlefield claims. They lied so much that we never knew when to believe them. And we didn't want to believe anyway.

McMillan. I'm sure the Vietnamese had seen black people, but they'd never seen black people like us. They came to touch our faces and rub our hair. Some of them were really astonished. Some made fun of us. And then we met some who sympathized because they had heard so much about racial discrimination in the States. Like on the trail we met one guy who gave us candy; and the guards let me buy some fresh fish with the money I'd received for my watch.

We reached a camp containing sixteen ARVN prisoners. We stayed here three weeks. Almost every day the VC called us for interrogation or gave us a political lecture.

They said, "We do not invade your country. Why do you come to bomb ours?"

We told them we didn't know. Really I hadn't thought about it till this time.

Davis and I talked about the Code of Conduct all the time, what would happen if we did this, if we did that. I could see nothing we did to violate the code. But the Code of Conduct—it's really hard to abide by once you're under pressure. What's more important? Your life or the possibility of a court-martial when you get back? I never had the feeling I would rather die than disclose information.

Watkins. Daly and I stayed at an interim camp till the first of March. Then we were taken to a prison camp that held six ARVN prisoners. On the way we were stopped in a village. A photographer took pictures of different guerrillas "capturing" us. A political indoctrinator at the camp gave us what he called a brief history of the Vietnamese people's struggle. He told us how the war started, how the Vietnamese had earlier fought off the Chinese, Japanese, and French.

The VC read from prepared lesson plans. They sometimes made us read the material and "analyze" it. They told us we were fighting for Lyndon Johnson to make him richer. We agreed with them. They were pleased and told us we were making progress.

Then one day they said Americans lived in fine houses but were dirty and filthy. Daly got into an argument with them about that. I thought the guard was going to shoot us.

Daly. They were interested in details of our earlier lives. The political officer asked, "Is everyone equal in the United States? Do all Americans live like you?" Then, "If you do not have true freedom in your country how can you come ten thousand miles to give someone else freedom?" There was no answer.

Actually I had had personal confrontations with overt racism only several times in my life. The first occurred when my brothers were transferred to an elementary school in Queens. White people marched around the school with signs saying, "Go home, Niggers, Go home." I was eleven.

Then during training in Louisiana I went with three white buddies to a bar in the small town near Fort Polk. A bartender leaned across the counter and said, "I'm sorry but we don't serve knee-grows in heah." He said it softly like he didn't want anyone else to hear. I just stood there because I didn't think I'd heard it myself. Meanwhile my friends had been served.

In several minutes another bartender came up. "We don't serve niggers in heah," he said loudly.

My friends said, "We're sorry. If we had known we would have never come here." They didn't pay for their drinks. As we left one said, "When we get ready to leave this shitty, two-bit town we're gonna bust it up."

I was raised to believe that regardless of color people are the same. There are bad black folks and bad white folks. The way the Vietnamese compared our situation, though, there was no argument we could really put up. I can't say how it was in the South, but Watkins gave the Vietnamese the impression that black people were treated horribly. I didn't agree with this. I'm not saying America is perfect—it's not—but you don't tell an outsider who has never been there all the bad things about your country.

It seemed that many prisoners tried to tell the Vietnamese everything terrible about America. For instance, at the permanent camp we had some guards who learned to speak a little English. One of them asked me about sex. I told him I was a virgin. He called me a liar. He said all Americans had sex by the time they were sixteen. I asked him how he knew. He said the other prisoners told him.

As for Watkins, I think he was being honest about his situation. It sounded as though he'd had a rough go in South Carolina. But from the very first he didn't offer the Vietnamese any resistance. And he didn't want me to say anything to upset them. Every time I spoke, he'd say, "Be quiet. They'll hear what you're saying." Rather than talk and have him tell me to be quiet, I just didn't say anything. It was a boring two months with him.

We were resting up before walking to the permanent camp. I had a minor wound in my right shoulder. I'd caught jungle rot before I was captured. A lot of soldiers were using bad feet as an excuse to get out of the field and the officers stopped sending them back till the pain was unbearable. A medic looked at my feet a couple of times and said, "Not bad enough." After I was captured the condition grew worse. My feet cracked and bled.

Watkins. The last of March we were moved to a village, where we waited till we were joined by three newly captured American marines. The marines were escorted by eight guards. One of the guards was a Caucasian. I thought at first he was a Russian. He carried an AK and wore rolled-up black pajamas. He had three Chicom grenades on a North Vietnamese belt, wore a bush hat and Ho Chi Minh sandals.

He asked us in fluent English how we were doing. We said okay. He didn't seem very friendly and neither were we. The group of us moved out. Daly and I were kept separate from the marines and not allowed to talk to them. The white VC led us down the trail. That night we stopped at a montagnard hootch. The Caucasian slung his sleeping hammock. He woke up later that night with an attack of malaria and sat shivering feverishly in the hammock. Finally he got up and came to sit by the fire with Daly and me. We ignored him.

Next day we arrived at the permanent camp. The camp commander and his translator came out to greet us. He embraced the Caucasian warmly, and they walked up hill arm in arm while the translator, Mr. Hom, gave us a briefing.

7

Frank Anton

U.S. Marine Pfc. Robert Garwood commanded the Viet Cong guard detail that brought Watkins and Daly to our camp. We weren't shocked to see the rifle-toting turncoat although he was, probably no doubt about it, the first American since the Revolutionary War to take up arms against his country. By this time we'd lost much of our capacity for shock; and, anyway, Russ Grissett already had given us a rundown on the defector.

Bob Garwood was captured in 1965. I think he was the first marine prisoner of war. He crossed over to the Viet Cong side sometime in mid-1967. Why he defected was hard to say. He was such a liar that we could never decide. A nice-looking guy, close to six feet tall, with regular features, brown hair, a full mouth, deep tan, he probably weighed no more than a hundred fifty pounds; but compared to us he seemed big and healthy.

Garwood had a half-dozen tales of how he was captured. The one we figured closest to the truth had to do with his taking a jeep to a village near Da Nang. Garwood was a driver for VIPs. He claimed to have been at one time the driver for Gen. Lewis Walt, marine commander in Viet Nam. What he was doing with the jeep that day we don't know, unless he was looking for a girl. He liked to leave the impression he was a lover. On the road he was stopped by the Viet Cong. Naturally he said he shot three or four before they pistol whipped him down. But we didn't believe that part.

Three of them were in the prison camp at first. Garwood, Grissett, and Eisenbraun. Later the two Puerto Ricans joined them. Eisenbraun was an army captain in the special forces when that unit deserved its name. According to Grissett, he and Eisenbraun fell sick after a few months. The captain developed a critical case of dysentery. Garwood had malaria but by some chance avoided the worst illnesses. Like us, they had to gather manioc and firewood and do their own cooking. Grissett said that Garwood used his fists on Eisenbraun, trying to make him work. On two occasions Grissett and the captain tried to escape; both times, he said, Garwood reported them to the Vietnamese, and they were recaptured after a few hours' freedom in the bush. One night Eisenbraun fell out of his hammock and injured his chest on the bamboo bed below. He was spitting blood the next morning, but the Viet Cong forced him to go on a manioc run. He died several days later.

Garwood seldom spoke about his decision to defect. We were gathering wood one time and he got a little philosophical. What he'd done had come about by Grissett and Eisenbraun not working, he said. The burden for gathering food was on his shoulders. He'd realized that sooner or later he would die from overwork, because he was weak and undernourished too. So he compromised and made a deal to go over to the VC side.

There was probably some truth in what he said. Garwood was not dumb; he was intelligent, and quite agile with his hands. Neither was he ideological. First and foremost he struck us as an opportunist. He had believed his life to be at stake. Therefore Captain Eisenbraun wasn't sick—he was lazy. I later saw this same attitude in our camp. Maybe it's the mentality of all forced-labor prisons. To prisoners able to work a sick man is a drain on their dwindling energies. There was a strong tendency in our camp to dismiss a nonworker as lazy, whatever his reasons might be. You had to have a lot of compassion not to get angry with him; and compassion, like food, was in short supply.

Garwood came to our compound and introduced himself around. He was friendly, quick to smile, and said, "I'm sure you've heard about me." He seemed happy to talk to Americans again. There was no question in our minds about whose side he was on. We listened silently as he told us about the Front's victories in the Tet offensive.

Davis. McMillan and I were convinced we were headed to Hanoi. The guards told us we would catch a plane and fly the rest of the way. They said, "In Hanoi you have many things. You have bath and music. If you have money give it to the gate guard and he will get you coffee and milk." It was the ambition of all guards in the South to go to Hanoi. Hanoi was heaven and a whorehouse all thrown into one.

When we came upon Anton and Harker's camp I said, "What liars!"

As we climbed the bank I saw a group of Americans staring at us, looking wild-eyed. Skinny and ragged. Faces the color of rice pudding. They began to pump us with a thousand questions about war news, sports, movies, broads, cars. I'd had a picture in my mind of a prison with big flood lights, high walls with guards patrolling back and forth. Here was this puny grass hootch with several pigs and chickens running around the yard.

Later someone brought out the food. Dr. Kushner sat on the ground with legs crossed picking absently at his rice. He passed what he didn't eat to Fred and Williams. Anton sat awhile and then got up and cussed the Vietnamese—"Goddamn motherfuckers!"—and sat back down only to pop up several minutes later and cuss some more.

Grissett quickly finished his bowl and hunkered down like a Vietnamese, waiting for someone to give him food they didn't want, putting a heavy stare on a likely prospect. When he received a gift he gulped it down, ran into the hootch, jumped on the bed, and pulled a blanket over his head.

I thought, "Jesus, I've been set down amongst some crazy men."

McMillan. They put us in a small shed that doubled as the medical and interrogation shack. The guys in the compound hollered to ask us what unit we belonged to.

We told them and yelled back, "How long you been here?"

They said, "One guy has been here two years."

I looked over and saw a man with gray hair, going bald fast, with a beard and a hairy chest. His arm was in a sling. He was big and looked like a starving ape. I said, "Christ Almighty! Two years and look at him!" Actually I was looking at Williams. I didn't see Grissett till later.

In a few minutes Garwood walked up behind us. He said, "How you guys doing?" He spoke fast with a sort of clipped accent. We were shocked to see him, didn't realize who he was.

I said, "What are you, a trustee or something?"

He said, "Yes, I'm supposed to go home soon." Davis and I had a small supply of rice and salt the guards had given us, plus two cans of condensed milk that was part of the payment for my watch. Garwood said, "We're gonna have to take the rice and salt but you can keep the milk." After he left, the guys in the compound told us through the fence about Garwood and warned us not to talk around him. They said he would rat on you, but didn't give us details about him being a crossover.

Garwood returned. He told us about the camp routine. He asked what unit we were in, how long we had been in Viet Nam, and where we were from in the States. Then he began to talk about himself. He said his parents were divorced, his father was wealthy and owned a printing shop in Los Angeles. He had established a trust fund for Garwood and his sister, and both were to receive eighty thousand dollars when they turned twenty-one. (Garwood looked to be about twenty-two.) Then he told us how he was captured.

He said he was driving for General Walt that day. He took him someplace and the general said, "I'm going to be here awhile so you can come back in two hours."

Garwood went to get a piece of ass or something. That's when the Viet Cong captured him. Garwood shot at them with his .45. This is downtown Da Nang, you know. Can you imagine? He said they told him they would release him if he crossed over. He said, "They lied to me, man. They fooled me. They said if I crossed over they would release me. Now they tell me I have to wait until a better time. They really fucked me over."

I said, "What are you doing now?"

He said, "I go down to the coast now and then to take pictures of military installations. Or sometimes I talk to the troops with a bullhorn to try to get them to stop fighting. But the only reason I do it is because I want to go home."

The guys later asked us what story Garwood had given us. He'd told them generally the same thing. It seemed like he did this every time a new guy came in. It sounded like an apology. I think he was trying to play both sides. Garwood was strong physically. He had a good build. And he was a pretty bright dude. He had a nice handwriting, a good working vocabulary, and spoke fluent Vietnamese. He could do anything the Vietnamese could with his hands. One time he fixed Kushner's glasses with a bit of fishing line. Did a good job too. And I saw him repair the VC's radio.

Garwood had a heavy rap. Still, I don't know what to think about what he said about crossing over because he thought they might release him. He looked sincere when he said it. But I really can't say. Garwood and Mr. Hom lived in the same hootch. They didn't like each other, I don't know why. I saw Mr. Hom lock BG's heels one day, made him stand at attention while he chewed him out. Garwood stood there and took it like he was a regular part of their army.

Daly. Garwood told us he crossed over because the VC promised to release him. In front of the VC, however, he would tell us they had released him in '67 but that he couldn't see going home while Vietnamese children were suffering and dying. He said he'd decided to stay and help do something to bring the war to an end.

Davis. Garwood wouldn't look you straight in the eye when he talked. He kept shifting his glance. I think he was ashamed of what he'd done. When he was up at the Vietnamese hootches he was very friendly with them. But when he was among us and the

Vietnamese guards got friendly, touching him or patting him on the back, Garwood looked uncomfortable and usually left All the Vietnamese except Mr. Hom looked up to Garwood. He was an American yet he could do everything they did. He could hump with them and build a hootch. Hom resented him.

Garwood talked to us about racism. There were five of us—Watkins, McMillan, Daly, Lewis, and myself. I think that was his job, to try to indoctrinate us. He sort of liked Joe Zawtocki, who was also a marine; but on the other hand he disliked Denny. Joe and Denny were members of a pacification team that had been overrun during the Tet offensive. Joe and Garwood became so friendly that they swapped rings, and Garwood lost Joe's. Then Joe said something one day about killing the Vietnamese. Garwood told the Vietnamese that Denny said it. Denny almost got punished.

I felt Garwood had problems growing up. He didn't seem to miss his family. There hadn't been a very good relationship between his mother and father. He spoke about his mother sometimes but never about his father, except to say he was a printer in California and had left him a trust fund. I thought he was a mixed-up guy. But I had to accept him as a Viet Cong. Take the time he escorted us on a manioc run. He carried an automatic carbine. The Vietnamese guard with us stopped in a montagnard ville and left Garwood to take us to the field. Garwood talked casually with us while we picked. Still, he was standing there with a weapon in his hands. Whether he would've shot us had we tried to escape I can't say. Who wanted to try him to find out?

Strictland. Garwood occasionally gathered firewood. Mr. Hom told him to do things and he obeyed without argument. Garwood was tidy, I have to say that for him. He kept his gear in shape, did PT every morning with the guards, and shaved daily. His dark brown hair was short on the sides and long on top like the Vietnamese. He sometimes wore green shorts. He didn't especially like Vietnamese food. He talked about American food and about returning to the States after the war.

He was in and out of camp all the time. He didn't trust us a bit.

When he got ready to leave he left. He didn't come down and tell us or say, "See you guys later." While in camp he called prisoners up to his hootch for interrogation. He was looking for someone to rat on the others. He called me up once or twice. He would lay his tobacco on the table and motion for you to have some. He knew we liked to smoke and seldom had tobacco. He learned that technique from the Viet Cong. It was like one of them interrogating you.

We sometimes asked him how the war was going. He never gave a direct answer. I don't think he believed the VC would win. He thought the U.S. would just eventually withdraw. When he said something we questioned or disagreed with someone might say, "Oh, come on, Bob." But everyone was careful. No one really tried to argue with him. It was a tight situation. We called him Bob to his face—and a lot of things behind his back. He was a pretty intelligent guy. What I'd call swift. If he had been on my side of the fence and had done his share of the work, I would have liked him a lot better than I did some of the guys there.

McMillan. The other prisoners were glad to see Davis and me and the milk especially. Someone heated water and prepared eighteen cups of milk-diluted water. Everyone told us how they were captured. We went to bed at nightfall. We had no lamps, there was nothing else to do. Usually we talked for two or three hours in the dark till we dozed off or the guards came in and told us to shut up. Talk about how we'd fought and what we would like to do to the Vietnamese. Anton said he'd like to get them in his sights one more time. Garwood sometimes would sneak down in the dark, listen outside the hootch, and go tell the Vietnamese what we were talking about. We caught him at it two or three times.

Russ Grissett's attitude about Garwood we couldn't figure. After Garwood jumped the fence he apparently told Russ he would do all he could for him and Captain Eisenbraun. In fact he did just the opposite. How Russ could have faith in Garwood I don't know. But he still did. When Garwood came to the compound he and Russ would go off by themselves to talk. Russ would tell us, "Don't anybody join us when Garwood comes down. Let me talk to him and he'll tell me what's going on." They would go to the side of the compound and hunker on their haunches like Vietnamese. Everybody learned to sit like that, I did after I'd been there awhile. Russ got the Vietnamese habit all around though; everything he did was like the gooks. He ate like them, rolled cigarettes like them, and smoked like them, with it dangling wetly out the corner of his mouth.

Davis. When Garwood left we'd ask Grissett, "What did you talk about, Russ?"

"Nothing, nothing," he'd say, and walk away. We knew then that Garwood had come down and shot his head full of bullshit. I guess he thought that by being friendly with Garwood it would help his chances of getting out.

McMillan. The camp commander called Davis and me for interrogation. Garwood was his translator. I wasn't ready to believe it yet about Garwood, so I said, "If I cross over will you let me go home?" Garwood translated.

Slime said, "You have to make progress in order to go home."

I said, "Maybe five months I will make enough progress?"

He said, "Maybe." I used to beat around the bush with them like this.

Ol' Ratface, this guy from North Viet Nam, told me one day, "Okay, you cross over and we'll let you go home."

I said, "You let me go home and then I'll cross over."

He said, "No, no, maybe you get home you join back up with America."

There was no way I could ever cross over, no way. How could Garwood do a thing like that? How could he turn his back on his family? That's what the guys in that camp were to me. Family. I mean, we got into arguments and fights all the time. But it was the sort of thing that comes into the natural relationship between man and wife.

Harker. We continued to improve the camp. The Vietnamese made us build outside eating tables, which we did half-heartedly because none of us knew how to work with bamboo. I was carrying grass one day when my back began to hurt. I couldn't straighten up. Back at the compound Kushner asked had I fallen or strained myself. I didn't think so. He examined me but saw nothing unusual. I started running a fever. I ate a little rice from my bowl at mealtimes and returned to bed.

A Vietnamese doctor arrived to treat Williams and Cannon. He drew a dotted line with a ballpoint pen on Williams' arm and told him he would amputate the next day. Williams suddenly began to say he had a weak heart. I couldn't blame him. The doctor decided not to cut. He treated him with heavy doses of penicillin and each day took him to the medical shack to pick out bone splinters. Williams' hand began to look better and didn't smell as bad. Cannon's wounds also improved but he grew steadily weaker.

The doctor examined me. He turned me on my stomach and felt my back. The pain made me rear up, but he could find no cause for the it. He left and returned the next day. This time he felt my back inch by inch. At the lower right side he made an indentation. He realized then I had an infection. He gave me a shot of novocain, sliced my back open, and ran a hemostat in to clean out the pus and establish drainage. It started healing and my fever went away. Kushner said the bayonet I had been stabbed with was filthy and had caused an inward-pointing abscess. The Vietnamese doctor was crude, but I owed him my life.

McMillan. After a week in camp I got an infection in my foot from a rock cut. It got worse but I kept it to myself. I'm afraid of doctors working on me, I've always been. Finally I told Kushner about it. He said I'd better let the Vietnamese look at it. My whole leg began to swell up. It started bothering me at night, I couldn't sleep, so I said, okay, I'll let them work on it.

Two Vietnamese came to the compound. One of them looked evil and mean. He was the one who was supposed to work on me. I told him, no, I wasn't going to let him do it. I wanted the other guy. He seemed to be a more pleasant dude. He pulled out a rusty razor blade.

I said, "You're not gonna cut on me with that?"

He said, "Ya." They gave me a shot of novocain. It killed the sensation a little, but I could still feel the cutting, felt it as the blade touched the bone. I screamed. The fellows had to hold me down. I passed out. When I came to my foot was bandaged and I was in bed. The VC medics changed the bandage every day and treated the cut with blue ointment. If I stand on it too long it still hurts. But within a month I could walk again.

Davis. Our schedule, such as it was, started at daybreak. Mr. Hom beat a bamboo gong and ran to our hootch and yelled, "Get up! Get up! Do PT! Do PT!" Some guys tried to stay in bed by telling him they were sick. Some of them really were.

Strictland. We did five or six stretch exercises, bend and reach, things like that. Garwood sometimes came down and made us do them when Mr. Hom wasn't in camp. I took the exercise period seriously. I thought it was helping me. To some of the other guys it was just a joke. Then I ran down to the creek and washed up. The Vietnamese did that. I guess I took the habit from them.

Davis. After exercises we returned to the hootch, ate a little rice, and waited for it to get completely light. A manioc run came up twice a week. If you were going you got ready. We wore our short pants on a run and a couple of pairs of boots were saved for this purpose. You picked out a pair and put them on, then got a bamboo basket and adjusted it, being careful to put a piece of cloth under the shoulder straps to keep them from cutting into your back.

We tried to leave by 6:30 and get to the field before the sun burned off the fog. The fields were in different spots. It usually took an average of two hours to reach them. The trails were under foliage or camouflage. The fields, however, were on the open mountainsides and if the fog was gone we had to worry about spotter planes. We ran for the nearest bushes when planes came over and hid till they went away. We were in enemy territory and dressed like Vietnamese. A bomb couldn't tell the difference.

Harker. Only three or four men at a time were permitted to go on a run, accompanied by two armed guards. The guards, who had asked the montagnards beforehand, told us which section of the field to pick from. The manioc bush looked like a slender tree about six feet high. The top was of green leaves, the stalk was grooved and rough on the hands. We hacked off the top, left about two feet of stalk. Manioc is a tuber like sweet potatoes and it was easier to pull them up this way. You grabbed the stalk and worked it back and forth to loosen it. A young plant came up easily, an old one hung on forever. Killing work, if you were weak.

The manioc looked like a long, fat root. Sometimes it was round and oblong; had a brownish-red outer covering similar to a sweet potato and a pink inner peeling. The edible part resembled an Irish potato but had a peculiar taste unlike that of a potato. It was an ancient and quite common food among the poor in parts of Asia.

Davis. A basket of manioc weighed about sixty pounds. If a weak man went on a run you would have to pull yours and probably his too and wind up carrying his basket back to camp. Depending on how far the field was you'd usually make it back by midafternoon. Tired, sweaty, bruised, and cut, irritated with those who weren't working hard enough, you ate some cold rice and took a bath and talked about what you had seen on a run. I was usually in a bad humor for several hours after I returned. Everyone learned to let me cool off before we talked.

All of us were having a hard time trying to live with our hunger. As a teen-ager I'd often eaten a quick hamburger and taken off with an empty feeling in my stomach that I thought was hunger. It wasn't. Hunger takes over your body, dominates your mind. You crave for meats and think your imagination is driving you crazy. Some prisoners spent hours making up elaborate imaginary menus. Some actually got into fierce arguments about whose menu was best. The only thing you could do was drink water with the meal and try to psych yourself out, tell yourself that you were full.

Harker. A small condensed-milk can was our measuring cup for food. Each prisoner got a can and a half of uncooked polished rice per day, approximately thirteen ounces. At first Grissett was cooking a can per person in the evening and the remaining half can the next morning. His theory was that you should have a full stomach before trying to sleep. We cooked the manioc separately and left it in a pot so we could eat it cold at noontime. We decided to split it down the middle, to cook three quarters of a can in the morning and three quarters in the evening. Russ objected violently. He thought we were trying to put him in his place as a punk lance corporal. Maybe that entered in on it, but much more was involved. We had to try to establish a system that could be voted on by the majority.

We received sporadic rations of nuoc mam and cooking oil. The cooking oil was usually soy bean oil and on several occasions U.S. peanut oil. We mixed the cooking oil and nuoc mam and heated it. There was enough for two small dippers of sauce per person, enough to wet our rice. We knew it had protein value. Some prisoners literally tried to drink it. But we never had enough to do us much good, and in fact the nuoc mam's salt content was harmful when beriberi hit us.

We didn't try very hard at first to gather wild greens from the jungle. None of them tasted good, and our hunger hadn't driven us to eat them. Later we realized they were necessary if we were to live. The Vietnamese showed us which ones were edible. In the evenings we tried to have some sort of vegetable. Often we stripped a wild banana tree down the middle and ate the pulpy substance. On trees with nonedible fruit we ate the banana flower. Once we had papaya and at other times breadfruit, which we got from the montagnards. All regular food such as rice, manioc, and vegetables was split into precise and equal shares.

McMillan. When food was dibbled out everybody's eyes were there. Nobody wanted more or less, they just wanted their share. The cooked rice made three small bowls per person each day. You can pack a bowl with rice or you can put it in light and fluffy. It makes a difference when you're hungry. Cooking chores were rotated among two-man teams. It was tacitly accepted that the cooks packed their bowls a little tighter than everyone else's.

Harker. Several other rules about food were passed on by Grissett and adopted by us. The first was the extra-benefit rule —"extra bennies" we called them. This included any small items of food collected by the individual. They belonged to him. It was not required that he share them though in many cases he did, usually with his best friends. Extra bennies were something like red peppers or a little dried corn you might get from the montagnards when you went on a manioc run. It was an incentive to pick manioc, which was hard work nobody wanted to do.

Davis. On a manioc run we had to pass through a montagnard ville. We always stopped in a few minutes on the way back and asked for tea.

Some of us picked up a few words of the montagnard dialect and combined them with the scanty Vietnamese we'd learned. Pfister was good at this, and he would say, "Got bop? Got ut?" Corn and pepper. "Give us breadfruit, give us something."

The yards would crowd around, laughing and saying, *"Cai gi? Cai gi?"* (What?) They often asked us for a manioc or two. We picked from their fields and sometimes they didn't have enough for themselves, so we could hardly refuse. Depending on how wealthy was the montagnard whose house we visited, he might give us a little corn or peppers or maybe some tobacco. But the yards were usually hurting worse than us.

Harker. Another rule was called "the lion's-share principle." Whoever killed an animal or bird got his choice of the meat and the amount he wanted. The principle was modified somewhat the day Watkins and Davis brought a mountain goat into camp. The goat had been killed by the VC. They gave a large piece of meat to Watkins and Davis, who had helped them move supplies, and a smaller share to the rest of us. Someone said, "Why should they get more? It was just luck they happened to be with the VC when the goat was killed."

Another added, "Yeah, why don't you two divide this around equally?" Davis tossed his in with the group's. But I don't think Watkins ever did.

Six of us were forced to carry rice for the VC. On the way back Davis opened his bag and filled my fatigue pants pockets full.

When we returned to camp the VC brought out tea and invited us to sit with them a few minutes. They were all smiles, we had done their work for them. As I sat down the rice trickled from my pockets. The VC medic girl spotted it. I lamely explained my bag had a hole and I was saving the rice for them. They knew I'd tried to steal it, but they didn't hassle me, and I gave it back. Obviously I lacked Ike McMillan's talent. He could swipe the shorts off them.

McMillan. The guys all said I could steal better, so I always went to the Vietnamese kitchen to draw our rations. The kitchen was controlled by mama-san and Hannah, the other Vietnamese lady. Everyone said Hannah had a crush on me but I didn't care for her. I would usually go up and beg for something. I talked to her in English which she didn't understand and she would reply, *"Khong biet. Khong biet."* Then I'd point to what I wanted. Most of the time she would give me some. And I would be stealing something else while she was getting me that. One day I stole eighteen cans of rice. I've always been pretty good for stealing things, even in high school.

Anton. McMillan was returning from the kitchen with our rations one day when a small ocelot ran across the compound. Ike dropped the supplies and shot up a bamboo tree like a rocket.

Harker. On a rainy night I was returning to the hootch before the guard arrived to make a head count. Suddenly someone pushed me from behind. I felt flapping wings under a raincoat. Garwood handed me the coat and said, "Here cook this and save me the two legs." He was gone.

Anton. Garwood wanted us to think he was trying to help us. But he also wanted chicken. The only way he could get it was by stealing from the VC. He demanded the two drumsticks and left the remainder to be split among eighteen prisoners. He was taking a big chance though. Anything could have happened to him had the VC found out.

Daly. We left one morning on a manioc run about 7:30. Joe Zawtocki, Denny, Weatherman, Sherman, and myself. The VC for some reason sent only one guard with us. The other one, I think, stopped off at a montagnard ville.

Anyway, we were walking along and Sherman said, "Today would be a good day to make a bird. What do you guys think?"

Denny said, "Yeah, you're right."

Weatherman agreed and asked Joe Zawtocki his opinion.

Joe was reluctant. He said, "I think it's a good idea but why don't we wait till we get back and try to get everybody to make a break at once."

The others pointed out how ridiculous this would be with sixteen armed guards around the camp.

"No," someone said, "This is the best time to try when we've only one guard."

The group asked me, "What do you think about it, Daly, since you're a conscientious objector?"

I said, "I'll go along with the majority."

"Do you think you could kill a guard?"

"Right now I want to go home. I think I would do anything to get back to my family."

We discussed the best time to make our move and decided to wait till we reached the manioc field. Joe Zawtocki was still not convinced. He hung back at the hilltop away from us and began filling his basket with manioc. We talked about who should jump the guard. Everybody thought it should be Weatherman, since he'd been a prisoner longer and therefore had a stronger motive for escaping. But Weatherman said, "I just can't kill somebody in cold blood. He's got to do something to me to make me want to kill him." Everybody said the same thing. Finally Weatherman agreed to do it.

The guard sat under a tree. His SKS carbine was propped nearby. Weatherman walked over and asked for water. The guard gave it to him. Weatherman began to play with the camp dog, which had followed us on the run. The guard was nervous. He looked as if he was too scared to make a move to get his weapon. You could tell Weatherman was nervous too. He finished the water and rejoined us. He said, "I just can't kill anybody in cold blood."

Denny said, "Well, if you can't let's forget about it."

As he said that Weatherman spun and went back to the guard. He asked for more water. The guard was positively jumpy now. Weatherman drank the water and returned. "Forget it," he said. "Let's get the manioc so we can get back to camp."

I started pulling manioc, a little relieved that Weatherman had decided not to try it. But unseen by me he had gone back to the guard once again. This time he jumped him. Next thing I knew he was calling for us to help him. Denny ran over. He and Weatherman beat the stew out of the guard, who was pleading for them to stop. Weatherman told Sherman to get the guard's weapon and shoot him.

Sherman said, "No, I can't shoot him."

Denny shouted, "Open the bayonet and stab him, Bob!"

Sherman flipped out the bayonet and stood with the weapon in his hands. He said, "No, no. I can't. I can't." He ran to me and said, "Here Daly, you take the weapon and do it. I can't."

I said, "Bob, I can't either."

Weatherman screamed, "Stab him, Bob! Stab him!"

Sherman threw the rifle down. At the same moment the guard broke free and ran. Weatherman and Denny chased him across the field, brought him down with a tackle, and began slugging him. Then they let him go, grabbed his weapon, and ran to where we were.

"Come on! Let's go!" said Weatherman.

Sherman said, "I'm not going."

They looked at me. I said, "If Sherman's not going, neither am I. You let the guard go. He's gone to get help. There's no way we can get away."

Weatherman said, "Bastards! Dirty cowards!"

Denny said, "I'll get you for this, Daly!"

They headed down the mountainside.

Joe Zawtocki came down from the other side where he'd sat the whole thing out. He said, "Let's wait awhile and give them time to get away."

I said, "There's no use hanging around here. We were too

damn yellow to go. Now if we don't get back to that montagnard village before the VC get here we're going to wind up getting shot anyway."

We ran for the ville. The guard had alerted the montagnards. They had their warning system of gongs going. When we entered the village it was like King Kong coming. Women ran and screamed and grabbed their children out of the way. As we passed some kids in a hootch they reached for an old musket and pointed it at us. They were holding it on us, as scared as we were, and I was praying for them not to pull the trigger. The villagers soon calmed down and came to tie us up.

Harker. Guards ran from the camp. We knew something was up. Garwood came to the compound and said, "A tiger's loose in the area. Everybody stay in the hootch."

The VC always told us we had to be careful in the jungle because a tiger might get us. I knew that was not it. I got a sick feeling inside. I said a prayer that they'd made it. At dusk the guards brought three of them back. They moved like machines, with blank stares. The VC pushed them in the compound. Joe Zawtocki was made to tell us what happened. Voice trembling he said, "We tried to escape today. We weren't successful. Weatherman was killed. Denny was shot in the leg."

The camp commander said, "If any of you try to escape you will be shot. The guards have their orders."

Later Denny told us he and Weatherman could hear the montagnards searching for them. They hid in some thick brush and decided to lay low till nightfall. A montagnard kid stumbled upon them. They had the guard's rifle but they chose not to shoot the kid. He scrambled out and ran away. A bunch of yards arrived a few minutes later, told them to come out with hands up. They left the rifle behind and crawled out. Denny was a little behind and to the right of Weatherman.

Weatherman stood with his hands in the air. A montagnard armed with an old Mauser approached. Denny heard Weatherman say, "No!" A bullet took off the back of his head, splattering Denny. The montagnard pointed the rifle at Denny and pulled the trigger. It misfired. Denny turned and ran down a creek bed. The montagnard shot, wounding him in the fleshy part of his calf. The yard was coming to finish him off when VC guards arrived from the camp. They saved him. He was taken to the montagnard village, and held for three days without food in a small shed where rats gnawed at him during the night. The yards spat on him and beat him. They undoubtedly thought he would have brought U.S. bombs down on them had his escape attempt succeeded. Garwood brought a written "confession" and advised him to sign it. He signed. The VC returned him to our compound.

Daly. On the way back to camp Joe Zawtocki said he was going to tell the truth. I said, "What do you mean, Joe? Look, Weatherman is dead. The guard's alive. He knows that Denny beat him and that Sherman had the rifle in his hands. Denny and Sherman are going to be punished no matter what. We don't know what they will do to us. But there's no use admitting we planned to escape. Why should four people get beaten?"

The VC held a day-long trial a week later. That was when Ratface, the North Vietnamese, arrived to become a camp director. Joe told the truth about his nonparticipation. I said I didn't go because I thought we couldn't make it. Denny was given ninety days in stocks and Bob Sherman sixty days. I got thirty days' suspended sentence. Joe Zawtocki was let off with a warning. The VC said this showed the lenient and humane policy of the Front because each person got something different.

I don't guess it was a bad punishment for what we did, if you want to look at it that way. But Sherman did lose his mind while he was in stocks. They were placed in a special hootch below the compound. They couldn't move and had no protection from mosquitoes at night. When Sherman got out he had a faraway look in his eyes. He talked crazy, couldn't remember his name at first. We took turns feeding him. He didn't want to eat. He knew how people were about food. So when it came your turn to feed him he would offer you the food. But nobody took advantage of him. If you turned your back he would throw it over the fence.

Actually Denny and Sherman didn't finish their whole term in stocks. Mr. Ho, a VC honcho, came to camp and pardoned them so they could attend his indoctrination class.

Strictland. The escape attempt occurred April 1, 1968. That's what they were too. Fools.

Anton. We talked little about escaping after Weatherman was killed. It was a subtle thing. We began to speak about holding out till the war ended.

Daly. I was on a manioc run a few months later with Denny and some other guys. We came across some orange trees that apparently belonged to the montagnards. Our guard was off some place out of sight. Everybody started scrambling for oranges. I went to a tree but couldn't reach any. The guard ran up and saw peelings on the ground.

He asked the others had they taken any.

They said no.

He asked me.

I said, "Daly no do."

He asked Denny had I taken the oranges.

Denny said, "Maybe he did, maybe he didn't. I don't know."

The rest of the guys then said the same thing. So the guard gives a stick to Denny and tells him to beat me.

I said, "Wait a minute, Denny. You're not going to beat me for nothing. You know damn well I didn't take any oranges."

He said, "I'm not going to hit you hard."

I said, "That's not the point. The point is the guard thinks I'm guilty. If you hit me you are saying in effect that I am."

The guard got impatient with our arguing. He grabbed the stick and hit me in the head. I screamed bloody murder and cursed him. He got scared and backed up. I moved toward him calling him MFs and everything.

The other POWs yelled, "Better shut up, fool! He'll kill you!"

I said, "Let him kill me but he'll stop breathing before me." I began to worry he really might shoot. I turned and ran to the camp.

I was telling the camp commander what happened as Garwood arrived. He said, "You stand at attention when you talk to an officer." I gritted my teeth and braced at attention.

I said, "The guard hit me for no reason."

Garwood said, "He didn't. Even the POWs say you took the oranges."

I said, "Listen, Garwood, I don't care what they say. Whoever told you that is a damn liar. Let them say it to my face."

That afternoon the VC held a trial. The other prisoners said I was guilty. What could I say? The VC ordered the POWs to suggest a suitable punishment. Denny told them I should go five days without food. The Vietnamese said, "Five days without food and he might die." Then they went down the line asking the other prisoners. The punishment was reduced to one day without food. Everyone said that was fair.

8

David Harker

Russ Grissett awoke early one morning in late June and yelled, "Everybody up! Let's do PT!" He hopped outside and began exercising vigorously, counting off at the top of his lungs, then swept the yard and made himself busy cleaning the compound, ordering us to help. Besides this activity, his attitude toward the Vietnamese, whom he usually called "fenderheads," underwent an overnight change, and he became almost respectful. This was how we learned Mr. Ho was coming. Garwood had told Grissett, and though Grissett didn't tell us we knew by his actions that something important was up. Mr. Ho had given Garwood and later the two Puerto Ricans a political course before they were liberated. Russ associated him with freedom. He was determined to give the impression that he too was progressive and deserved to be released.

Anton. We watched Grissett and said to ourselves, "If he's wrong about being freed he's in deep trouble." We knew it would be a terrible blow. All of us wanted to believe there would be a release.

"Maybe we'll all go."

Grissett said, "No, just two or three."

We tried to guess who it would be.

Grissett naturally said, "It's me."

We thought it would be him too, and we talked about who else might go.

Ho arrived with an entourage of four assistants and body-guards. One of them cooked for him, another washed his clothes. He brought along special canned meats and Ovaltine. Mr. Ho was thin, about five foot eight, very squirrely looking, with gray-flecked hair. He had a pair of brown-rimmed glasses of the old-fashioned type. He wore faded blue Permapress slacks and a mottled green camouflage silk scarf. He had once been a profes-sor of English at a Da Nang lycée. His wife, he said, worked as a nurse at the Da Nang hospital and was a spy for the NLF.

Ho had taught Garwood to speak Vietnamese. Garwood looked up to him like a father. He said Ho had the equivalent rank of two-star general in the National Liberation Front. He was one of their top political cadres. We later saw VC pamphlets confirm-ing this. Mr. Hom also idolized him, tried to copy his sayings and mannerisms. His eyes lit up when he talked about Ho.

Harker. We were issued new black pajamas before the indoctri-nation course began and ordered to take a bath and cut our hair. The guards became more friendly, as if they were worried about what we might tell Ho about them. During the two-week course we didn't have to gather our food, which was a badly needed break from the hard work, and a pig was killed. We needed the meat, for by this time we all looked bad. Dysentery had spread. The compound was dotted with droppings of pus and mucous. The smell was overwhelming. Fred had lost a lot of weight; Can-non was like a skeleton, down to ninety pounds. Dr. Kushner was seriously ill.

The Vietnamese built a small classroom. It was the usual open affair with four rows of planed bamboo benches. Slogans on the wall: "Viet Nam is one. The Vietnamese are one." "The Viet-namese will surely win, the U.S. will surely lose." "Freedom of speech is necessary in debate." We stood at attention as Ho came in with his retinue. The class began at 7:00 and ended at 11:00. The afternoon session lasted from 2:00 to 4:30.

"First I will read my documents to you," Ho said. "In the afternoon you'll be broken down into three study groups. You'll be free to say what you think."

The course's theme was the four-thousand-year struggle of the Vietnamese people. He started with the ancient Chinese invasion and slowly, very slowly, worked his way up to U.S. involvement in Viet Nam. He told us about Viet Nam's historical heroes, the Trung sisters, Tran Hung Dao, Nguyen Hue, about the *Kim Van Kieu*, the epic poem of Vietnamese literature.

Anton. What he told us was unbelievably detailed—and basically true, though we didn't know it at the time. I didn't believe anything he said because of my lack of knowledge about Viet Nam and inherent distrust of the communists. Under these circumstances it became terribly boring. We just wanted to get out of class as quickly as possible. I got off to a bad start with Ho the very first day. I had a chronic case of diarrhea. I went to the latrine anywhere from twenty to a hundred times a day. Half the time I went in my pants. It got to be a psychological thing. I couldn't make it to the latrine because I told myself I wasn't going to make it. I would get one step away and feel a warm stream running down my legs. I sometimes sat down there hours at a time.

Anyway, thirty minutes into the first class I felt an urge to go. Ho was into one of his long lectures where he took off his glasses, waved them around, put them back on, and paused to take a sip of Ovaltine from his glass. I raised my hand. He looked at me but kept talking. Ten minutes later I was squirming around and waving my hand in the air. He scowled at me. I said, "That's it." I stood up and ran backward out of the classroom and headed for the latrine.

I was fixing my pants as I returned. Ho was reading from his documents about the unjust Chinese invaders.

He stopped, took off his glasses, laid them on the table, put them back on again, and said, "You! You could be shot!"

I said, "Shot?"

I raised my hand and tried to explain about my diarrhea. He wouldn't let me speak. He said, "You are very arrogant and that is a sign of a lack of discipline."

A guard took me to Mr. Ho's hootch after class. Ho chewed me out. He told me again that I lacked discipline. "You're an officer," he said. "You should set an example for the other men." This was the only time they mentioned anything about officers. The VC told us no rank existed in the camp, and they were alert to any signs that it did. They took pains to show distaste for Kushner, Williams, and me because they figured we were the authority bloc and believed if anyone gave them trouble it would be us.

Ho's assistants led the afternoon study groups. He floated from group to group to check on progress. The VC tried to include a little Marxism in the indoctrination. Our study-group leader typically posed a question like this. He said, "A man works in Detroit. He makes cars for General Motors. But when it comes time to buy a car he must pay for it. He is not given the car. Why? What is your opinion?"

They usually called on Kushner, then me, and Williams third. Kushner stood at attention and spoke for ten minutes without saying anything. I said something a little different and sometimes disagreed with Kushner. Williams obliquely turned his comment into a joke and shifted the answer to something about the food we'd like to have. Whoever followed would usually say I agree with so and so and sit down. This went on the first few days till the VC caught on. Then they started asking the other POWs first. At night we talked about the course among ourselves. The VC heard we were doing this—maybe Garwood told them—and next day Mr. Ho read us the "Free speech is necessary in debate" slogan and emphasized, "but only in debate!"

Harker. The study-group leaders said the U.S. had broken the 1954 Geneva accords and that we were criminals of war. We didn't argue. We said, "I think the Vietnamese people have a just struggle. They kicked out the Chinese, Japanese, and French. It is something they have a right to do."

The group leader asked why we thought the war was "illegal, immoral, and unjust"?

We responded, "All wars are illegal, immoral, and unjust because innocent people are killed. Everyone should learn to live in harmony without fighting." That got us around the problem of condemning the U.S.

Davis. They went over everything again and again. It was impossible not to learn something. I found the part about the Trung sisters interesting, Viet Nam's twin Joans of Arc who mounted elephants and led the battle against Chinese invaders. The VC were braggarts about their history. They said they had kicked out the French and were now doing the same to us.

"We have water buffalo and you have jets. You are bigger than we are physically. Yet we fight you and win."

Silently I was saying, "And if I had a chance I would wring your fucking neck."

Strictland. You see, we thought Ho was crazy. A fanatic eaten up with communism. He read endlessly to us about how U.S. capitalists used people. I guess some prisoners believed it and some didn't. I mean about capitalism. Now, you know, I'm not saying that all rich men use people. But some guys do try to get way ahead and don't care who they step on doing it. Everybody knows that.

McMillan. Mr. Ho had stateside Kool-Aid, orange juice, and peanuts. This dude was like a king. Served on a bamboo tray. This is in the middle of the jungle, you know. He had people carry his clothes and sleeping gear, had a special cook. Our mouths were watering for his goodies.

He put the five blacks and Denny into a separate study group. Denny had a little Indian blood and claimed to have more than he had. Ho rapped to us about how the blacks had been enslaved and how Custer had done the thing to the Indians, said, "The white man sent you here to kill two birds with one stone." I learned a lot about the four-thousand-year history of the Vietnamese. I thought it was stupid as hell. They should have given up a long time ago. After class we joked about how we wished all the Vietnamese had been killed when the Chinese or French or Japanese were there.

Most everybody went along with his program, though. You disagreed with him and that was it. He asked one question and told us not to discuss it among ourselves. "Do you think the American people as a whole are gaining or losing from the Viet Nam war?" Some guys said America was losing as a whole. I felt this way too. The ones who said we were gaining—oh, man. Ho went into details explaining and said, no, you can't be gaining. Eventually everyone started agreeing with him.

Daly. Everybody hated to sit in class. I disagreed with something during the political course and we argued a whole day. At the end everybody told me, "Whether you agree or not, tell the man you agree."

Davis. Garwood told us Ho had the power to liberate or eliminate you on the spot. Give you the lean and mean treatment of the Front. Ho said, "This isn't your fight. Your fight is in America. We're yellow and you're black and we should join together to fight our common enemy." We agreed. I believe he intended to cause a split between the whites and blacks, thinking the blacks would turn to the Vietnamese for help and guidance. It didn't work. After Ho finished we told them everything he told us.

McMillan. The blacks didn't sit around and have racial conversations. We referred to the whites by our special names and told jokes. Watkins spoke about it because he was discriminated against quite a bit in his life. He had seen a lot of shit. All Davis talked about were the white guys who lived near him in Alabama who were almost like brothers to him. Daly talked a lot about the gangs in New York. I don't know who was prejudiced against who because the way he told it blacks were beating blacks and whites were beating whites.

There really wasn't much prejudice among whites in our camp. I was once sleeping between Dr. Kushner and Fred. The VC had just split us into two hootches. Daly and I were the only two black guys in this group. Kushner said, "Ike, let me sleep where you're sleeping." He wanted to talk to Fred at night but I thought he was trying to move to a better position. I said, "No, man, your place leaks when it rains." Kushner jumped up and started calling me all kinds of sonsofbitches and motherfuckers. Grissett took his side and I thought they were all going to fight me.

I told Watkins and the others that the white dudes were going to do me a job. I said, "I'm the only black guy down there cause Daly's not going to help. Watkins came with Davis and asked Kushner what was going on. He said he was just teasing. After living awhile with Kushner I learned that was the way he was. He would call you a dirty rotten motherfucker in a minute. But he didn't mean any harm by it.

There are several types of prejudice. A certain kind of man wants to be mean and cruel. Then there's the ignorant who doesn't know any better. I think Cannon was like that. One day he wanted some manioc and Watkins wouldn't give him any. Cannon walked up and said, "Will, goddamnit, I want to know why I didn't get no motherfuckin' *co mis.*" Cannon wasn't wearing any clothes because he had a bad case of diarrhea.

Watkins said, "Cannon get out of my face. You're spoiling my appetite."

Cannon said, "Goddamnit, motherfucker, why didn't I get anything to eat?"

Watkins pushed him away. He didn't push him hard but Cannon was weak and he fell over backward. Cannon came to our hootch. Daly and Cannon were buddies. They shared cigarettes and everything. Cannon said, "That goddamn nigger."

Daly said, "What did you say, Cannon?" Daly had a girlish voice. "Are you prejudiced?"

I said, "What's going on?"

Cannon said, "That goddamn nigger almost broke my arm."

I said, "I guess I'm a nigger too, huh?"

Cannon said, "No, you ain't no nigger. It's that goddamn Watkins."

Cannon wasn't really prejudiced. He couldn't even spell the word.

During the political course the VC told us to write about the racial incidents we had faced in the army. I said, "I'm not going to do it." Eventually I told them a lie. If I had told the truth they wouldn't have believed me because I really didn't have any dramatic incidents to tell.

Back at Fort Benning I had this tight buddy, Lawrence, and both of us liked to booze it heavy. One night we got drunk and returned to the barracks about 3:00 A.M. Everybody was mad when we woke them up. Me and Lawrence liked to fight. We pulled out our entrenching tools and offered to take on the whole bay area, but nobody would fight. A big inspection was scheduled at 7:00. We were still in bed when the officers came around. They found a case of wine in our footlocker. The first sergeant threw us on KP for a week. Lawrence said he wasn't going to pull KP and went AWOL. Me, I did my duty.

I wrote about this incident for the VC, leaving out the booze part. I told them I had been given an extra week's KP because of racial discrimination. The VC seemed happy. They wanted to know what KP was. I told them kitchen police. They still didn't understand. They asked Garwood if he thought my story was true. I think he said yes. In a way Garwood sympathized with the brothers. It puzzled me, it really did. I don't know whether it came from the fact the VC naturally sympathized with blacks or what.

Each of us had a line to tell the VC. Except Watkins. He wrote it out just the way it was. He spoke about the prejudiced company commander he'd had at Fort Benning. He told the VC about that in class.

Daly. I tried to explain that if a black man had money he was considered equal. They couldn't believe there were middle-class blacks in the States. They asked me to list my family's possessions after I was first captured and then called me a liar when I said we had a television and a stove and a refrigerator. I think Watkins and I were the first blacks the VC had ever seen. They felt our skins and were all ohs and ahs. They touched our heads and jerked their hands back as if expecting to get shocked. Mr. Hom told me the reason I hadn't visited Niagara Falls was because all of America's sight-seeing spots were closed to us.

Anton. Each day Grissett took a seat at the front of the class. He sat stiff-backed, listened attentively, and volunteered answers to questions. On the fourth day Mr. Ho said, "I want to make one thing clear. I did not come here to release anybody." You could see Grissett wilt. Ho went on, "If you think that is the purpose of this course, you have misinterpreted. I am here to educate you, to make you learn." Any interest Grissett had before evaporated from that moment, although he continued to nurture a half hope that maybe Ho was kidding and would release someone after all.

Harker. Mr. Ho drew a distinction between what he called the U.S. imperialist government and the American people. He said he didn't hate the American people. Each hour we had a ten-minute break and he came around to talk to us informally. He told us that after the war he hoped to visit Disneyland.

Anton. The political course was built around one key incident. We thought it was spontaneous at the time but it wasn't. It occurred midway through the course. Garwood was there. Normally he didn't attend but this day he did. He and Hom sat on either side of Mr. Ho. Ho asked Williams a question. Williams in the course of his answer used the term "ARVN."

Ho looked up fast and glanced at Garwood and Hom. He said, "What did you say, Williams?"

Williams said, "ARVN troops."

Ho yelled, "They're puppet troops! Not ARVN! You are trying to sabotage this course, Williams!"

Williams was dumbfounded. He said, "But that's what we call them. It means Army of the Republic of Viet Nam."

Ho said, "I know what it means. I also know you are trying to sabotage my course. Class dismissed! Everybody back to their hootch!"

The VC continued to harangue Williams during the noon break. He apparently told them he was sorry and would say puppet troops from then on. He was told that wouldn't be good enough. Later in the afternoon we were called back to class. Mr. Hom launched an attack on Williams. Then Garwood began. He spoke in biting tones. "You have come here to kill innocent Vietnamese people, Williams. Now you have sabotaged this course. You think you know more than everybody else. I've always hated you." He continued in this vein a few minutes and ended, "I spit on you, Williams."

Davis. The VC wanted to make an example out of somebody. They tried to get the most influential man in camp. Williams was infantry and had won the Silver Star in Korea. Whenever someone had a question they went to him. The VC told us we would have to criticize Williams in class. We got word to him and told him not to say anything, just to sit and take it. When it came my turn I stood at attention as was required and said, "Williams, I'm saying this not to hurt you but to help you. Constructive criticism is good. You were wrong to sabotage this class. You should understand this."

Daly. Everybody criticized Williams. I did too. We gave him some hard blows. It was the first time we'd really criticized one of our own. Nobody thought about it much till later. After his death we looked back and we were sorry. I think it was done because we had to do it. Everybody knew one thing. If you didn't criticize the way the VC wanted it would only prolong things.

Anton. Mr. Hom came to our hootch our first month in camp and made us sit in a circle. He said, "Now I want you to criticize each other's actions." I criticized Lewis for sleeping in the daytime. He in turn criticized me for some small thing. Someone then criticized Harker for a minor infraction, and so on. We laughed at first but stopped when Hom got angry. But we continued to treat it as a joke even though we were required to hold weekly sessions for nearly a year till the VC gave up on getting us to take this old communist technique seriously. The Williams thing was different. But here too no one was trying to even up scores.

Williams stayed in our hootch but we were not allowed to speak to him. He didn't talk. He was worried about what was to happen to him. Ho called him to the camp commander's hootch, where he remained till nightfall. He didn't say much when he returned, but told us the VC had made him write an apology. At first he wouldn't put in the strong stuff they wanted. They made him write it thirty times. They hit his wounded hand, held a gun to his head, and threatened to shoot him.

Next day he had to sit at the front of the class. The VC continued to humiliate him. Williams said he would apologize. He was a big man with a strong voice but now it had turned to a squeak. He said, "I apologize to the Front and realize my mistakes. I understand now that I planned to sabotage this course. I apologize again and promise to try very hard in the future." He looked shriveled. He snuffled like a kid.

Harker. He looked very old. Old and tired. He had a runny nose and seemed as helpless as a little child. I remembered how he had kept fighting after he was wounded, how he pulled us through those first days after our capture. I hated the VC.

Strictland. Williams would've been better off to have kept his mouth shut. If the VC said something, he should have said "blah-blah-blah" and agreed with them. Eventually he did anyway, so why not then? You know, if the VC say shit, you say, "What color?"

Anton. Williams was taken to the VC hootch the following day and forced to write again. Soon they told him he was finished. Next day he volunteered to go back and write more. The VC were giving him cigarettes, and he was a chain smoker. For cigarettes he would have written more of their lies. We were upset at him for this. Actually he'd begun to drift and perhaps we hadn't noticed it. Earlier he'd said he was going to cross over to the VC side and then escape. At the time he could hardly walk.

Harker. "What can you do to help the Vietnamese struggle against foreign aggression?" Mr. Ho asked us at the end of the course, and supplied the answer. We could make tapes for broadcast around the world; write GIs and urge them to refuse to fight; write American government officials to condemn U.S. actions in Viet Nam. "You have committed war crimes. You are subject to being punished as criminals of war. But we have given you the right of rebirth," he said. He added that we could very easily find ourselves dead if we didn't cooperate.

Anton. We refused to write at first. Grissett pleaded with us. "We have to write," he said, "otherwise no one will be released." We hung on our refusal.

Ho called us to class. He pointed a finger at us and said, "Maybe soon you can go home. But in order to do this you must write. Do not have a wait-and-see attitude." We thought he was lying. Yet maybe . . .

He called Kushner and me to his hootch. Kushner was sick and needed medicine. Ho said, "You write and I'll get you the medicine. It is very easy to die in the jungle. No one will know." He said this quietly. We returned to the hootch and thought it over.

He called us back and we said, "Okay, what do you want us to write?"

He outlined it simply. "Write what you think. You want to go home. You have been here a long time. You want your family to know you are alive." He ordered some Chloromycetin from a field hospital for Kushner and the others. It arrived in several days.

We wrote: "We have been captured a very long time. We want the war to end so we can go home." Everyone signed. The VC changed their minds. They did not want everyone to sign, only representatives from the marines, First Cav, 196th, blacks, and the Indian.

We rewrote the appeal and turned it in. Mr. Ho tore it up. "This is no good," he said. "You must tell the truth."

"What is the truth?" we asked.

"That Nguyen Van Thieu is a puppet of the U.S. imperialists. That U.S. troops are killing babies and raping women in Viet Nam."

We tried to bargain with him, and said, "Okay, we'll put in everything except the part about U.S. soldiers killing innocent civilians and raping women." He agreed. We wrote it as mildly as we thought we could get away with.

McMillan. Dr. Kushner said every man should make his own decision whether to write. Mr. Ho told us he could do anything he wanted to us. He said we could be buried right there. Weatherman had already gotten blown away and all that. I didn't think we had much choice.

Anton. During Ho's course Garwood was promoted to the rank of cadre of the National Liberation Front—the equivalent of lieutenant. He was given the name Huynh Chien Dao, which they told us meant brave liberation fighter. We were ordered to call him Mr. Dao. The VC stopped us from calling Williams Top and Kushner Doc. From now on it was to be simply Williams and Kushner. We were also informed that we had been given a promotion—from Criminals of War to Prisoners of War.

Ho told us the montagnards had heard about our progress. "They want to give you a gift," he said. "But they are very poor because the U.S. bombs their fields and defoliates their crops. They can only give you some bananas." They gave us thirty bananas and a cucumber apiece. To us it was a big deal.

Harker. I was politically unprepared for Viet Nam. It wasn't up to the army to indoctrinate me, though I think they could have familiarized us with the country's language and customs before sending us over. The material was in every public library. I was an average citizen, and the average citizen knew nothing about Viet Nam. I hadn't read a single book on the country. At first I found Ho's political course interesting. It put a little doubt in my mind. I said, "Maybe the VC have something." At the same time I thought I was hearing only one side of the argument. I began to ask why wasn't an election held in 1956 as specified by the Geneva agreements. Was it the Viet Minh's fault? Or Diem's? I also began to dislike the French for not putting Viet Nam on a better economic footing while it was their colony. Why hadn't they improved the life of the peasant farmer? They had educated an urban elite and these were the ones we were stuck with. They weren't at all representative of the Vietnamese.

The difficulty was, the VC quickly began to repeat themselves. They told the same story over and over so monotonously that it seemed they needed reassurance themselves. As it was repeated so many times I realized I was hearing an account of four thousand years of warlike backwardness. You can't get around it no matter how much you might sympathize with the Vietnamese. They like to fight. Struggle is a part of their life. I wouldn't try to draw any slick Freudian conclusions, but it's a fact that they are a people with a negligible sex drive. Even when the ARVN were at their most undisciplined, you heard about them stealing chickens but never about them raping women.

Anton. A certain amount of what the VC said seemed true. They always threw up the 1954 Geneva agreements to us. They said we had broken the agreements and had shipped Diem military arms. Kushner had read a little about Viet Nam. He said he couldn't remember for sure but thought the VC were distorting the facts. All the while we were in the jungle we believed they were misrepresenting the 1954 document. But it turned out they weren't. They later gave us a verbatim copy. It was just as they'd said—they hadn't misquoted a bit.

Indoctrination classes continued sporadically after Ho left, conducted by the camp commander and Mr. Hom. Our opinions began to change somewhat, though most of us continued to back U.S. policy in terms of what we'd thought before being captured. Our debate was along the lines that maybe the VC were right, they had caught a rotten deal—but, still, they were sonsofbitches. It was an attitude made up partly of our racism (we're all racists, I mean, to a certain extent), our contempt for their lack of material development, and the fact that they were our captors and almost starving us to death. Everyone said, "All these thousands of years and this is all they've got—they don't deserve anymore. Look at the Japanese."

The VC continued to demand certain ones of us write antiwar appeals. They once told Cannon to write his autobiography. He came to me and said, "I can't write too good. You write yours and let me borrow it to give me ideas about what to say." He copied my autobiography word for word, wrote his name across the top, and turned it in. The Vietnamese never asked him to write again. Ike McMillan and Lewis and several others got around the problem by having Pfister write their propaganda.

McMillan. It wasn't that I was scared to write. I'm going to tell you now, I just don't like to write. One time the VC told us to write an antiwar letter to our buddies fighting in the Nam. I said, "I don't have any buddies."

They said, "Then write your relatives."

I said, "I don't have any of those either."

They said, "Write anybody." I told Pfister to write for me and just tell a lie about something. He knew he would get some cigarettes out of it. The reason we got Pfister as our ghost writer was he had a nice handwriting. If you didn't write well enough to suit the VC they made you do it over.

THE AMERICAN VIET CONG

1st Force Recon Company (Rein)
Phu Bai, RVN
DTG 151630 July 1968

Operation Order: 305-68
Operation: Houston
Patrol: Dublin City (C-2-2)
Debriefer: Cpl. W. D. Kearney

Patrol Report

1. *Composition:* 10 enlisted.
   Special Attachments: None.
   Comm. and Observation Equipment: Two PRC-25s, one 7 × 50.
   Special Equipment: One M-14, one M-79.

2. *Mission:* Conduct reconnaissance and surveillance operations within your assigned haven to detect possible VC/NVA troop movement or arms infiltration in the vicinity of Hill 273. Particular emphasis is to be placed on locating and fixing enemy storage areas, fortifications (trench lines, bunkers), harbor sites, and the direction and trafficability of trails in the area. Be prepared to call and adjust ARTY/Air on targets of opportunity in support of Operation Houston.

3. *Time of departure and return:* 130700H/151630H.

4. *Omitted.*

5. *Synopsis:* 51 hours of patrolling and observation resulted in two contacts with estimated 25 VC/NVA.

6. *Observation of enemy and terrain:*

145

A. *Enemy:* 151230H (YC 925987)—Patrol was taking a break when one member of the patrol saw two VC/NVA, twenty meters away, carrying AK-47s, dressed in green utilities, and wearing cartridge belts. The patrol opened fire on the two VC/NVA killing both. The patrol heard one of the VC/NVA say in clear English, "Help me!" when he fell. The patrol states that this enemy was Caucasian with brown hair, age 20–25, 5'9" tall, round eyes and was wearing green utilities and spoke distinct English. The team then threw M-26 grenades at estimated 20–25 VC/NVA moving toward their position from the north. When grenades were thrown patrol heard two more VC/NVA scream and fall. The patrol broke contact and began woving NW up Hill 273 vicinity YC 9299. Team heard movement and suspected that enemy was following them.

151400H (YC 915995)—The patrol was breaking bush when the team leader spotted one VC/NVA lying on his stomach looking at the patrol. The patrol leader shot and killed this VC/NVA. At this time, the patrol began receiving a heavy volume SA/AW fire from an estimated 25 VC/NVA, resulting in one USMC KIA and one USMC WIA (minor) in the initial burst of fire. The patrol returned fire as the VC/NVA began moving toward the patrol's position, killing four VC/NVA with small arms. Gunships were requested and immediately arrived on station.

Marine gunships began rocketing and strafing the area. Marine fixed wing was requested and received. After fixed wing was utilized, all movement around the patrol's position ceased. As the team was being hoisted out, they again received S/A fire. The team members on the ground returned fire resulting in one additional VC/NVA KIA. At 151630H hoist extract was successfully completed under fire.

B. *Terrain:* Steep with heavy undergrowth. Canopy was 30–50 high. Movement was difficult.

7. *Omitted.*

8. *Results of encounter with the enemy:* Two probable KIA VC/NVA by S/A. Seven confirmed VC/NVA by S/A. One USMC KIA by S/A. One USMC WIA (minor) by S/A.

9. *Condition of patrol:* Good.

10. *Conclusions and recommendations:* Patrol leader thinks that the VC/NVA they had contact with were going toward Delta Relay.

11. *Effectiveness of supporting arms:* Gunships and fixed wing did an outstanding job.

12. *Comments by debriefer:* Four patrol members saw and definitely identified one enemy as Caucasian. All patrol members distinctly heard the enemy cry "Help me!" This action took place in the same general vicinity where an enemy battalion-size base camp had been previously located (see patrol debrief record no. 224 and Flag Dip no. 283) at vicinity YC 927987.

13. *Select munitions:* Yes.

14. *Patrol members:*

CPL House, C. H.	CPL House, C. H.
LCPL Gordon, P. C.	2nd PLT, CO. "C"
LCPL Shafer, D. W.	1st Recon Bn.
LCPL Wilker, J. A.	Patrol Leader
LCPL Sweeney, D. J.	
PFC Olenski, P. F.	
PFC Ayala, W.	
PFC Wall, W. E. (WIA minor)	
PFC Brown, C. G. (KIA)	
PFC Beard, J. A.	

Patrol Leader Charles House. *It was around noon the third day of the patrol. We were tired, out of water. We stopped by a swift-flowing stream in a boulder-strewn clearing to fill our canteens. Then set up all around security by sitting in a circle with each man facing outward. We began to eat C rations. We communicated by hand signals. Thirty minutes passed. Perry Gordon stood to put on his cartridge belt. He looked at the stream. Suddenly he got the damnedest expression on his face. I thought, "What the shit?"*

Gordon lunged for his rifle. He said, "Oh, my God, he's going to shoot me!"

I looked and saw a white man standing on the other side of the stream.

A North Vietnamese walked out from behind a boulder. Gordon yelled "Gooks!"

He pumped off four or five rounds. The white man and the gook fell. We all began to fire. The Caucasian tried to get to his knees. I heard him say, "Help me!"

I saw fifteen or twenty more gooks coming down the ridge. I shouted, "Let's get out of here!"

Perry Gordon. *At first I thought he was a team member refilling his canteen. At the same time I knew that couldn't be because we'd already done that. He wore knee-length dark-green pants. Across his chest was a red sash like the kind beauty contestants wear. It looked to be made of silkish ao dai material. Maybe he wore it to keep the VC from firing at him. His brown hair was close-cropped on the sides but long on top. He was of average height and weighed maybe a hundred forty or fifty pounds.*

He looked at me. His AK was slung over his shoulder and pointed to the ground. I was astonished. I expected him to open fire. My rifle was on the ground. When the North Vietnamese walked from behind a boulder, the white man turned and looked at him. Then he turned and looked at me. He didn't seem to be shocked. He just stared at me curiously.

By this time my rifle was up and ready. I cut loose with five to eight rounds of semiautomatic fire. The Caucasian went flying into the creek. All this happened in a matter of seconds.

Everyone opened up. Wilker's M-16 jammed. He threw a grenade at two more NVA who stepped from behind the boulder. I changed magazines and fired again at the white man, who was trying to get up on one knee. He said, "Help me . . . help me . . ." The other patrol members began to break bush while I and the M-79er covered them. Then we took off too.

Several hours later we ran into an ambush. Our point man, Brown, was killed. As he was hit Brown fell backward, knocking over the duece point and saving his life. Corporal House wasted the gook who got Brown. We radioed for marine gunships and jets. They worked over the area. North Vietnamese were all over the place. We reached a bombed-out area and called a chopper in to extract us. We took more fire as the chopper hovered overhead. The first two men were lifted up the hoist, and one accidentally dropped a grenade on our heads with its pin out and safety spoon off. Wilker picked it up and tossed it away before it exploded.

On the chopper back Phu Bai we talked about the white man for the first time. I think we were too shocked to mention it earlier. None of us believed our eyes. I felt bad about it at first. But I decided it was either him or me. Even if I'm not too hot about killing VC, I'd kill another American like that, one who was working for them. But I hope I don't have to do it again.

Strictland. No, Bob Garwood wasn't killed by the marine patrol. He left our camp in July. That's when this guy Ho was there. It was strange that Garwood would leave with Ho there, but he did. I could never figure it out, unless Ho sent him on an assignment. He was gone three or four weeks. He went to the hospital during this time. The reason I know—well, I don't really know but this guard at the camp, a young kid about fifteen, got sick and they took him to the hospital. Garwood told us when he returned he had seen the kid and he was okay.

There was nothing to indicate Garwood had been wounded. He told us he'd been down.to the coastal plains. He had a portable loud speaker and would go down to talk to American GIs about crossing over to the Viet Cong. He said while he was gone he got fired on and the VC saved his life by jumping in front of him.

Author's note. Bob Garwood disappeared in September, 1965. At the time I was executive officer of the army's special counterintelligence organization in Da Nang. Our counterparts in marine intelligence asked us to be on the lookout for information about the young private. They were somewhat reticent about the circumstances of Garwood's disappearance, perhaps fearing embarrassment for the Corps, but it was clear that his was no ordinary case.

The following telegram was sent to Garwood's father four days after he was reported missing:

Regret to confirm that your son Private Robert R. Garwood USMC has been reported missing 28 Sept 1965 in the vicinity of

Headquarters Battalion Motor Pool when he departed in a Mighty Mite vehicle to report to the Division G-2 section. He was discovered missing during bed check and further investigation reveals that he failed to report to the G-2 section. Extensive search operations are in progress and every effort is being made to locate him. You will be advised when additional information is received. I extend to you on behalf of the United States Marine Corps our deepest sympathy during this period of great anxiety. His mother has been notified. R. C. Mangrum Lt Gen USMC Acting Commandant of the Marine Corps.

A few years later I visited Garwood's father in a midwestern city. Mr. Garwood is a short, stocky man with wavy and receding gray-black hair. He used to be a mechanic, but for the past fifteen years has worked as a commercial printer on hourly wage. The Viet Nam war had almost ended when we met, and Mr. Garwood got us a beer and talked about his dislike for the antiwar protesters who were then in the news. He didn't support the war however, he quickly pointed out, because the U.S. had failed to win it.

As for himself, he said he was a man opposed to violence. "In that respect Bobby was like me. He would get up and walk away from a fight." Later, after another beer, he added, "It really wouldn't surprise me to find he was helping the VC. He was weak. He'd do whatever anyone wanted if they stuck a gun to his head."

Bob grew up in a lower-middle-class neighborhood. Mr. Garwood divorced his first wife for infidelity, was awarded custody of young Bob and his brother, and later remarried a waitress who bore him six more children.

At the beginning of his son's last year in high school, Mr. Garwood clashed repeatedly with Bob over his wish "to run around with a wild crowd and stay out till three o'clock in the morning." Bob Garwood was an average student—he had a turn for math—but he dropped out of school and ran away to live with his girl friend and her mother. Mr. Garwood retrieved him from the girl's house, and had him placed in a juvenile home for delinquent children.

Bob's real mother was an underlying point of friction in the dispute between father and son. Bob had renewed contact with her when he had trouble with his father. His former wife, Mr. Garwood told me bitterly, had acted as if Bob didn't exist after the divorce, never came to see him, never sent a Christmas card. After the relationship was resumed, she began to visit Bob and to give him occasional pocket money.

The family crisis was compromised by the appearance of a U.S. Marine recruiting sergeant, who, not untypically, relied on the juvenile home for help in filling his monthly quota. Bob asked for and got his father's permission to join. On October 11, 1963, he was sworn into the marines. He was seventeen. After basic training at Camp Pendleton, California, he became a driver for high-ranking marine officers. Later he was shipped to Okinawa, and then to Viet Nam.

Bob sent his father a conciliatory letter from Viet Nam. "I should have had more respect for you but I never felt I could talk to you. . . ." He apologized and said he'd meant no harm to anyone, especially his stepmother. He wrote home sparingly in 1965. He never indicated he was in any sort of trouble, nor did he speak much about the war. His last letter, dated September 11, 1965, was a typical hasty note.

Dad, family, all

It is a long time no see, hear, or write, how everyone at home? Me well I'm fine. I just got out of the field hospital and stayed there [to be] a little better. I had a week with a disease called Tropical Malaria. This is not as bad as general Malaria but can be if they don't do anything about it. I'm OK now so don't worry. All I need now is some decent American food.

I have not got really much to say but I'll do my best to finish this page at least OK. How Gran Ma C—— getting along? Fine I hope. How the people in Michigan getting along, well I still haven't heard for sure yet the day I'll be coming back to the States. I'm sure [it]

will be good to get back I've never missed any thing in my whole
life as much as I've missed the States and really almost forgot what
it's like to be among civilized people and places. There is been a
little rumor that maybe I'll be back in the States by November don't
worry I should be home for the holidays, anyway that's what I'm
praying.

Hey if it's not too much to ask how about a line or two from
somebody back there. I'd still like to know if everybody [is OK] I'd
writing again as soon as I can so until I hear from you, take care
all and may God be with you all always.

Hoping to hear from you real soon.
Love from your son.
(signed)
Bob

PS   I have not told you anything about Viet Nam as it's still in about
the same situation as when you had heard from me a little hotter is
about all. How much do you hear about Viet Nam back in the States,
I'll bet they really build the Marine Corps up don't they. Believe me
none of it is peaches and cream although I wish some of it was. Take
care all and write soon.

U.S. Marines operating near Da Nang picked up enemy propaganda leaflets signed by Garwood not long after he disappeared.
In May, 1967, the National Liberation Front made a brief announcement via radio that Garwood had been freed. But he failed
to show up at friendly lines, and no further explanation was
given. Then in July, 1968, four members of the marine recon
patrol described above identified Garwood from file pictures of
missing Americans as the Caucasian they had encountered and
believed to have killed in the jungle west of Da Nang. A marine
intelligence officer without authorization disclosed Garwood's
name to the press, and his father was then quietly alerted that his
son was perhaps a defector. The next official word about Garwood came more than a year later when three POWs were freed
by the Viet Cong.

Department of the Navy
Headquarters U.S. Marine Corps

4 December 1969

Dear Mr. Garwood:

This is to confirm information previously provided you concerning your son, Private First Class Robert R. Garwood, 206 96 69, U.S. Marine Corps.

The three recently released U.S. Army Prisoners of War reported conversing with your son on October 24, 1969, the day before they were released. Your son made no specific requests; however, he did state that he would like for you to know that he is okay. The three returnees reported that they saw your son in the Prisoner of War compound frequently and that he appeared in good health.

I would like to remind you not to release any background information regarding your son's personal history or military service. Release of such information could adversely affect his welfare since it may be used for coercion and propaganda purposes. Also, this will serve to protect you from any harassment by peace groups and anti-war demonstrators.

In the event that any additional information becomes available concerning your son, be assured that you will be notified.

Sincerely,
(signed)
G. E. Lawrence
Colonel, USMC
Head, Personal Affairs Branch

Bob Garwood dropped out of sight in late 1969 after saying he was leaving for Hanoi. There were indications that he did in fact reach North Viet Nam's capital and later rumors that he had been sent to study in Russia. A black American soldier, who operated in the central highlands around the Cambodian border, was also detailed by U.S. intelligence reports in the latter part of the war as a defector. The black soldier at last word, however, married a Vietnamese woman and ceased actively aiding the Viet Cong. Another handful of Americans, in-country deserters left behind after the Paris cease-fire, has reportedly helped the VC as a matter of expediency.

After the POWs were freed in 1973, I asked a group of Pentagon intelligence officials what was to happen to Garwood.

"He didn't come back!" they said with relief.

Robert Garwood is listed by the Defense Department in a special category called "Prisoners of War Unaccounted For."

9

Frank Anton

Willie Watkins slowly took over as camp leader. He was the strongest. When there was work to be done he did it. From there it grew to his having the crucial say about what and when to cook. He then began to make other decisions too. It was never outward that he ran the place. He didn't say, "I'm the chief." But he was. I guess you would call Watkins a good-looking Negro. He was a little over six feet tall, lanky, with very dark skin and penetrating eyes. He kept his hair short and himself neat. He was wiry and hard as a rock, could carry two sixty-pound baskets of manioc easier than I could walk. And he seemed never to get sick.

At the beginning Kushner, Williams, and myself got together and discussed what we should do. The person who led the camp had to be physically strong. None of us was. We decided to try to use our influence as a group. We made no attempt to create a military organization. The VC warned us individually several times that if we did we would be punished. Moreover, we weren't sure of our legal rights in the matter. Kushner was a captain but a doctor and therefore a noncombatant. I was a warrant officer, a pilot with no command responsibility. Williams was a first sergeant but wounded.

Eventually Watkins let us know that since we couldn't work our

155

decisions would be limited. Some of the others followed him, saying, "That's right. Anybody who tells me what to do has to work at least as hard as I do." Willie had the Negroes organized on some questions. He got them off to the side and spoke to them about what they should do. I don't know what they talked about, but it was bad for our morale. At times they took care of each other. At other times they were split.

No racial comments were made in camp, although a couple of guys didn't like Negroes. Joe Zawtocki, for example, didn't talk about Willie being a Negro but being Watkins. "I hate that black sonofabitch," he would say. Strictland got along with the blacks okay because he could work. Harker did too but he didn't like Willie. Actually it came down to who could work and who couldn't.

The Vietnamese went to Willie when they wanted to know something about the camp or to organize an activity. Watkins got the information from them and told us. In this respect he had pushed out Russ Grissett, who served at first as our communications link with the VC because he'd been there longest and spoke a little Vietnamese. But the VC hated Russ and they liked Willie. They liked him mainly because he worked hard and never talked back. Willie, unlike most of us, always called Garwood Mr. Dao, as the VC ordered us to do. He hated Garwood, that was obvious, but he kept it to himself. He was very secretive.

Daly. Russ Grissett told us when we first got to camp, "In the jungle the lion is king. To survive you must live like an animal." Kushner and I tried to argue that it didn't have to be that way. But eventually it was exactly as Grissett said. We fought and carried on. We lived for a time like dogs. I even took part in it myself, yes.

Anton. Watkins could have whipped anybody in camp—that was the point. Everyone thought so. Davis, who was several inches shorter and also very strong, had a certain influence over Watkins. Frequently Davis disagreed with him but they never fought. Willie liked Davis. He would bargain and barter with him before it came to blows. Several people tried to fight Willie. Lewis was one. Watkins took care of him with a single lick.

Daly. That's true. Everybody was afraid of getting beat. Watkins once pounded the stew out of Joe Zawtocki. Kushner and Anton swore they would make Watkins pay for it if they ever got back to the States. They didn't say this in front of Watkins, though. I thought since we were a military group the leadership responsibility should have been Captain Kushner's. He always said the obligation was not his because he was a noncombatant. He said the one who should be in charge was Sergeant Williams. But Williams was wounded. Many people felt Kushner was using this as an excuse to avoid responsibility.

We all admired Captain Kushner. He helped us with his medical advice. But the man was lazy. The first time we argued was when I told him it was his turn to sweep the hootch floor. He refused. He said he hadn't gone to college for so many years to sweep floors. I said, "Wait a damn minute. I didn't go to school for twelve years to sweep either. But everyone has to take his turn." He also said that before he would carry manioc he wouldn't eat them. You couldn't believe he was so lazy. But he did change. Anton never did.

Harker. Dr. Kushner was an intellectual caught in a situation where physical strength was the chief virtue. He was, as his wife Valerie said in *Life* magazine, the type of guy who would tell her to mow the lawn because he didn't want to mess up his hands. I was famous for jumping on his back. I guess I was letting off steam. Davis was the serious type. He believed, like Watkins and Strictland, in working or else. He would get into hassles with Kushner but Kushner would sweet talk him out of it. It was true that Kushner and Anton were sick. But we were all sick. And sometimes you simply had to push yourself beyond your limitations.

Watkins. Kushner was a nice guy, easy to get along with, but he was soft, and I was especially suspicious of him. I felt he was strong enough to pick manioc. All of us felt that way. We thought it was mainly laziness. He said he couldn't go. We said, "If you don't bring back more than two or three that will be helping." He said walking was bad for his feet, that he could hardly make it. We said we felt the same way. Still, if we didn't pick them we would probably starve. Finally we told him, okay, no work, no eat.

Anton. I didn't like Watkins but I had respect for him. What he did was wrong. Yet he didn't do it with malice. He did it because he was strong and lacked judgment. He took over without really trying. He did a lot for people who were sick, so much that I would have to overlook the bad part. He helped people when they were down and did not say anything about it whether he thought they were faking or not. Willie hated Williams. Why we could never figure out. Yet he helped Williams. He carried him to the latrine when he was down. He was that type of guy; he could hate but still help you.

Everybody at first tried to work. That's my opinion. Right away people got sick. I myself was sicker than the others because I didn't eat rice in the beginning. Kushner and I went down fast. We remained weak after that. At first we went for firewood. We had to get it every day because we could never get enough, and there were no complaints. Then my load got smaller and smaller. If I carried a piece the other prisoners wanted to know why I couldn't carry ten pieces. If ten pieces, why not twenty? When I carried none I heard the snide comments, "Last time you carried some, why can't you do it now?" I didn't mind it so much when it was said to my face. But I knew they were talking behind my back. I couldn't pick manioc at all.

Kushner didn't think that being a doctor excused him from working. He was sicker than everybody realized. All they understood was that "I'm doing all the work and he's eating half the food." That's the way it was. Kushner confided to me he felt terrible about not being able to help more. He would get depressed and go off by himself. The VC jumped on him more than anybody else. Some of this, of course, was his own fault. He would argue with anybody about anything.

The Vietnamese saw what was happening to us. I don't know whether they planned it. But there were signs they encouraged our antagonisms. I remember Mr. Ho said that so and so doesn't work yet he eats as much as the others. He told Watkins and Davis they should have more because they did half the work.

Yet it was not the VC but a skin disease that pushed us into our darkest period and caused a near-fatal split between us. Daly came down with it first, which was unusual since the blacks were less susceptible than we were to disease. But he was lighter-skinned than the other four, a coffee-and-cream color, and though big, perhaps more fragile. It quickly spread, some catching it worse than others.

Harker. The disease was probably caused by a lack of vitamins and oil. It was unlike anything ever seen by Dr. Kushner. The epidermis cracked open with water-blister-type sores that first ran clear serum and then pus. Scratching was almost sexual in its relief but only made the disease worse. The pus dried, gluing our pajamas to our backsides. The pain was horrible. Eighteen of us were jammed together on the bed. It was excruciatingly hot. But we had to sleep under our blankets to ward off hordes of mosquitoes. Men cried out at night, "Kill me! I want to die!" Guys began to schiz out in the daytime by pulling blankets over their heads to shut out the world. The disease was combined with our growing dysentery and malaria. The hootch smelled like a septic tank. It was best not to get up at night unless absolutely necessary. Probably you would step in excrement while walking down the aisleway.

The skin disease broke out before Mr. Ho arrived. It jumped from man to man. Ho saw the condition we were in. It was he who ordered the VC to build us another hootch. The VC had divided us several months earlier into two nine-man squads. At the time it meant nothing. The squad leaders were mostly responsible for giving the VC a head count in the mornings and evenings. Now Watkins' squad was moved to the new hootch. Our squad, headed by Strictland, who replaced Grissett, stayed in the old hootch.

Ho possibly had ideas about Strictland, and maybe that was why he was made a squad leader. All of us thought constantly about being freed. But even though you wanted to go along with the VC for this reason things sometimes got so ridiculous that you questioned them before you could catch yourself. "You don't understand," the VC would say. "You imperialists have aggressed us."

"Oh, yeah, how could I ever forget?"

Strictland made few mistakes of this sort. He was quiet and went along without arguing. He was rather short, boyish-looking, with cool blue eyes and light freckles. He was strong as a bull and a hard worker. He had been brought up on a tobacco farm in North Carolina and was drafted after high school. That's what the VC liked about him. Their idea of a "progressive" was someone who killed himself working.

Strictland. I did anything they said. Other guys argued with them. Some they'd have to hit in the head to make them get out of bed. The VC might come to the hootch and say, "We need five guys to carry grass to build us a house."

I'd say, "I'll go." Watkins and this guy Davis, we'd go do it. I didn't mind. I felt like I was just getting by. Surviving.

Anton. The VC separated the two nine-man squads into two hootches and it just so happened that most of the strong and healthy men were concentrated in one squad. Watkins, Davis, Denny, Joe Zawtocki. In fact myself and Long, who was captured when a special forces camp was overrun, were about the only ones in our squad who couldn't work. But almost everyone in the other squad was sick with the skin disease or other ailments. Harker and Strictland were the stronger members of the second squad. Harker had a terrible case of the skin disease. Strictland had serious kidney trouble, he was pissing blood.

Separating us into two hootches turned out to be like putting us into two different countries. We became enemies. At first there was a compromise about work. Watkins told the other hootch, "You send two guys on a manioc run and we'll send three or four." Then it got to the point where we'd send three and they'd send just one. Resentments built up. I irritated the other squad because I wasn't working, yet my squad was complaining about them. No one said much about Long because he was ill from the moment he arrived in camp.

The VC killed a pig on September 2 to celebrate North Viet Nam's Independence Day. Before going to eat with the Vietnamese, Grissett said, "Let's show them today how Americans act. No reaching and grabbing. Two people serve and no one eats till everyone has his food." Everyone agreed. The food was placed on the table. Grissett and someone else began politely serving the others.

Suddenly Grissett said, "Fuck this," and dumped half a plate of meat into his bowl, squatted on his haunches, and began to shovel it in. The meal deteriorated into the usual reach and grab.

That's where we were at this point. Our mental condition had begun to match our physical condition. We had no shoes, toothpaste, soap, or mosquito nets. All of us had bed sores from the hard bamboo. Rats ran rampant through the hootch at night. They were unbelievably brave. Sometimes they crawled up and sat on our arms. I guess they sensed we were one of them.

Davis. The split began one day in my hootch. Watkins, Denny, and Joe Zawtocki were talking about the guys in the other hootch being lazy. Everybody had the skin disease. We returned from manioc runs with our hands swollen and bleeding. Petty irritations became hard resentments and then anger. Some of my squad thought some of the other squad were goofing off. Some thought Dr. Kushner had too much education to work. Everybody was sick and feeling sorry for themselves, that's what it was. So we said why don't we split up and let each hootch worry about itself.

Harker. We hadn't had to work while Ho was there. The Vietnamese had done everything for us so we could attend class. The quality and quantity of our food was a little better during this time. The vacation ended and we had to face the reality of scrambling for ourselves again. The skin disease and the separation into two hootches opened the way for the breach.

The split started the day after the September 2 celebration. The other hootch said they had taken a vote at the end of August and had decided that my squad must henceforth gather its own firewood and manioc and do its own cooking.

We said, "You're crazy. Somebody will die."

They said, "This is the way it's going to be."

I was mad at Watkins. I later found that Denny had a big say in the matter too. It was like a slap in the face. I thought Watkins didn't understand the situation. A lot of men in my squad were deathly sick.

The decision to split apart was theirs. But we played the game like them. All of us played. Things became competitive and petty. Some of my squad were in the Vietnamese kitchen after the September 2 celebration and saw a pot of leftover pig fat. We brought it back to our hootch. Instead of going eighteen ways, it went nine.

Anton. We had one kitchen, a small shed with a mud-packed stove and an underground chimney to disperse the smoke. During the split we took turns using it. The other squad took an extra long time when they cooked. Whether on purpose or not I don't know. In retaliation the people cooking for us also took an extra long time. We ended up eating only two meals a day instead of three. And for about a week each group had only one meal; one group in the morning, the other in the afternoon, because they couldn't get into the kitchen till then.

Harker and Strictland did most of the work for the other squad. Harker had lost a lot of weight and like myself was very thin. He was of medium height, with a shock of brown wavy hair, a full mouth, and teeth that could have used braces when he was a kid. He was basically a loner. He and I simply ignored each other at first and seldom spoke. He was a hard worker, though, and good with his hands. Everybody respected him for this.

Davis. There was animosity. Some guys from one squad didn't talk to the other squad while the split was on; but I did.

McMillan. My foot hadn't completely healed. A lot of people said I was shamming. They thought I should have gotten up quicker. But I couldn't walk well, it was impossible to hump up and down the rocks. Kushner would go on a manioc run and couldn't bring back but two or three. He wasn't built for it, he just couldn't do it. Daly couldn't carry a heavy load either, would stumble and fall and tear up two manioc baskets before he got off one run. Fred could do nothing; he was swollen with edema. Even Grissett had fallen very sick.

Watkins did a lot of things to piss people off. It wasn't that he was sympathizing with the VC. But, goddamn, he was trying to cover his ass in the long run. He didn't do that much to be progressive. Kushner did everything to be done because he was an officer and the VC were always on his back—they forced him to do it. Watkins didn't do any more than Kushner. But the fact was Watkins was truthful about the things he did. He was honest. That was one reason why the Vietnamese liked him.

But he didn't understand our situation. Even before the split Watkins told Kushner, Daly, and myself that either we worked or he would cut off our chow. In fact he did cut us for one day. It surprised me as a black man that he would do that to another black man. I said, "This dude must be crazy." Any man in his right mind could have seen we weren't able to work. If he had a little sympathy he would have known.

Will didn't look at things that way. He was hard. One day I walked into the kitchen to get some water when he was cooking. He told me to wait a few minutes till chow was ready. I tried to get the water anyway. He said, "If you get it I'm gonna knock your teeth down your throat."

Damn, man, I'm looking up at a big dude, almost twice as big as I am. Plus that he had once boxed in the Golden Gloves. I said, "Okay, man, if that's the way you want it."

Davis was in that squad with Watkins and Denny. Davis wanted to get along with everybody and he did; everybody liked him. But as I said to Kushner, "If a man tells Davis to jump off a mountain, he'll jump." I told Davis this to his face. I said, "If I'm in a situation where a man told me not to cook your rice and said he would beat me if I did, I wouldn't cook for you. But I would at least take some of my rice to you."

During the split, don't get me wrong, some guys were talking to each other. But I wasn't speaking to no damn body.

Davis. I didn't want any part of the camp leadership. I didn't want to be always hassling others about what they should do. We

were all men. I was about as strong as Watkins. If it had come
down to a fight it would have been a pretty good one. He never
gave me any static. Maybe because we were both black and there
was a mutual respect.

Harker. I got up before dawn early in September and went to
take a leak. When I returned I saw Cannon lying on the floor near
the firepit. He often sat up at night and slept in the daytime. He
was in terrible pain and there was so little room on the bed that
his movements disturbed the others. He was making a strange
noise. I went to investigate. He said, "I'm trying to get back on
the bed." But he wasn't moving. I realized he was in a sad state.
He went into a coma later that day, and passed away after a few
hours.

The VC made a bamboo coffin. We dug his grave. They came
to the hootch and said, "Here are some white clothes to bury him
in."

We said, "Take your clothing back. We don't want anything.
You didn't give him anything when he was alive." They were
insulted, and left.

They must have realized that we felt very strongly about it for
us to talk back to them. Later they called us to a meeting. The
camp commander said, "Why do you think Cannon died?"

We said, "Because he did not have proper medical care or
adequate food."

The VC said, "No, he died because of his wounds and because
he didn't clean himself."

We argued with them. They became irritated. We backed off.

Anton. Williams had grown weaker after the political course.
He had a bad case of edema. The fluid had swollen his testicles
to three times their normal size, they were unreal, watery looking;
his legs and stomach were swollen and the fluid had begun to
press toward his heart. If Kushner had had the simple diuretics
available in any pharmacy, he could have saved his life. It was
especially hard on him watching men die whom he knew he could
save if medicines were available. But nothing was available, or if

it was the VC waited as usual until it was too late.

Williams lay fatally ill some days. Watkins carried him to the latrine, others washed him. The VC gave him a can of condensed milk. Kushner warned him not to drink it without diluting it because it was too sweet in concentrated form and would complicate his dysentery. By this time, however, Williams was practically incoherent. He drank it straight. One morning several weeks after Cannon died we awoke to hear Williams breathing strangely. In a couple of hours he was dead.

A few weeks after Williams it was Sherman's turn. He had never recovered from the time spent in stocks after the escape attempt. He had hung on the following months like a walking zombie, sitting outside when the sun was out, inside on the bed when it wasn't. We reminded him of his Marine Corps stories, trying to make him talk and take an interest in living. He couldn't remember them. Sometimes he laughed and smiled. But he wasn't there. And finally he died.

McMillan. Usually the two squads didn't talk to each other but that night in November we did. Joe Zawtocki was up by the kitchen when he called me. Me and Joe got along pretty good because Joe blew pot. All the guys who blew got along, I associated with them. Anyway, Joe says to me, "Hey, Ike, want some pussy?"

I said, "Yeah, man."

He said, "You're gonna have to eat it."

I went to see what he wanted. He had the camp cat with him. Grissett, Harker, and Strictland had planned to kill the cat and eat him. Trouble was, nobody could catch him. I returned and told everyone we had the cat.

Somebody asked, "Who's gonna kill him?"

I said, "I'm not gonna kill him. I've done had enough of bad luck with cats."

They said, "What do you mean?"

I remember when I was small I used to aggravate cats—set them on fire, shoot them with my BB gun. I'd do this for devilment. My grandfather used to beat me. Ohhh, did he beat me! One time I caught this cat and poured kerosene on his back and lit him up. He looked like a shooting star. That night when I was asleep, that same cat jumped on my bed. I grabbed a window stick and started beating him. He didn't move. I got a Coke bottle and threw it at him. He still didn't move. I screamed for my grandmother. When she came the cat disappeared. I knew I had seen the cat, but now he was gone.

You can ask my wife. If a cat crosses me I'll turn around and go the other way. Any cat. That's me today. I respect cats. And it went through my head that I shouldn't bother this VC cat. But I said, "Hell, I can't have no worse luck than I'm having right now."

Davis. I didn't want them to kill it actually. I liked the cat and thought it was bad luck to kill one. I also knew the camp authorities would miss it. I told them to let me hold the cat. They said, "No, you'll turn him loose." And I would have too.

The cat was miaowing loudly. He knew something was up, all the guys were gathered round petting him. They tried first to drown him in a pot a boiling water. But he jumped out scratching and spitting and almost got away. Then Grissett said, "I'll kill him."

McMillan. Russ took the cat outside. Two or three minutes later we heard this *ka-loomph!* He returned. The cat's head was bashed in. Someone got a rusty razor blade and began to skin it. Kushner was detailed to hide the fur and entrails in the latrine. Strictland watched for the guards.

Some guys from Watkins' hootch were there and we said, "Hey, there are too many of us here. Somebody should go." They left.

We started jiving around, wondering how it would taste because it was all lovely pink meat.

"Jeez, look at those thighs!"

Strictland whistled a warning. We stashed the cat. A guard arrived. He asked us what we were doing.

"Boiling water," we said. "We're thirsty." It looked strange because we weren't supposed to have a fire at night. He told us to go to bed. Then he left.

We resumed our work. Ten minutes later a guard we called College Joe slipped in without Strictland seeing him. He walked up behind us, scaring us half to death. He saw the cat but didn't recognize it. He said, *"Tot lam,"* and laughed. He thought we had killed some sort of wild animal.

Then Qua the montagnard guard came in and began poking around.

He spotted the paws, which we hadn't been able to skin, and shouted, *"Meo! Meo!"* All of us ran from the kitchen and left the cat laying there. Went to our hootch and jumped on the bed.

The VC and Garwood arrived with lamps. They ordered us outside. Fred was the only one from our hootch who hadn't been in the kitchen, he was too sick. Before we left the hootch we agreed that no matter what happened we wouldn't admit anything. Outside, they called me and Harker to the front.

"Who killed the cat?" Mr. Hom asked.

"I don't know, Mr. Hom," I said.

He asked Harker.

Harker said, "I don't know, Mr. Hom."

He went down the line asking each person. Everybody stood firm.

Anton. We watched from our hootch. It was an eerie scene. The lamp light distorted the Viet Cong's features and made them appear even more sinister.

They said, "You have killed the camp's cat. The camp commander loves his cat. All the guards love the cat." It was ridiculous. They had loved the camp dog too. Yet one day several months earlier when meat was in short supply they had beaten their lovable dog to death with sticks and eaten him. They had had a pet parakeet they were going to teach to talk. It too had disappeared into their pot. "The baby loved the cat." The younger cook, Hannah, had a two-year-old boy who ran around the camp bare-assed. "You must tell us who killed the cat."

McMillan. We stood firm for half an hour. Then Russ said, "I killed the cat. I heard a noise by the john and I threw a rock and accidentally killed him." That wouldn't wash. The VC jerked him out of line. They kicked and beat him. He fell to the ground. They pounded him terribly.

Harker. Garwood came down the line and punched me in the ribs. He said, "Somebody's gonna pay for letting Russ take all the blame." The blow stunned me. Not because it was thrown hard but because I was weak. I stumbled backward. A guard removed Kushner's glasses and slapped him brutally.

McMillan. The VC tied us up. Daly and I were fastened to a pole so tightly as to cut off our circulation. I started vomiting. The medic girl ran to see what was happening. The VC untied me. Several hours later they untied everyone but Grissett. Several guys were made to bury the cat. Next morning the supply director worked Grissett over with a cane. It was his cat, brought to camp to keep the rats out of the rice supply. As the guards passed by they kicked Grissett and pinched his ears. Around noon they untied him. The camp commander called us to a meeting. He asked for our opinions about what had happened the night before.

Kushner told him the guards were cruel savages. The camp commander had this slinky look on his face. That's why we called him Slime. He giggled like the Vietnamese do when they're nervous and asked the others what they thought. Everyone said the same thing. Then Slime apologized for the beatings we'd received. He said if he had been there it wouldn't have happened. It was true—he wasn't there. Ol' Ratface, the North Vietnamese, was in charge. He didn't care what happened. Slime was like that. When someone died he came around and apologized. The ARVN POWs told us he was dangerous, that he would execute you, and we believed he would. But at least Slime seemed to show a little sympathy. The rest didn't.

Anton. We could not understand why Grissett confessed to killing the cat. It wasn't necessary. He never recovered from the incident. Perhaps he'd been hurt more deeply than we realized when he lost his influence over us as Watkins assumed the role of camp commander. I know his failure to be released after Ho's indoctrination course hurt him. And then taking that terrible beating must have made him give up all hopes of being freed. He became quiet and meek. He quit talking about going home, stopped eating, and began to regress. He lay on his bed all day long in the fetal position with a blanket pulled over his head, sucking his thumb and whimpering like a baby.

Strictland. After we learned the camp routine we didn't want Grissett to tell us what to do. Someone like him needed to have authority. A lot of guys said that was what caused him to go downhill.

If Grissett decided not to work, he wouldn't even though he might be in better shape than others. Some mornings he said, "I'm sick." He'd tell so and so he could have his rice. If someone offered you rice, you grabbed for it. You always gave your rice to someone in your squad. You looked after them first; that was natural. Anyway, after the other guys went to work Grissett would get up and say, "Where's my rice?"

We said, "We thought you were sick and gave yours to someone."

He said, "I'm better now." He had a morning sickness called work disease. He was the type of guy to take his rice back.

Grissett would get hungry and say he was going on the next manioc run.

"Okay, I'm going too," I'd tell him. Manioc might not have done me any good but I was sure going to carry them so I could eat them.

Russ would get a basket of manioc. When he returned he wouldn't let anybody touch them. He would eat them himself. And when he finished he wanted somebody else's.

Then we said, "You didn't let us eat any of yours. Now you can't have any of ours."

At the last Grissett squatted in a corner of the bed with a blanket pulled over his head. The medic girl had four or five dull needles. She bulled them but it didn't do any good. When she gave a shot, half of it wouldn't go in. She gave me one and my shoulder got infected. I still have a hole in it. The VC brought doctors in when people started dying. Kushner told them what the prisoner needed to survive and after the guy was about dead they brought the medicine. When Grissett was unconscious they let Kushner give him I don't know how many shots. But it was too late.

Davis. Everybody pitched in when someone was really down. Personal differences were forgotten. Russ had dysentery very badly. We washed his clothes and brought food to his bed. He developed a case of bronchial pneumonia. We thought he was gone. Suddenly he popped out of it. One morning he awoke and began to move around, did some exercises and looked like his old self. He said he was going to be all right. Then several days later he sank back into it. We tried to make him eat, make him get up and move about. We were fighting against impossible odds. At a certain point in starvation a lack of vitamins brings a loss of appetite. A man will ultimately lie down and die staring at food piled in front of him.

Harker. Russ went harder than anyone. Kushner and I stayed up all night with him. He fought it so. He knew he was dying. He asked us to tell his sister that he loved her. He passed away about 3:30 in the morning the day before Thanksgiving. The medic girl came to the hootch. At first when we got to camp she had been cool toward us. But as people fell ill, as she saw she could do nothing to help because of her lack of knowledge and equipment, she became sympathetic; and we began to consider her our friend. We could see she was truly sad that Russ had died.

Several days after Thanksgiving it was Bill Port. You could tell by his bone structure that Port had once been a very big guy. He was from the First Cav. He was taking a squad from LZ Baldy to reinforce a unit getting hit. Just as they jumped from the choppers mortars started coming in. And then a ground attack. There was mass confusion. Port remembered seeing Viet Cong darting around the landing zone. He was hit by a mortar round. One of his ears was half blown off, his toes were completely ripped away, and his left arm had a deep wound that drained continually. He had powder burns on his face and severely limited vision in his left eye. At dusk he would be almost blind and someone had to lead him to the latrine. After he was first captured the VC took him to a field hospital. There they treated his wounds and fed him eggs and monkey meat regularly. He improved a little. But not enough to justify their transferring him to our camp. Why they did that we never knew. Through it all Port kept a good sense of humor. He was taken in his sleep.

McMillan. The split between the two squads lasted till people started dying like hell. Nobody brought it up to anyone's face. But the people in the other squad who wanted the split saw what was happening. They started thinking. They could see others were run-down and might die too. It didn't end all of a sudden. We gradually got back together in early December. The Vietnamese had something to do with ending it. They moved us five blacks into another hootch, making it three squads instead of two. They also told us we had to have two permanent cooks. After the split was over and we were back together I didn't say anything about it. But I was still mad. I intended to get even with some of those guys.

Harker. The VC half-stopped it in a way, and we did too. The split was so absurd and should never have happened; and didn't. No one spoke about it.

Daly. The Vietnamese separated us into three groups because they could see we weren't getting along. From the very first moment they reorganized us, people got together and things began to change. The VC tried to make us black fellows think they did this because we were sort of special. Mr. Ho had given us this idea one night in July when he called us to his hootch. He didn't say so directly. But he asked had we heard of the Black Panthers and when we said no, he told us all about them. That's all Ho talked about, black this and black that, how the Front sympathized with the blacks. He said, "You should be in the States to tell of your experiences. What would you do if we released you?"

We said, "Oh, good night! We would tell about the war and

what's happening over here and everything!" We thought when they moved the blacks together in a third hootch that maybe they were preparing to release us.

During the split everything was filthy. It wasn't so much the fault of the Vietnamese as our own dirty sanitation. One group would cook and wouldn't wash the pans. The other squad would do the same thing. Overnight rats and bugs ate what was left in the pans and we got up and cooked out of them again. Nobody wanted to wash the rice before cooking it. If you didn't wash it sometimes almost half the ration was rat feces. Still, people cooked without washing it. The Vietnamese claimed that was why people were getting sick. So they said they wanted us to have only two cooks. And mama-san was assigned to teach us how to cook properly.

The POWs voted for whom they wanted as cooks. Harker and I were elected. Since I had prior cooking experience I became head cook. The assistant cook was responsible for preparing the fire and making sure enough wood was on hand. Harker didn't mind the work but he hated to get up at 3:00 A.M. After several weeks he quit. Lewis came on. He lasted till he had an argument with mama-san. Lewis didn't eat manioc. Sometimes when mama-san cooked she mixed them with the rice. She was doing this one day and Lewis said, "No, no, we no eat this way." She continued what she was doing. Lewis pulled off the pot top. Mama-san went hollering to the VC area. Mr. Hom came down and chewed Lewis out. The VC removed him as assistant cook. McMillan took over.

We had three large pots. One was for boiling water, another for cooking rice, and the third for manioc. First thing each morning we made drinking water. We had washed the rice and cut the manioc and covered it up the night before, so everything was prepared. The rice took about ten minutes to cook. Some guys wanted manioc and rice together, others wanted them separately. Some wanted a few, others forced themselves to eat a lot just to be full. Occasionally if we had extra cooking oil I cooked manioc patties or manioc soup. We ate with chop sticks we carved ourselves. Later we received American-made spoons.

Every day, three hundred sixty-five days a year, someone came to me and said, "What're we having for lunch?"

I started cussing. "What do you think we're having? Manioc and rice!"

There were times we cooked three times a day, times we cooked twice or once, and times we didn't cook at all. It was sort of an unwritten rule when it came your time to cook under the old rotation system that you screwed everybody else. But the truth is, when I became permanent cook I never took any extra. Guys kidded me about tasting the manioc soup too much. I guess everybody thought I looked surprisingly healthy. I never lost much weight like everybody else. I was five foot eleven and most of the time weighed about a hundred seventy. But that was the story of my life, it has always been like that.

Anton. I practically went into a state of shock when people started dying. Most of those who died had beriberi to some extent, and I had it too. Beriberi is primarily caused by a severe deficiency of vitamin B_1. The disease is inevitable when you have a steady diet of polished rice. It killed many American POWs in Asian camps during World War II and Korea. You get dysentery at the outset, then a swelling called edema, which is caused by a retention of body fluids. My legs ballooned up. My testicles looked like baseballs. I moved in slow motion. The edema retarded respiration. The VC gave me B_1 and iron shots. I received a hundred shots in two months. None I thought did any good.

McMillan. Anton was lazy long before he got to Viet Nam. He said after he graduated from warrant officer's school his father, an air force colonel, told him that was the first successful thing he had ever done. Anton was tall and so skinny that we called him Bones. He weighed about a hundred ten pounds. He had a thin mouth and bushy black eyebrows that moved up and down like dark thunderclouds when he grumbled, and he talked in a nasal tone. He thought we were down on him because we tried to make him get up and do. He lay under his blanket all day long. If we hadn't pushed him and made him get up, he would have died. All of us knew that.

Harker. We had a small celebration Christmas Eve. The VC gave us a banner with a star on it. We hung it behind the bed in Joe Zawtocki's hootch and found a little tree and decorated it with bits of paper. We listened to Radio Hanoi that afternoon. Several pilots held in Hanoi read beautiful warm messages about how they missed home and the children who were growing up without them. We allowed ourselves to linger over thoughts of our families. The VC returned to Watkins his New Testament, and he read the Christmas Scriptures. We said the Lord's Prayer and sang a few carols. Bob Garwood was there, he was a friend of Joe's, and he sang with us.

The camp commander made a brief speech. "You are allowed to enjoy Christmas because of the Front's lenient and humane policy. We are sorry you are not with your family. But Johnson prolongs the war. Maybe next year you will be back home." He didn't promise but he sounded almost certain that Nixon, who had been elected the month before, would end the war. We clutched at his optimism. Our spirits rose.

Anton. The Vietnamese gave us some candy. We divided it into equal shares. Garwood saw we had split it up. He reported us to the Vietnamese. The camp commander told us collect the candy, said we had to eat it community style.

"Put it in the middle of the bed and you can have it at midnight."

We said, "Midnight?"

They wanted us to stay up because captured U.S. pilots were to sing Christmas carols over Radio Hanoi at 12:00.

The pilots already had read messages saying they had ham, turkey, and cranberry sauce. We said, "If we could have but one bite of it!"

We tried to be happy but couldn't. People were showing tears. Anyway, when the camp commander said we couldn't split the candy we said, "It's our Christmas. If we can't divide it the way we want, you keep it. Or give it to Garwood."

Finally he gave in.

Harker. We received an extra can of rice for our Christmas meal and two chickens. On New Year's we had another celebration, with extra rice and several cans of U.S. Army B-ration ham. But if our spirits were rising, they suddenly fell the next day.

Anton. Fred was captured on his first mission. He had been in Viet Nam six days. He was on the tail end of the patrol and fell asleep from exhaustion during a ten-minute break. The others were gone when he awoke. He seemed to think they had left him on purpose because they didn't like him. He didn't smoke, didn't drink, didn't swear. He wasn't an average marine. He had been an excellent student and had won a scholarship to Notre Dame. He was having problems at home. He considered his father weak. His mother wore the pants in the family. Instead of going to Notre Dame, he joined the Marine Corps to prove he was a man.

Harker. You watch the changes in him. His legs swell with edema. You see his hair becoming frizzy, it stands up on his head. His eyes begin to bulge. Before he was a nice-looking guy. Now he looks foreign, strange. Kushner punched me one night. Five of us were in the hootch, McMillan had built a fire, and we had let Fred come over to sit by it. For being a good boy that day. It gets down to the ridiculous but you try to develop some sort of incentive for making them want to live. "Fred you can have your blanket if you wash yourself." Or "Fred you can sit by the fire if you don't crap in your pants today." He had that faraway look in his eyes. When he saw us watching he smiled gently. I wanted to cry.

Anton. He began to make a lot of noise at night, crying over and over, "Mama, oh, Mama . . . I want my Mama."

Once in the middle of the night someone, I don't remember who, yelled, "Die, motherfucker, die!"

No one was shocked. Several people laughed. It was that kind of situation, so pathetic, but the realism of the moment because nobody could get any sleep. Later people talked about it and said what a rotten thing to do.

Harker. You could confront him with it. "You're dying, Fred. You've got to try. You've got to get back. Your mom wants to see you, your dad does too. You mean so much to them."

He'd reply, "Yes, I want to. But I can't. I just can't."

"Why? You can. All you have to do is eat."

"Doesn't taste good."

"The food doesn't taste good to any of us. But you've got to eat to live. You ate it before."

"All I want is to be warm. Please let me sit by the fire."

Prison didn't change him as it did others, didn't make him harsh and nasty, foulmouthed like many of us became. He kept his manners through the hardest of times, always said thank you for the smallest gestures, and remained a devout Catholic when others had their faith shaken. When he died the day after New Year's all of us realized that some part of ourselves had died with him. He was nineteen.

10

David Harker

The Viet Cong gave us our first canned goods when prisoners started dying. They began to kill a pig every week or so and our rice ration was increased. There were three or four large hogs in the camp and a varying number of smaller pigs. There were also thirty or forty chickens scratching around the camp area; some of them wandered into our compound. After a few weeks of extra food, however, our ration was cut back to its usual marginal subsistence level. Only the very sick were put on a special diet prepared by the Vietnamese cooks.

Several months after Mr. Ho departed we began to receive certain luxuries. We were given two bars of strong lye soap which had to last the group at least a month, got a sporadic ration of toothpaste and a toothbrush, and afterward, best of all, were given green army mosquito nets, which not only saved us from being eaten alive by jungle insects but protected us from our rodent roommates. Later on we received thin, bamboo-woven sleeping mats and a pair of black-rubber Ho Chi Minh sandals cut from old car tires. We usually had one or two dull Arabian Beauty razor blades and a plastic razor. Our beards had practically stopped growing because of the poor diet. A little scraping every several weeks did the job. Hair clippers were always available;

after a few rough scalpings several POWs became adept barbers.

We settled into a routine suffocating in its sameness day after day. We got up at daybreak, ate breakfast, and if we weren't working, sat around till it was time to eat lunch. From 11:00 to 1:00 or 2:00 was our nap period, in accordance with Vietnamese custom. (The war almost completely stopped all over Viet Nam from 12:00 to 2:30 during country-wide siesta time.) This was the only time we were supposed to be on the bed in the daytime though we constantly broke the rule and the VC were constantly on our backs about it. Davis could mimic the high-pitched voices of the guards and he came in one day and said, "Kushner! Get up! Get up!" Kushner shot straight up; he didn't think it was so funny. Men usually sat outside in the compound in the few spots of sunshine that broke through the trees. Friendship cliques had naturally formed, and groups of two or three were scattered here and there.

We made a chess set of bamboo. There was talk of making playing cards from the camp rules, which were posted in the compound. (The first rule: "Don't make loud noises with same guys in your camp.") But Pfister, in urgent need of rolling paper, smoked the rules before we got around it, much to the vengeful dismay of the Viet Cong. They eventually gave us a deck of cards and we quickly wore them limp. At 5:00 each afternoon we were required to listen to Hanoi Hannah. The VC had a two-band Panasonic transistor in a brown-leather carrying case. Mr. Hom brought it to the compound and made a big show of pulling up the antenna; and then ordered us to gather around. Hanoi Hannah played several popular American songs during her half-hour English-language broadcast, the main attraction for us. If Mr. Hom had his back turned Ike McMillan danced by himself to the music. Anton listened to the program more attentively than anyone. He thought he could pick up facts by listening between the lines of the propaganda. Occasionally we did find nuggets of news buried in Hanoi's lies. We learned of the lunar landing when Mme. Nguyen Thi Binh criticized the U.S. government for being able to put a man on the moon but unable to stop the war.

On rainy nights Garwood sometimes brought the radio to the

blacks' hootch under the guise of letting them listen to another propaganda program that came on about 9:00. While someone watched for the guards, we listened to the Armed Forces Radio Station or Voice of America. But Garwood was nervous about getting caught, kept switching the dial back and forth, and we never learned much, although we were always fairly well informed about the ups and downs of the peace negotiations. Our only reading material was several VC propaganda newspapers and the New Testament. So we talked to each other; and then talked some more, long after we knew each other's personal stories by heart.

Daly. The average person exaggerates. We all do. Many guys made tales of their captures sound like John Wayne. I could understand. But then a few of them told personal stories and a month or two later repeated the same tale, only this time they changed the facts completely around. And guys sat there and listened as if they believed them. It burned me up. I had to say something. Then whoever was talking accused me of calling him a liar. I'd say, "No, I'm just trying to tell you what you said before."

Anton. Daly couldn't do normal labor but he worked hard as a cook. He spent five or six hours every day in preparation. When we had rotated cooking chores the food was lousy. But after Daly got used to doing it he cooked well. He did a good but unintentional imitation of Aunt Jemima, rolling his pajamas to his knees and tying a rag around his head. We often talked about the possibility of receiving packages from home (which we never got). Daly would say in all seriousness, "I would like to receive some Minute Rice." We groaned and cussed him. Daly and McMillan were the most reliable source of camp entertainment. They argued and fought nearly every day, mostly about religion.

Daly. Ike McMillan didn't give a damn about being a prisoner. He seemed perfectly content. I talked to him about religion and there were times when he listened and seemed sincere. But if I talked too long he got hysterical, started cussing, and screamed, "F—— Jehovah!"

I thought that as prisoners we should have been drawing closer to God. But it didn't work that way. Many guys seemed to drift farther away. Davis was the only one who listened and never said anything bad about religion. Dr. Kushner talked about being an atheist, yet said his prayers every night before going to sleep. I said, "I can't understand it, Kush. You claim to be an atheist but you pray all the time."

McMillan and I fought about a lot of things, not necessarily about religion. He woke up mornings on the wrong side of the bed. I knew no matter how much we argued he would never pass a lick unless I called him one thing. A black nigger. Good night! I bet the other prisoners had to separate us a thousand times.

McMillan. Daly was very religious, especially for a man of his age. He knew a lot about the Bible. He could quote chapter and verse. He cussed and carried on but he lived by the rules of the Jehovah's Witnesses. He could have never killed anybody. He was really a conscientious objector. I lived with him long enough to know that. Oh, he always said when he got angry, "I'll kill you. I'll stab you." But you knew he wouldn't.

I had a lot of steam in me from being cooped up. We fought all the time. I could jump up and hit him in the face two or three times before he could get to me. He was too big to wrestle, God Almighty, was he too big! Some of the others pulled us apart. It didn't bother me. Next day we would be back in the kitchen arguing again.

Davis. Daly and McMillan never hurt each other. They made a good cooking team because Ike was excellent at getting us extra food. He was a born chicken thief.

McMillan. The first time it happened was when I saw two little VC friers over by a tree in the compound. I threw them a few grains of rice and led them to a place out of the guards' sight. "Come here, babies! Here my little sweets!" I grabbed them by the necks, put them under my arms for concealment, and choked them as I walked casually toward our kitchen. They made not a peep.

Grissett had stolen a few chickens and Garwood had given us seven or eight, but I became the specialist. A chicken hawk and a weasel hung around our camp. Sometimes we heard the chickens squawking when the weasel got into the chicken house. The guards would run out and shoot at him. If the weasel struck in the morning I hit that afternoon. I was the weasel's brother.

We could terminate a chicken in three minutes. A pot of hot water was waiting and we threw him in and finished plucking while he cooked. Split the intestines with a sliver of bamboo, cleaned them, and put them back in the pot. Ate everything. Some wound up half done and tough as hell.

A man at the hootch door watched for the guards. The warning word was "checkerboard." If the word was given we hid the chicken in the fireplace. The door man tried to hinder the guard for several minutes. He asked the VC what was going on in the world, what Nixon was doing. It gave the VC enough time to tell him the "Vietnamese will surely win, the U.S. will surely lose"; and us enough time to stash the chicken. Once that happened I came out of the kitchen and bullshitted with the guards. I wasn't tight with them. But I laughed and shot the shit with them. Trying to get over, you know. Then the guards made a head count and left. And I went back to my work.

The VC had a big white rooster. I had my eyes on this rooster for a long time. He was smart. I knew the only way I could catch him was to get him down by the latrine. There was a hole in the side of the latrine where chickens went to eat maggots off the excrement. One day when it was raining hard I chased that rooster around the compound for an hour. I said, "I'm gonna catch that cocky bastard if it's the last thing I do."

I was standing there in the rain and saw him stick his head in the latrine. I made five fast steps, then stood like a statue. He took his head out, looked around, and said in his throaty voice, "*Ku-kwa-ku-koo, ku-kwa-ku-koo.*"

He stuck his head back in and resumed eating. I moved forward again, stopping when he took his head out.

"*Ku-kwa-ku-koo, ku-kwa-ku-koo.*"

I got right over the hole and froze. When the rooster was busy I stuck one hand in the shitter and grabbed his neck and with my other hand hit him from the rear so he couldn't escape. Broke his neck in three seconds.

I went to the hootch and said, "Okay, we're having bird tonight." They couldn't believe it. That's why the guys liked for me to cook. When I cooked we had chicken at least once a week. It was always split at least twelve ways, and wasn't much, but it was something.

The VC eventually began to suspect something was wrong. Later they gave us a few chickens of our own to raise. But we had no say over when to eat them. We were allowed to kill them only when they gave us permission. So the weasel would never strike our chickens but he often got the VC's. The weasel was great for that. The VC couldn't understand.

Davis. We burned nuoc mam to stink up the place and cooked the chicken in that. We took a bite and dropped it into the nuoc mam and looked to see if a guard was coming. Or we hid it under our rice and manioc. It didn't take much imagination to figure out what would happen if we were caught.

McMillan. The VC killed at least six pigs in a good year, usually on their major holidays, which were Tet, Ho Chi Minh's birthday, North Viet Nam's National Day, and the NLF's anniversary. They killed a pig once and gave us three small chunks of pork. I went to their kitchen to pick up our rice ration and saw this pork fat lying around. I stole a five-pound slab, stuck it down my pants, and carried it our hootch.

The holidays were the only thing we had to look forward to. Our lives revolved around them. Otherwise every day was the same. A few weeks before a holiday arrived there would be heavy trading on advances for the expected meat supply. Everyone got a tobacco ration every month or so whether he smoked or not. You might get fifty Vietnamese-type hand-rolled cigarettes from one ration. So the smokers competed with each other for the nonsmokers' tobacco ration. The rate of exchange depended on the size of the meat. An average piece was about a half-inch square. We called a piece gigantic if it was about two inches in size. On a big celebration we might get twenty-five average-size pieces per person. It was mostly pig fat and so greasy that it gave you diarrhea.

We traded everything. Rice for manioc, manioc for rice. Some people were interested in red peppers, which we got as extra bennies on manioc runs or stole from the yards. Dr. Kushner loved peppers. I don't have anything against the Jewish people, but he was like they say the Jewish people are, real tight. He drove a hard bargain. He would use psych on you in a minute, wind up swapping you one piece of meat for ten peppers.

Harker. Tet was the VC's biggest holiday. The guards and camp personnel put on a skit and we could hear their songs and laughter. Things grew quiet as they gathered around the radio to listen to Ho Chi Minh's annual message. A guard ushered in the lunar New Year by firing a clip from his rifle. The mountainsides around us echoed with rifle fire. Moments like these we sympathized with the Vietnamese. They were soldiers too. But such times were short-lived. The VC were unpredictable. We never knew when they would turn on us.

Anton. In February we noticed the VC were working on something below our compound. Even the camp commander was helping out. We thought maybe they were building a water-buffalo pen. We could taste the meat. Then we saw them taking food down there, much food, meat and eggs, things we weren't getting. We said, "They've got a high-ranking VC officer there, maybe Ho or someone higher." Our curiosity grew. One day we edged down that way to gather wood, hoping to get a look. Suddenly someone started throwing rocks at us.

Garwood told us a few days later that an American defector was there. He said the soldier had walked off his unit's landing zone, surrendered to the Front, and was now writing antiwar appeals. He said, "He's on his way to be educated in Hanoi." A few days later they moved him in with us.

Mr. Hom put us all in a circle beforehand and said, "I'm bringing up another American. You must be careful in your dealings with him because he can get violent."

We said to ourselves, "We'll break the sonofabitch. He's getting all that food and we're up here starving."

The American walked into the compound. His green fatigues were covered with blue peace symbols drawn with a ballpoint pen. He carried a folder of poems about love. He immediately began to tell us about the antiwar movement. He said, "We're losing the war. It'll be over by next year." It was Gus, a short midwesterner with long hair and a big nose. Our hippie.

Shortly after he was captured he had escaped and crawled through the jungle for two days. He said. Maybe he did, and he stuck to the story, but nobody believed it. He said he hadn't told the VC he was a crossover, that they'd tried to get him to write antiwar appeals, but he'd made them mad and demanded to come up with us. He threw rocks at us that day to attract our attention. He was probably confused like all of us after he was first captured and ready to say anything to get out of the situation.

McMillan. Gus was a regular pothead and we rapped strong. I thought he was a good guy even though we had our ups and downs. Gus was what Kushner called a smart-aleck punk. We went at it one time. We didn't pass licks, I put my dukes up, but we didn't go. That's the only time we got that way. Mostly we argued and I would say, "Okay, man, I can't take no more," and he would break away. We argued about a song that came out in the world. He said it came out at a certain time and I disagreed.

I said, "Look, man, I ought to know. I'm black."

He said, "I don't care. I've hung around with as many black people as you have."

I would get sort of pissed at this.

As Gus told me, he got the ass at his lieutenant. He already had a pot charge hanging over his head. The MPs in Da Nang had caught him. He had had his way when he was coming up. "Mama, I want this. If I don't get it I'm gonna run away from home." That type. Like he said he got drunk at the age of twelve and they had to pump the liquor out of him. He asked his mother for a drink. When she refused he and some other kids lifted a case.

The lieutenant gave Gus a ration of shit. Gus said, "No, I'm going to smoke my pot." The lieutenant didn't catch him smoking, but he was in some way harassing Gus. He picked up and walked off the LZ. When the VC captured him he told them something in their favor and that's the way they took it. Gus wasn't a crossover. No way in hell.

Strictland. One spring day we saw choppers overhead. We thought perhaps a patrol was being inserted into the area. The VC thought so too. Later that day artillery started falling on a nearby trail we used to get to the manioc fields. The VC said it was U.S. artillery. We suspected they had their own units fire because they thought a patrol was coming in. They were shook up. Next morning we packed our stuff and made ready to leave. We didn't go any place but sat around with our stuff packed for about a week.

Harker. The air activity increased. Our camp wasn't remarkably camouflaged. We worried about the possibility of bombs. In early spring the VC moved us to another site a day's walk away. I heard after we got back that a U.S. rescue team had entered the old camp the same day we left and found hot coals but no signs of where we had gone. Moving to a new camp was like starting over again. We were jammed once more into a single hootch. Our setup was similar to the other camp. We were on a mountainside with a nearby stream. We made a water line by running bamboo tubes to the camp. We were better camouflaged, under high trees, and gathering firewood was no problem. However, the manioc fields were further away. We had to cross "the long drawn-out hill" to reach the fields. Sometimes a run took all day.

The long war had begun to take its toll of the Viet Cong. We could see for the first time that they were hurting badly. Their supply lines had been cut—*our* supply lines—and the summer of '69 was to be one of our most difficult periods. Defoliation missions by the two-engined C-123 spray planes multiplied in our area. The tart smell of chemicals hung in the summer air. We caught a glimpse of the lumbering planes doing their work. The jungle around us browned out and peeled away. Montagnard villages magically appeared in the distance where they had once been hidden by thick green foliage.

The defoliation missions stirred a heated controversy. The planes, of course, were killing our food supply. Manioc became scarce. Leaves fell off bushes. Plants died. We had no choice but to eat them. It tasted like rubber. (Though we ate a lot of defoliated manioc we suffered no ill effects we could see.) But there was more to the group's arguments against spraying than merely our self-interests. Many deeply felt America had no right to kill the crops of civilians already almost starving.

Anton. The U.S. had put out news that it was only defoliating jungle. This is what I thought to be true. But I saw that the planes in our area sprayed nothing but crops, which, I guess, is a means of warfare. But we were dependent upon the crops as well as many people who weren't involved in the war. So we got very upset when they sprayed. For about a two-month period we had no rice. We ate manioc and weeds. Strictland was particularly upset. Maybe it was because he was a farm boy.

Davis. Guys at first wouldn't accept the reality of being in prison. This was a major cause of trouble. In 1969 we learned to cope, and just in time too. We learned to get by on a minimum of food, all the short cuts to survival. Every day I went through mental exercises to put myself in the correct state for working. I would say, "When I get back I'll have my food and a bath"; and suddenly a small bowl of dry rice and a cold, soapless bath became something important to look forward to.

At night I would say, "Okay, I'm home." I concentrated on everything I had done in my life, particularly the period when I was eighteen and nineteen and had a lot of girl friends. I could make it seem so realistic that I became dazed and my body seemed to float. I relived every minute I had been in bed with women. And I never got tired of it either. I awoke next morning with my pajamas plastered.

Kushner said, "What the hell do you eat to have so many wet dreams?" Harker and myself had a lot of them. Some guys took months to have their first one because of the poor diet. Although we talked about how many girls we would take on when we got home, sex was something surprisingly unimportant to us.

Kushner could never understand McMillan. Ike was always happy. He had the same ability as I to psych himself out. Maybe in a little different manner. When Kushner was depressed, Ike would start playing around and Kushner had to laugh.

Harker. Rica was standing by a hootch. She had just come from taking a bath. She wore blue culottes with white stripes. She was short, well stacked, a lovely girl with sandy hair and blue eyes. My God! She'll never make it! She looked at me and smiled warmly. On the other side of the fence two bearded men sat beside a tree breathing hard and rubbing their faces. Davis and McMillan were with me. We walked silently past them. We weren't allowed to speak to anyone new in camp.

Davis. We found out later they were German nurses from a hospital in Da Nang, sent to Viet Nam under West Germany's aid program. They considered themselves neutral because they treated all war-wounded Vietnamese without inquiring whether they were VC. They had taken a jeep drive outside Da Nang the last of April on a Sunday sight-seeing trip and were stopped by the Viet Cong. Five of them: Bernhard, Georg, Monika, Rica, and Marie-Luise. They were briefly held in a VC woman's house. She turned out to be a nurse who worked with them in the hospital.

Monika Schwinn and Marie-Luise had lagged behind on the trail. Garwood brought the other three ahead to our camp. A few days later Monika limped in crying hysterically. The VC had pushed Marie-Luise to walk without proper rest and food. She had died on the trail. The four Germans were placed in a new hootch on the other side of the compound fence. Why the VC had brought them to our camp we couldn't understand. Possibly the VC realized their mistake in picking them up. But they didn't want to admit it and lose face by releasing them. They often operated on a logic no greater than that.

Gus spoke a little German. We communicated with them

through him when the guards weren't looking. A few guys made joking crude comments about the girls that irritated me. I had nothing but sympathy for them. And I think most of us felt this way. I washed their clothes occasionally. Our rice ration had been cut back to half a can a day. They passed what food they didn't eat over the fence in a plastic shaving kit one carried. Denny visited their hootch at noontime and returned with some peppers. Bernhard later told us without rancor that Denny had stolen the peppers. When someone approached him about it, he said, "Hell, they didn't need the damn peppers anyway." Incidents like this turned people against Denny.

Rica was strong. She worked hard to take care of the other three. Monika, who was twenty-six, was plump but weak from the ordeal. Then one day Rica suddenly fell sick. She faded fast. It seemed she went in several days. Bernhard said a few words as we laid her in the shallow grave.

Harker. Georg, who was tall and slender, got sick after Rica died. We brought him to our compound and bathed him. He kept saying, "All I want is a piece of bread and some cheese . . . just a piece of bread." He had a heart condition before coming to Viet Nam, but had read about Vietnamese civilians caught in the war and had wanted to do something to help, so he concealed the condition from medical examiners in order to qualify for the hospital program. I put my hand over his chest. It felt like a kitten purring. We buried him beside Rica.

Davis. Monika would have died too if Bernhard had not made her exercise all day long. They were out beside their hootch early each morning. He had her walking back and forth and doing exercises. She became angry at him. I couldn't understand the words but I understood her tone. But he made her do it. He gave her the will to live, and at the same time made himself live. She grew stronger. She was still in danger of sinking into a fatal depression. When she wasn't exercising she sat vacant-eyed picking at her rubber sandals. Finally the VC let her help in the kitchen a bit. This gave her the needed stimulation to hang on. They were moved from our camp in September. Some of us thought the VC were taking them elsewhere to let them die so it wouldn't be bad for our morale. But they lived. They were moved to North Viet Nam and released in 1973 with U.S. POWs. That the Vietnamese had held German nurses for five years rated one sentence in the world's newspapers.

Anton. Five Vietnamese POWs lived in a hootch outside our compound. All of us liked Captain Nghia, an older, dignified Vietnamese who spoke English slowly but always chose the precise word. He was quite intelligent and very droll. The captain was a mercenary, as he was the first to admit in delicate ironical tones. He told us how he had worked first for the French and then the Americans. We discussed with him whom he would work for next, the Russians or Chinese.

He was in charge of a supply warehouse in Saigon and had been arrested for "releasing a truckload of cigarettes to the wrong party. That is to say," he added, "I was a bribee." Another Vietnamese POW told us it wasn't only cigarettes he sold on the black market, but television sets and anything else he could lay hands on. Anyhow, Nghia, possibly to appease the Americans, was sent to jail for a year. It wasn't such a bad life, he said. His wife was allowed to visit him every day. She brought him cakes and French pastries.

The good life ended when he was released in 1969 and ordered to the battlefield. He said he stepped off the helicopter and asked directions to his unit. Somehow he took the wrong trail and ran into the Viet Cong.

The VC said, "Do you *chieu hoi?*"

Nghia said, "I'll never *chieu hoi.*"

A VC raised his rifle and started to fire.

Nghia said, "Wait! *Chieu hoi! Chieu hoi!*"

A second ARVN POW was a young first lieutenant named Quy. Short and powerfully built, he looked like a miniature Green Bay Packers' fullback. He spoke Lao, French, and English. His father owned a nuoc mam factory. I never got along with Quy as Harker and Davis did. Quy worked well and resented people who were sick. He even resented Nghia. He beat up Nghia. In their part of the camp Quy was boss.

Harker. Three Vietnamese POWs were with us on a manioc run. We were crossing a swift-flowing stream dotted with rapids when one of them slipped and fell. He was swept away by the current. He had a heavy manioc basket on his back. It looked certain he would drown. Davis himself was weighted down with manioc. But he didn't hesitate. He rushed after the Vietnamese, splashed in, and pulled him free.

Davis. It's like David Harker, who was one of my closest friends in camp, to leave out his part. Both of us pulled him free. I doubt I could have done it without Harker's help. The Vietnamese told us with his eyes that he was grateful to us both.

Anton. Watkins still ran things. Joe Zawtocki, who had been one of the advocates of the split, became weak in the summer of '69. What he'd done came back to haunt him because Watkins cut his food one day and harassed him about not working. Things came to a head. Watkins physically pushed Joe around.

The Vietnamese put the sickest on a special diet. They sometimes gave us a small can of sweet condensed milk. I got maybe twelve cans total. That was much more than anyone else. The others resented Long and me for getting the milk. Nothing was said, it was just in the air, and made me feel bad sometimes. Occasionally those of us on the special diet got an extra half can of rice per day and a few bananas. We were given canned goods when they were available.

It was said to me that I was faking in order to get extra food. The first time someone told me this I was stunned, I couldn't believe he'd said that. Eating salt was bad for edema because it helped retain fluids. I was told I ate salt to keep the edema up, so I could stay on the special diet. I thought that was absurd. It was true I sometimes ate salt. I couldn't eat rice without it. From early childhood I've always had to put a lot of salt on everything I eat.

McMillan. Dr. Kushner warned the ones with that edema jive to lay off the salt. He said, "It may not kill you but it'll certainly make things worse." We found later that Williams was stealing salt from the kitchen because we were giving him bland food. It was hard to get down rice without salt. Anton and the others were doing it too. All of them could have passed it up. They just didn't believe they were going to die. Anton saw them dying and he wised up and stopped using it.

Davis. Long and Anton were the best of friends. Long brought a poncho liner along with him when he was captured. He and Anton lay under it all day. Long was an easygoing guy who listened to Anton's gripes. One morning everyone was up and around and even Anton was doing PT. Someone said Long was still on the bed, that he was grunting and breathing hard. We called Kushner. He ran to the hootch and examined him. He said it looked like a heart attack. He started massaging his chest. Long was going "Ugh! Ugh! Ugh!" Kushner pounded his chest. Long began to breathe easier.

Mr. Hom came and said, "Long, you must get up and exercise so you will not die." We successfully maneuvered Hom out the hootch. Kushner ordered Long to stay in bed and rest. I think Kushner saved his life that morning.

McMillan. I liked to harass the guards. At night they came in with a little lamp to make a head check. I rolled a cigarette and asked for a light. When they handed me the lamp I lit my cigarette and "accidentally" blew out the lamp at the same time. Then they had to walk back in the dark through the mud. Most of them couldn't speak any English. I'd say to them in a sweet quiet voice, "I would like to bash your stupid face in." They just smiled.

Some of them weren't so bad. Peaches was one of the better ones. He heard us talking about the boogaloo and thought it was some sort of American good morning greeting. He would come along and say, "How your boogaloo?"

I'd say, "My boogaloo is just fine, Peaches. How's yours this morning?"

You couldn't change their minds about what they believed.

Only one person could have done that—Ho Chi Minh. We told them that Ho Chi Minh had an illigitimate kid in New York, that we'd read this in a magazine. Mr. Hom said, "No, no. Cannot be. He do not like women. He do not have sex. You have very bad attitude." He got terribly upset. We didn't push it after that.

Harker. The camp directors and Mr. Hom occasionally called us to the classroom to tell us more about the "Vietnamese people's just struggle." Their thesis was that the U.S. had come to Viet Nam to exploit the country's raw materials. Like retarded pupils we were required to stand at attention and recite this formula reply when called upon.

Once when his turn came Pfister said, "We're here to get all your breadfruit and tobacco," two items particularly relished by us. Everyone laughed.

Hom said, "Do not make a funny." Such light moments were few and far between—and dangerous. Mr. Hom passionately hated all Americans. He never lost a chance to degrade us.

We wrote or signed infrequent antiwar appeals. We could no longer see any purpose in resisting. It was a constant hassle, they were on our backs, and not to may have gotten us thrown in stocks. They said, "If you do not write maybe you will break the camp rules and be punished." On the other hand, they applied no physical coercion to make us write other than the pressures of living on a near-starvation diet. They wanted us to write that Americans had committed war crimes. Here we made our last stand. We refused to write we had seen war crimes, and condemned them in a general way.

Anton. Our resistance to writing was focused on nuance. The VC insisted we write about the U.S. killing civilians. We made a big thing among ourselves of making sure we wrote only that the "U.S. should not kill *innocent* civilians." Then one day the VC brought us an article clipped from *Life* magazine about the My Lai massacre. Many guys were upset about that. A statement condemning My Lai strongly was written. I thought Calley was being made a scapegoat. Everybody else was against him.

Davis. We hated to see the VC bringing another appeal to us. Nobody wanted to sign. I felt guilty at first. Then I said, "I would like to put someone else in my position and see what he would do." Eisenbraun the special forces captain was supposed to be one of the toughest guys who passed through our prison camp. The VC broke him. Sergeant Williams was as hard-core as they come, and he collapsed. I thought it was a matter of survival.

Perhaps we didn't take it so seriously because we didn't take the Vietnamese that seriously. Most POWs thought the Vietnamese were stupid. America is so diverse that it's hard for a Vietnamese to analyze our country. The Vietnamese couldn't understand that we all had somewhat different attitudes because one guy was reared in the West, one in the East, and one in the South; that one was white and one black; one was Jewish, another Baptist or Catholic. They couldn't understand that one's taste in food might differ from another's, that not everybody in the world ate only rice and nuoc mam. Nor could they understand that though we might not love and respect our president as they revered Ho Chi Minh, this did not necessarily mean we hated him.

Yet we probably understood them less than they understood us. Most of the time we underestimated them because guys thought, "Oh, he's just a gook." In irritation you called them gooks, as a white guy might say he's just a nigger, or a black man he's just a hunk. Racism shows itself in anger. You must understand a man's culture before you can understand his race; and we knew nothing about the Vietnamese.

Harker. Strictland and Watkins began to attend a special indoctrination class with a new prisoner, a Tennessean with a serious shoulder wound who had joined us in March. A big guy about six four and with huge arms, he began to fade away after a few days in camp like a leaking balloon. For the first time the VC turned up with blood plasma. They gave him transfusions and treated him with drugs. Kushner reflected that if he had had the same medicine he could have saved Fred and the others. The Tennessean had not received any political indoctrination. So when the three of them began the course we didn't think much about it. The VC told us Watkins and Strictland were taking part to show the new man the "correct study methods." The three of them were tight-lipped about what was going on. They said only that it was the usual propaganda.

Watkins. The camp commander asked Strictland what he would say if he was released, what he would tell the world about his captivity.

Strictland, trying to figure out what the VC wanted to hear, said, "I'll say nothing. There's nothing to tell."

The camp commander said, "No, no. You must tell how well you have been treated by the Front and about U.S. aggression in Viet Nam."

Strictland said, "Oh, yeah. Of course."

A big antiwar rally was scheduled for Washington in November. They asked if we were released would we take part and speak against the war. We said yes. We began an intensive two-week course. We had to stand at attention and repeat how the U.S. was bombing and killing innocent people. I said it back to them in their own words. After a while they told us we didn't have to stand to recite. They gave us extra food. We received our meals from the Vietnamese kitchen and ate separately from the other prisoners. I made a tape recording which was to be played over their radio. Then I came down with malaria, and I wondered if I would be allowed to leave.

Harker. We were called to a meeting and told the VC had submitted a request to the Front for their release. We were dumbfounded. How could we have been so stupid not to see it coming? At first we were angry with Strictland and Watkins for not telling us. We couldn't understand. We were their best friends. Nobody should hold secrets like that. Later we thought it was amusing. They had been prisoners too long. We would have probably reacted the same way.

Why the VC had chosen Strictland and Watkins was not difficult to figure out. They had worked hard and kept their noses clean. The VC liked them. As a black and a white they provided a racial balance. And both were in fairly good physical shape. The choice of the Tennessean was more subtle. We always thought that if a release came, Joe Zawtocki would be included. He was a hard worker, had a personality the VC liked, and had served time as a squad leader along with Watkins and Strictland. But Zawtocki had become very ill in the summer of '69. The National Liberation Front's public image would not have been helped to release someone who looked like he just walked out of Dachau.

The Tennessean, on the other hand, had received relatively good medical attention, showing the lenient and humane treatment of the Front. Besides, Dr. Kushner told them he thought the Tennessean had contracted serum hepatitus. I think they were worried about another prisoner dying. As we later learned, Hanoi had begun to improve the treatment of POWs held in the north around this time, probably because of world interest in them. The policy undoubtedly was passed down to the VC.

Strictland. When the camp was called to a meeting someone always asked the VC, "Well, when are you going to release somebody?"

They said, "You make progress."

We played along with it. It didn't bother you. You would say, "I'm getting me out." You didn't think you were being dishonorable to America. I didn't tell them anything of importance. I didn't know anything. Nobody told them anything that would help them or hurt us.

The North Vietnamese guy had taken over as camp commander. Slime was transferred to another assignment. He told us not to tell we were going to be released. When it was announced at the meeting I was smiling from ear to ear. I could tell some guys were pissed because they weren't going. The VC moved the three of us outside the compound into the hootch the Germans had used. They gave us meat with every meal for the first time since I'd been captured. I guess they were trying to fatten us up. We waited around for a few weeks. I began to think maybe they weren't going to let us go.

Anton. Strictland and Watkins were given candy and extra food. They secretly passed some of it over the fence to us. We were depressed. In a way, though, we thought maybe there would soon be another release. We knew why those three were being freed. It wasn't for being progressive. Nobody was progressive in the conventional communist sense of the word. Kushner and I did most of the writing. For that reason we took the brunt of the VC's propagandizing. Some guys were really rotten about it when they got home. They said, "I haven't written anything," and pointed at Kushner and me. The military intelligence people asked us about it. Kush and I told them the same thing: so and so didn't write because he was too goddamn stupid!

Harker. No VC honchos were at the celebration meal. We became a little excited and said, "Maybe we'll get two big meals out of their release." That's what happened. Another ceremony was held later. We heard Willie Watkins' speech on the radio. It was on before he left. He thanked the Liberation Front for releasing him and talked about racism in America. They played Aretha Franklin's "Respect" along with his talk.

Strictland. High-ranking officers, including a VC province chief, attended the second ceremony. The camp commander gave a speech in Vietnamese which was translated. We also made a little talk. We ate at a table with six officials and Garwood, who had come for the occasion. We had seldom seen him after we changed camps in the spring. He had gone from bad to worse. He sometimes came in and said hello. But it was clear he didn't particularly care to talk to us anymore. He asked me to tell his mother he was alive and well and to write him in Hanoi. He said he was leaving soon for North Viet Nam.

Harker. They left the next morning. It was raining. The three of them wore bamboo coolie hats and had their pajamas rolled to the knees. We said, "Good God, if anyone sees them they'll be killed." The VC had taken their measurements and sent to the Front supply office for a dark-green NVA-cut uniform. They wore it at the ceremony and carried it with them wrapped in plastic to put on shortly before returning to friendly lines. We watched them walk down the path. Something hung in our throats. It was an empty night.

Anton. Harker was told to give a speech at the ceremony thanking the Liberation Front for its generosity in releasing the three. He made a mild speech, it was barely adequate if anything. Harker had an obstinate attitude toward the VC.

Strictland. The interpreter, a guard, and a girl VC escorted us to friendly lines. We walked ten days. As we reached the coastal plains we walked at night and slept during the day. Once we were about to cross a road. The VC thought a U.S. ambush team might be on the other side. So they fired their rifles in an attempt to spring it prematurely. The three of us didn't know what was happening. We ran the other way. They had to call us back.

We stopped at a village near an ARVN outpost. The VC shook hands and hugged the government Popular Forces in the village. That was Vietnamization for you. They told two small boys to lead us across a wide paddy to the ARVN outpost. They turned back. The boys led us halfway across, got scared, and ran away. We asked an old man to help us. The soldiers at the outpost had been firing all morning. They were shooting at nothing, just scared.

As we moved closer they fired at us. Watkins and I were looking out for ourselves, we were ahead of the Tennessean. We took cover behind a blown-up bridge. The ARVN continued to shoot at him. If I had had an M-16 I would have killed me a few ARVNs. I didn't know whether we were going to make it or not. I thought, "We went through all that trouble to get killed a few steps from freedom." The firing finally slacked up. We yelled to them in English, and made our way cautiously to the outpost.

The VC thought when we left the jungle that we were going to Washington to take part in the antiwar demonstration. I may have thought the same thing, I don't know. I didn't go to Washington. Neither did Watkins. I sort of regretted later that I hadn't gone to speak out against the war. I guess if I had people would have said I was brainwashed.

Harker. Things returned to the usual grind for us. The manioc fields in our immediate area were depleted or defoliated. We had to use the camp's fields, a day's walk there and back. A week before Christmas we got word to move camp. The VC made Davis, Pfister, and me carry salt to the new site. It was raining. We left at 7:00 and got there at noon by walking slippery, narrow trails and across a swift river. The camp was half completed. The kitchen was without the usual mud stove, undergrowth hadn't yet been cut away from the compound. It would have been depressing had there not been a good manioc field a hundred meters away and plenty of hardwood to burn.

We moved camp next day. Joe Zawtocki was too weak to make it all the way. We left him in a montagnard village. Davis and I went back to get him. He sat by a fire the montagnards had made for him wrapped tightly in his blanket. We smelled something and saw that he had singed the blanket he was sitting so close. His eyes had that familiar faraway look. We gave him a pep talk. He was the only son, he had three sisters, and we told him he had to carry the family name forward; shouldn't disappoint his relatives, for Watkins and Strictland had told them he was alive. He said, "No, I don't want to. But it's so hard." After everyone talked to him he said he would try to get his food down.

We were listening to carols on Radio Hanoi late Christmas Eve. Somebody returned from the hootch and said, "Joe's dead."

Dr. Kushner spoke to us. He said we had lost another comrade, that we were in the jungle and had to pull together, we would soon be back with our families and all this would be in the past, would not be a reality but something to be buried in our minds.

The VC gave us a can of condensed milk. We heated water to dilute it into twelve cups. After Kushner was through Daly talked about what Christmas meant to him. He went on and on. Someone said, "Don't you think it's time we quit. The milk's getting cold." We sang a few carols, drank the milk, and went to bed. There was no speech by the camp commander.

Christmas morning we dug Joe's grave. Others gathered bamboo for a casket. It was a rocky area and hard digging. We didn't get it very deep. It was close to lunchtime. We carried him down wrapped in his blanket. Kushner said a few words. We repeated the Lord's Prayer. Then we returned to the compound, washed our hands, and ate.

Anton. Mr. Hom came to the compound with tears in his eyes. He said the camp commander had given him strict orders not to let Joe Zawtocki die but Joe had done it anyway and spoiled everybody's Christmas.

Daly. After Strictland and Watkins left we never saw Bob Garwood again, which was fine with us. Of everyone I knew he was the only person I believed to be a traitor, unless what they said about John Young was true, and I have no way of knowing if it was.

11

John Young

Some Americans at the Lang Vei U.S. Special Forces camp later suspected I had given the North Vietnamese information about the camp's defenses. There's no way I can defend myself. It was an assumption bound to be made because I was captured before they were and the attack against Lang Vei was successful. The camp was overrun the night of February 6, 1968. Obviously the North Vietnamese wouldn't hit a special forces camp on three or four days notice. It was something that evidently had been planned a long time. They weren't stupid. I think half the South Vietnamese soldiers at Lang Vei worked for them anyway. I later talked to Brandy, a Green Beret captured at the camp, and he said that a lot of desertions occurred two days before Lang Vei was attacked.

Lang Vei first entered my thoughts the evening of January 26. I was at the Da Nang Special Forces B Team headquarters. A clerk came by and said, "The sergeant major wants you out on the first flight tomorrow morning. You'll be going to the Laotian battalion."

I said, "Okay," and went to find out more about the assignment. Nobody was in the ops center; they were all in the club. I looked up Lang Vei on the map. I saw that it was a small camp astride Highway 9, several miles southwest of Khe Sanh and edging the Laos–South Viet Nam border. Along with Khe Sanh, it was the American outpost closest to North Viet Nam in the country's northwestern sector.

The U.S. had tried for a few years to monitor infiltration from North Viet Nam by using helicopters to insert small special-forces reconnaissance teams on the strategic border mountains overlooking the dozens of north-south trails and small dirt roads collectively known as the Ho Chi Minh trail. The North Vietnamese had driven the teams off the mountains with larger forces and inflicted heavy casualties. Another tactic involved sending a U.S.-advised battalion of Royal Lao troops to try to control infiltration by launching operations into Laos from the South Vietnamese side at Lang Vei. It was better, of course, to have Laotians operating in Laos than South Vietnamese. Still, the fact that Laotians were based inside South Viet Nam was its own cause for secrecy under terms of the war, and little publicity was given to the work of the Royal Lao Brigade's Thirty-third Battalion.

I checked around and found several troopers who were familiar with Lang Vei. They told me that the three noncommissioned officers assigned to work with the Lao battalion had quit and returned to Da Nang because they said they couldn't get the Lao soldiers to go out on patrols and operations. Two new replacements had already been sent to the camp; I was to be the third. The choice didn't surprise me. I was a weapons specialist. In the month I'd been in Viet Nam my job was to work with Nung security forces in Da Nang. The Nungs were mercenaries of Chinese extraction whose reputation for fierceness was not undeserved. They provided the guards and security patrols for the Da Nang base camp, which was headquarters for special forces operations in the First Corps area. It was my duty, supervised by an officer, to see that they carried out the assignment properly.

I returned to my quarters to put together my equipment, which included a carbine and a .45-cal. pistol, binoculars, ammo vest, web gear, two pairs of camouflaged tiger suits, two pairs of regular fatigues, some underwear and T-shirts, three pairs of canvas-vented jungle boots, shaving gear, and a camera. Next morning I hopped a resupply chopper at the Marble Mountain air base. We went up the sandy white coast and cut inland near Hue toward the west. As we passed over Khe Sanh I looked down and said to myself, "Boy, am I glad that's not where I'm going to be." I could see bunkers dug into the red clay adjoining the airstrip and almost feel the tenseness of the marines moving around below. I didn't like the positions of any special-forces camps I'd seen. They were usually in valleys because a level airstrip was necessary for resupply, despite the fact this violated all military concepts of commanding the strategic terrain—the high ground —and made them extremely vulnerable.

I could see as we approached Lang Vei that its position was better—but not by much. It sat on a low hill at the lip of a valley. When I got off the chopper I saw no one I knew. It was late morning. I walked to the team house to get something to eat. The unpainted wood-and-tin building was heavily sandbagged and lowered half underground. I got a cold beer and sat around for a while, then walked down by the heliport and along Highway 9 for a few meters to have a look around.

Lang Vei was garrisoned by a reinforced Special Forces A Team, maybe twenty Americans, plus a number of South Vietnamese soldiers, montagnard irregulars, and the Laotian battalion. Everyone was busy, and no one seemed to notice me.

Finally I spotted the sergeant major, who had choppered out with the colonel from Da Nang. I went over and said, "Am I supposed to go straight over to the Laotians?"

He said, "Yeah, go ahead."

I stopped off in the ops center to look at the intelligence map. I realized why no one had paid me any attention. Lang Vei was surrounded by three North Vietnamese divisions.

It hit me in the pit of my stomach. I wasn't going to make it out. I knew it. I had earlier got the feeling I wouldn't be coming back when I finished at Fort Bragg. I wasn't superstitious, and I'd tried to brush it off, but it wouldn't go away. I told my wife before leaving that I probably wouldn't return. It sort of disappeared after I got to Da Nang. I wrote to tell her not to worry, that Da Nang was fairly safe. I didn't mention we were getting rocketed quite often. Now as I looked at the map and saw the small red rectangles marked in grease pencil surrounding Lang Vei, I said to myself, "I was right after all."

The Laotian battalion had set up a perimeter where the old Lang Vei camp had been, about a hundred fifty meters southeast of the new camp along Highway 9. The old camp had been overrun in mid-1967, a fact which I think was kept secret from the press. The old camp was positioned a little higher than the new camp and was maybe sixty meters in diameter. Nearly five hundred Lao soldiers were squeezed together in dugout firing positions which had poor fields of fire because the area in front was overgrown with weeds. Outside the perimeter was an old mine field. The map key for the field had been lost. No one knew exactly where the mines were laid, and no one was anxious to venture out past known safe areas.

There were many sandbagged holes but no real bunkers. What passed for a bunker was the corner of an old building that had collapsed under repeated rocket and artillery attacks. The still-standing corner was reinforced with sandbags. It provided shelter for a sergeant, a medic, our Vietnamese interpreter, and a Laotian. I got a piece of tarp and set it up outside as my hootch. A colored medic was there when I arrived. I introduced myself and he grinned and said, "Man, we're in trouble."

I went to talk to the lieutenant colonel who commanded the Lao troops. He was the only one of them who spoke English. I made him a gift of my binoculars and we began to speak casually about our families and then moved to the situation at hand. I learned he was no more optimistic than I about our chances. The Lao were equipped with an array of old weapons ranging from communist AKs to French BARs. They were limited to one grenade per man and that grenade had to remain on the perimeter at all times. Camp supplies were mostly airdropped. The Americans at the new camp grabbed them first; the Lao got the leftovers.

I began to collect the Lao's old weapons, replacing them with M-1 carbines scrounged from the A Team. At least they would have weapons that fired the same ammo. The next day, January 28, I repaired machine guns. Most of them were old and in bad condition from lack of care. That night the A Team at the new camp received a ground probe from NVA commandos who set off trip flares. Everybody went wild; there was lots of unnecessary shooting.

On the twenty-ninth I continued to gather and repair old weapons. The day was mostly taken up by the doctor from Da Nang who came to give the Laotians a cholera shot with an automatic gun. Everyone at first refused the innoculation. The lieutenant colonel volunteered to start things. The troops lined up behind him and went through. The colonel moved slightly as he got his, causing a few drops of blood, and was given a piece of cotton for his arm. Every Lao thereafter demanded a piece of cotton whether bleeding or not.

I received a call on the radio that evening to report to the A Team. It had begun to turn cool as the sun fell and I could feel the layers of heat working up from the powdery red dust as I walked to the operations bunker. The A Team commander, a captain, had returned that day from a thirty-day leave in the States. The situation was desperate, he realized, but he hadn't had time really to figure out what was going on. I think he was just anxious to get things moving. Action for the sake of action.

He walked to the big map on the wall, and said, "Young, I want you to take a patrol out tomorrow morning to recon this village right here." He pointed to a small ville nearly two thousand meters northeast of Lang Vei. "Get your radio and anything else you might need."

I said, "Who's going with me?"

He said, "Nobody. We can't spare anyone."

That was the end of my briefing. I knew the marines at Khe Sanh couldn't get two clicks from their perimeter without a battalion, and he was telling me to take a small patrol out.

I asked questions around the A Team about what things were

like out there. They said, "Well, there's the map. You can see the
NVA are all around us. You'll just have to be careful." There was
nothing else to say, so I left. To get back to the old camp I had
to walk through eight rows of rolled concertina wire that surrounded the new camp. All the gates were closed for the night.
It was pitch black. I was scared. I felt somebody was going to
open up on me any minute. As I walked down the road I whistled
loudly as I could without being obvious, hoping the ARVN would
know I was leaving and the Laotians would realize it was I coming
back.

When I returned I told the lieutenant colonel I needed some
men for a patrol. I hoped he would give me a company. He said
he could only spare seventeen men, less than two squads. The
sergeant who technically commanded our three-man group was
frightened to death and wouldn't leave the camp perimeter. He
and the medic suggested that I sandbag the patrol. I did not think
one minute about not carrying out the assignment. I began to
prepare for the morning.

Shortly after sunrise we moved out in a column of twos along
the road leading to Khe Sanh. The heat settled on us like a wet
blanket. As I worked out the stiffness in my legs I thought of the
long day ahead. We passed several Vietnamese civilians. I started
to stop and interrogate them but remembered I had nobody with
me who spoke the language. We walked the road about forty-five
minutes and then cut north through jungle scrub.

The point man was twenty meters in front of the column. We
had scarcely cleared the road when he took the first round. Firing
erupted all around us. I ran to get him but saw it was no use. He
had taken it through the head. I turned to give a signal to the
Laotians. There was no one to signal. They had fled.

I ran three steps. Got caught in a volley of fire. Took a round
in my lower left leg. Another grazed me. As I fell I took two more.
The bullets shattered both bones in my lower leg. Didn't feel
anything. It was as if I was running and my leg suddenly gave out.
Tried to jump up again but couldn't. Rolled over and looked at
it and said, "Oh, my God!" Pants leg was blown away. Blood all

over. Pieces of bone sticking out. Crawled to a gully.

I tried to calm myself. I knew I was hit only in the leg, I wasn't dying. Bullets splatted in the dirt around me. I tried to call Lang Vei headquarters on my Prick-25. "Spunky Hansom, Spunky Hansom, this is Twenty-Bravo. Over." No answer. Tried again but didn't have time to finish. The area was too hot. I went through two thirty-round magazines, firing the carbine on automatic.

The NVA were thirty-five meters away. I saw my rounds blow away the heads of two of them manning a machine gun. Thought I got another, but I couldn't see well because I was spraying and trying to duck their fire. I inserted a third magazine into the underbelly of my carbine. Suddenly I felt two sharp points pricking my back. Two NVA had outflanked me unseen, approached from either side. They carried SKSs with flip-out bayonets. One of them said in a heavy accent, "Surrender or die." He handed me a small calling card. One side was in English. It said I had been captured by the National Liberation Front and would be treated humanely.

They snatched my rifle, grabbed me under each arm, dragged me a little past their lines, and leaned me against a tree. They removed my pistol belt and web gear but left my ammo vest intact with sixteen magazines in it. Later before they moved me out they remembered to remove the ammo. A medic arrived almost immediately. He gave me a shot of tetanus and penicillin but no morphine. It wasn't needed. I felt no pain for two days. I was in shock.

A captured Laotian had a leg wound identical to mine. The North Vietnamese put us in green-canvas hammocks stretched across bamboo poles and moved us off the high ground into the jungle toward a valley. Three hours later we were almost caught in a bombing raid. The NVA heard the hiss of the falling bombs and dropped me, ran for cover under rocks. The B-52s walked a mountain above us. When the earthquake started I crawled to the rocks faster than I would have thought possible. The attack over, the soldiers returned, dusting themselves off and laughing.

I was surprised to find them so cheerful. I could see on closer examination that they were a mixture of VC and North Vietnamese.

We moved awhile longer and stopped. I spent the night in a hole in deep jungle. I was exhausted. Before dropping off to sleep I thought about what had happened and wondered why I had made it this far. From everything I had heard about the enemy, I knew it was only a matter of time before they would kill me. I was told during my training that the VC showed no mercy to special-forces soldiers. The Vietnamese woke me next morning with a cup of powdered milk. They pointed to the hammock and motioned me to get in. We continued to move. It felt like we moved for two days. But I'm not certain because the pain had started, making it difficult to concentrate.

We reached a jungle camp. It was made up of underground bunkers. The number of soldiers in the area told me it was at least a battalion or regimental headquarters. It was obviously very secure; soldiers walked around weaponless. A Vietnamese came to interrogate me. He looked to be about thirty-five. He told me he was a math teacher in a Hue high school before joining the Liberation Army. He spoke politely and had a sort of British formality about him.

Some soldiers sat me on the edge of a bunker, with my legs hanging over. The interrogator explained why he was going to question me. "I am a Vietnamese fighting for my country. The Americans are here as aggressors. They are foreigners fighting against my people. You must understand why I have to ask you questions. It is not that I want to but because I must in order to help my country."

He began to quiz me about Lang Vei.

I told him my name, rank, serial number, and religion.

He said, "You do not need to say that. I have your dog tags."

I said, "I just got to Lang Vei three days before I was captured. I was with the Laotians. I never really went to the new camp. So I can't tell you anything about it."

He said, "You're lying. We have ways to make you talk."

They definitely have ways. He started with my wounded leg. He and two soldiers first pulled on it, then kicked it viciously. I passed out.

When I came to the interrogator told me that if I didn't talk he would have the wounded Lao killed. The Laotian sat on the edge of a hole a few meters away, facing the other way.

I said, "I can't tell you anything because I just got there."

He gave a signal. A North Vietnamese shot the Lao in the back of the head with a TT-33 pistol. The Lao pitched forward into the hole. I was stunned. He ordered another Laotian brought up. I couldn't tell whether he was from my patrol.

"You will be responsible for this man's death too if you do not talk."

I again told him I didn't know anything. A soldier executed the second Lao in the same manner.

The interrogator showed me a regular 1:50,000 army map on which U.S. positions at Khe Sanh and Lang Vei were marked in detail. He had a dozen five-by-seven snapshots taken with a 35-mm telephoto lens of Lang Vei's mortar pits, gun positions, and team house. He pointed at the pictures and asked me to identify the obvious. He was seeking verification of what he already knew.

I pointed out the helipad and said, "Highway Nine runs through here and the Vietnamese and Americans are over here at the new camp."

He asked how many men were in the camp, the locations of specific firing positions.

I repeated that I didn't know. Which was actually true.

He raised his pistol even with my eyes, and said, "This is your last chance."

I said quietly, "I can't tell you anymore." I guess he either accepted it or didn't feel like killing me. He lowered the gun and motioned for them to take me away. The interrogation had lasted six hours.

Next day a doctor opened my wounded leg, cleaned out the multiplying maggots, removed some bone splinters, then put in drainage tubes and fitted me with a ladder splint. He gave me a tetanus shot and some penicillin and morphine. I was moved a few meters up the hill and placed in a dark bunker. The interrogator came every day or so to see how I was doing. Once he brought a reporter from the Liberation News Service. The reporter had a tape recorder but no camera. He asked my name and the circumstances of my capture.

On February 6 the interrogator stopped by for a few minutes. He was unusually cheerful. He said, "Would you like to watch us overrun Lang Vei tonight?"

That evening I could hear North Vietnamese artillery whistling overhead toward Lang Vei. I reckoned I was about three clicks directly from the camp. In the distance I heard the unmistakable clank and rumble of tanks. The sky southward was lit with flares. Several jets flew over. There was less air traffic than I thought there would be, possibly because the Tet offensive was taking place all over South Viet Nam simultaneously. The sound of gunfire died out next morning. I knew the attack had been successful when I saw Sergeant Thompson being led into our camp.

We moved out three days later. Vietnamese medics put a regular hip-length plaster cast on my leg. It would have been perfect if I had not had an open wound. No hole was left in the cast for drainage. Several soldiers carried me in the hammock. When we reached the top of the first hill I saw Thompson, who was unwounded, and five ARVN who were captured with him. Thompson gave me a blanket. We moved south-southwest toward the Laos border, reaching a small montagnard village that evening. Thompson and the ARVN slept in a hootch elevated on stilts. I slept below on a bamboo platform.

Thompson and the others were gone when I awoke. My guards pulled me to another hootch, gave me some penicillin, and disappeared. Medics later came to remove the leg cast. It had turned soft and started stinking. The house belonged to a family of the Bru minority. For the following two weeks I was to be continually shocked by the treatment I received. The Bru respected the house as if it were mine. They brought me breakfast and supper of soup and rice balls. I was given my own private basket of potatoes and manioc. Villagers returning from the fields always made sure the basket was full. The younger women were bare-breasted, the older wore sarong-type dresses, and the men were interchangeable with peasant Vietnamese except for their darker skins. They were gentle farmers. And I began to re-examine my thoughts about the war.

During my two weeks in the Bru house I realized I knew little about Viet Nam or why we were there. I was not even very familiar with the country's name until I got to Fort Bragg. Laos and Cambodia I knew were someplace in Asia, but I certainly couldn't have placed them on a blank map if I had to. Nor was I familiar with the definition of communism. I had been told in general terms at Bragg that it was something bad, something we had to fight against. That was good enough for me. I considered myself 100-per-cent red, white, and blue.

An interpreter arrived at the Bru house. He was upset. Apparently a mix-up in orders had caused them to leave me alone two weeks. I was taken to a makeshift camp where I joined two other Green Berets. Thompson and Brandy had tried to escape before I arrived but had been recaptured. Brandy had a wounded leg; he'd taken grenade fragments at Lang Vei. We began to move northwest up the Ho Chi Minh trail.

It was my worst time. My leg was killing me. I put three bamboo splints on it and tied them together as tightly as I could. The ARVN POWs carried Brandy and me in hammocks. I tried to slide down the steep inclines and the pain was unbearable. We came to a camp in northern Laos after a few days. We stayed there two weeks, resting up. I was unable to eat and had dysentery, was swollen with edema. Two more American POWs joined us—McMurray, the radioman at Lang Vei, and Ridgeway, a marine from Khe Sanh who was taken in an ambush. Unknown to us, the Marine Corps sent Ridgeway's "remains" to his parents and they buried him, only to discover five years later he was still alive.

We resumed our march and reached a river. It may have been

an extension of the Ben Hai, which separates North from South Viet Nam, for shortly after crossing it we were put on trucks. We drove through areas that looked like the moon, the jungle was completely leveled. As we got deeper into North Viet Nam we saw that almost every village had been destroyed. Rice fields were churned up and cratered. Suddenly jets flashed out of the sun. We took cover beside the road.

Ted Guy

I landed at midnight from a mission in Laos. We were short of aircrews so I scheduled myself to fly next morning. I went to my sleeping trailer and had a bucket of popcorn and a couple of drinks with my roommate, Col. Ross Carson, the squadron commander. I got several hours sleep, awoke at 4:30, and went to the club for a breakfast of scrambled eggs and toast.

At 6:30 I was in the squadron room doing some paper work. A major who had been in-country four days walked in and said, "Colonel, when am I going to fly?"

I said, "How about right now?" My regular back seater was supposed to go on the mission with me. But he had been shot down recently with another pilot, his wife was having a baby, and because of the dual circumstances we had managed to get him a stateside leave. I told him to skip the flight and leave early for the U.S.; I would take the eager major with me instead.

I thought it would be a good mission for the major's first. It was scheduled for a sparsely populated area of Laos. We wouldn't have to worry much about the accuracy of our bombs. The mission had come down from Seventh Air Force in Saigon. Normally we got a prewarning frag about three o'clock the afternoon of the day before the mission was to be run. About 10:00 the same night it was finalized and my aircrews notified. It was to be a two-plane flight. In the front seat of the lead plane was a young captain later killed in Viet Nam. Flying his back seat was a colonel getting a routine instructor-pilot check. I was flying number 2 as the captain's wingman, but as squadron-operations officer I had overall command. The mission was what we called "a dollar ride." Theater indoctrination.

The briefing began before 7:00. When we were airborne we were supposed to establish radio contact with Hillsboro, code name for the flying control center that coordinated bombing missions in the south. Hillsboro would then direct us to operate under the instructions of a small propeller-driven spotter plane west of Khe Sanh. That's all we really knew about the target. The prop-driven Forward Air Controller (FAC) would give us the specifics when we got there. We carried four 750-pound high-drag bombs. A high-drag has four large fins that open on its back to slow its descent. We can deliver it very low and very fast with excellent accuracy. I had flown my first high-drag mission in Laos in November, 1967. Now, five months later, I considered myself an expert with this type of ordnance.

The weather briefers told us the monsoon was creating a heavy haze below ten thousand feet. The intelligence officers said over forty thousand NVA troops were massed in the Khe Sanh area. They showed us map locations of known flak sites and where our best bail-out areas would be in case of a shoot-down. The brief was finished by 7:15. Take-off was scheduled for 8:30. We returned to the squadron office. I briefed the major on emergency procedures in the event we got hit. I'd tell him to eject at once and he'd better get out fast because I would be right behind him. I explained his crew duties. He was my RTO, primarily responsible for radar navigation—what we pilots informally called a GIB, guy in the back seat. I had been hit on two occasions. Neither was particularly serious. I lost an engine near the Cambodian border and had to land at Saigon. I lost another engine one day down in the Delta and recovered at Bien Hoa. Small-arms fire both times.

Before Viet Nam I'd never flown two-engines. I'd always wanted to be a single-engined fighter pilot where you only had yourself to worry about. I volunteered five times for the war, beginning after the '64 Tonkin Gulf incident, but was not released from my job at Randolph Air Force Base until early 1967 so I could go. I hoped to fly single-engined F-105s from Thailand into North Viet Nam—that was my first choice. Da Nang was my second choice, and Cam Ranh my third. I would have had to wait two months until a new replacement-training class started in order to get F-105s. Headquarters told me I could get into F4s in one month, so I took that instead. My GIB and I graduated number one in the F4 class, as top gun out of thirty-five crews. Then I was sent to Cam Ranh Bay.

I changed my mind about two-engines after I flew the Phantom awhile. The F4 is a good weapons system, a very stable missile platform, and a capable fighter-bomber. Below 350 knots it handles like a truck. Get above mach one and it flies super. There are two hand throttles on the left side of the cockpit that move back and forth and control speed as well as the extrathrust afterburner. A stick in the center of the floor controls steering. It is studded with an assortment of firing buttons. You're flying with the left hand on the throttle and the right hand on the stick and in front is a small radar scope. There are many, many subsystems with scores of switches and dials. It's a complicated piece of machinery.

I wore a flying suit, a G suit, survival vest, and a parachute harness. I carried a .38 Police Special strapped to the small of my back. A survival knife was fastened to my leg. I also carried two emergency radios and a tree-lowering device. Before going on a mission I usually took off my wedding band, removed my wallet and other personals. For some reason I did not do that this morning. We went to the airplane and strapped in. Ross Carson came to the flight line just before I took off. I was starting the engines. He had held a helluva party the night before. He smiled bleary-eyed at me and waved good-by. We took off and were refueled by a KC-135 tanker near Plei Ku. Then we continued to Da Nang and contacted Hillsboro. The control center gave us the code name of our FAC and told us to contact him by flying fifteen miles on a 270-degree radio due west of Khe Sanh into Laos.

Frankly, I hadn't realized we had a war going on in Laos till I got to Viet Nam. I had read a little about it, a few excerpts in magazines, but not much. On my first mission we had tried to knock out a NVA supply road. We cratered the road with our bombs. Which, of course, they fixed thirty minutes later. That was why we had such a large air effort in Laos and Viet Nam. We knew they had up to thirty thousand people out there repairing roads all the time. The bombing was a great deterrent. First of all, it took away a large part of the labor force from North Viet Nam; and second, the factor of harassment was always there. We worked out tactics where we tried to find out where they were repairing craters and then we hit them. If we hadn't had the bombing, a lot more supplies would have been moved into South Viet Nam.

Still, I suppose I did not think some aspects of what we were doing were totally effective. We often worked with FACs on road cuts and truck parks. Sometimes when they told us there were truck parks and troops concentrations on the ground, I'd say, "Bullshit." There was nothing, just jungle. But as I walked up the Ho Chi Minh trail, I found there were a lot of truck parks in these areas, and I saw some of the damage we had caused.

We ran a lot of missions around the Tchepone area, which was a major junction of the Ho Chi Minh trail. In fact that's where I got my first Silver Star. I went to Tchepone one night when the weather was twenty-five-hundred-feet overcast. The FAC wanted us to come down and hit a river fording. Other flights had not been able to get below the ceiling. Like idiots we broke through and took what the FAC later estimated to be three thousand rounds of automatic weapons fire. There were numerous trucks on the road and we hit them. Six days later I got another Silver Star for going after automatic-weapons positions.

Of my hundred twenty missions, most were in Laos and fifteen were in North Viet Nam. We seldom went north from Cam Ranh. We wanted to get to North Viet Nam, very much so. Those missions were what we called a "counter." Everytime you went north you got two points toward an air medal, whereas a mission in Laos or South Viet Nam counted only one point. It took twenty points to get an air medal, and you could get one twice as fast flying north. Of course, I don't think air medals were the main reason. The main reason we wanted to go—and there were some guys who didn't—was the challenge, the excitement of flying into North Viet Nam. I had already made up my mind to extend my tour to get an assignment flying north when my time at Cam Ranh was up.

We passed over Khe Sanh and reached our area. A flight of F-105s was working the target, doing the usual dive bombing from twenty-five thousand feet. And, of course, hitting absolutely nothing. I'm kidding. But it looked to me like they were getting no lower than that. The FAC called and asked what kind of ordnance we carried. We replied four seven hundred fifty optional select bombs. He asked if we would go high-drag and try to hit a ZPU, a 14.5-mm antiaircraft gun. The captain radioed and asked what I thought. We didn't like to get into pissing contests with guns. But this site overlooked Highway 9. The FAC said it was important. He had tried to get rid of it for two days. I said, "Okay, we'll go."

My policy was to try to get there and give the FAC at least twenty minutes of work. From Cam Ranh to target and back usually took anywhere from an hour fifty minutes to two hours and a quarter. Sometimes, though, we went the 335 miles to Tchephone, made one pass, and came straight back if we didn't get refueled. And if a lot of missions were being run into North Viet Nam from Thailand, we didn't get refueled because the tankers were busy.

We were flying a floating-wheel pattern. As we circled the target, Lead went one way and I another to distract the gunners below. There was no reported flak or ground fire. Going around on the first pass I lost sight of the captain as he rolled in but saw his bomb go off. The FAC told me to put mine fifteen meters to the east of Lead's. I rolled in and released the first one. The FAC said it was very long. This upset me a little because I'm a pretty good bomber.

I called him and asked, "Are you sure?"

He said, "Roger that. It was two hundred meters long."

I should have known right then something was wrong. Looking back, I think I had a malfunction of the bomb-ejector rack.

Lead radioed and said, "Next pass we're going to deliver two bombs." I acknowledged. Lead made his run and dropped. The FAC told me again to put mine fifteen meters to the east of Lead's bombs. I rolled in and pickled the first and then the second. I was delivering at five hundred knots in a ten-degree bomb angle and releasing at about two hundred feet, which put me about fifty feet off the ground when I pulled up. Right after I released the second bomb and began to pull up the airplane was shaken by a violent explosion. I later figured out the bomb-ejector malfunction caused me to get caught in my own bomb blast.

I looked to my left where automatic weapons fire was coming from ground troops. Then I saw two ZPUs firing. I wasn't worried. If you can see muzzle flashes that means they aren't hitting you because they aren't leading.

I called my GIB and said, "Did you feel that?"

The major said, "Roger, I felt it."

The Phantom has a taletell panel with about twenty-eight lights that go on when something is wrong. I looked down and it said, "Check hydraulic systems," which give power to the landing gear and flaps. It was a common failure with the F4s. We sometimes lost our hydraulic resevoirs. It meant when you returned to the base you had to make a careful approach and then a cable-arrest landing like on navy carriers. I'd had two of them in the last month. I didn't consider it a major emergency.

I pulled up in the downwind leg, and said to the major, "How does everything look back there?"

He was very gung ho, said everything was fine.

I said, "If it's all right with you I'm going back to get the damn gun."

I had a phobia against automatic weapons. I thought we ought to get it while we could. I called Lead and told him I had the gun in sight. I said I would mark it with my 20-mikemike cannons and for him to put his last bomb on it. The gun was in a bunker on a bare hilltop. At the base of the hill were the gooks who were shooting at us with rifles. As we circled around I lost all control of the airplane for a moment but regained it. I went in on the final approach. I started firing about four thousand feet out, could see my tracers cut through the middle of the target. One thousand rounds. The cannon firing so fast I could hear only a loud vibrating whine—*ssszzz.*

Halfway through the pass the airplane suddenly felt as if it was sitting on top of a ballpoint pen. I pulled back on the stick. Nothing happened. We were heading straight for the hilltop. I went into max afterburner. It gave me just enough extra thrust to lift me over the hill by five feet. I radioed the emergency distress signal: "Mayday! Mayday! Mayday! This is Phantom Eight-Two." No response.

The taletell panel was lit up like a pinball machine. I had almost three quarters of aileron stick left to hold the wings level. I had, to the best of my knowledge, no elevator control at the time. I had a failure of the hydraulic systems, later lost the pneumatic system, and was losing fuel at the rate of three to four thousand pounds per minute. I had also lost the radar system. I told the major to call Lead. Our radios were dead. I told him we would try to make it to Da Nang. I didn't want to try Ubon in Thailand because we would have had to go clear across Laos.

The afterburner increased thrust; as speed builds up the airplane tends to climb. With my little aileron and rudder control I thought I could make it to Da Nang. The major couldn't see the front cockpit, and I chose not to worry him with everything going on.

He said, "Colonel, this is the most fun I've had in years."

I said, "Negative. We're up the creek without a paddle, buddy." We got to ten thousand feet and started the turn toward Da Nang. I didn't want to bail out at that point because I knew forty thousand NVA would be waiting to greet us. I was about to tell the major to take out his UFC-10, which is the emergency radio, the beeper, when the airplane rolled over on its back and started a nose dive to the ground.

I yelled, "Eject now! Eject now!" I looked down and saw my

pocket containing the escape and evasion gear, the maps and escort chits, was unzipped. I zipped it, then reached down to the seat lowering switch. Next thing I remember is a red and white parachute blossoming above me. The airplane blew up and somehow triggered the ejection mechanism. The major didn't make it. I didn't see another chute, didn't see a seat, didn't see the airplane. It was 9:32 in the morning.

I was in beautiful shape coming down. I took out a cigarette and lit it with my Zippo. I remembered I had been told that the gooks can smell tobacco from a great distance, so I put it out. A strong wind began blowing me westward deeper into Laos. The chute was swinging back and forth. I tried pulling on the risers to steady it. I looked down to find some high ground to land on. Everything looked to be dense green jungle. I could imagine myself dangling three hundred feet up, that was the size of trees in the area. If I had to use my tree-lowering device, I knew I would probably hang myself in the process.

I drifted down and the wind abruptly stopped. I prepared for tree penetration by putting hands over eyes and pointing toes downward. When I opened my eyes I was swinging to and fro. I looked down with dread. My feet were two inches from the ground. I'd fallen through the only hole in the triple canopy probably in all of Laos! I unbuckled my harness and opened my survival kit. Normally you do this coming down. But it's a bright yellow color and I thought if I opened it in the air the enemy would see it. It opened with a loud hissing noise as the dingy inflated with compressed air.

As the hissing began I heard a rustle of movement to my right. I took out my emergency radio and yelled, "Mayday! Mayday! Mayday! Phantom Eight-Two. Anybody read?" I ran a hundred meters and put the radio on automatic beeper. I stopped out of breath behind a large tree felled by lightning. Heard a noise behind me. Turned and saw seven men in green uniforms, carrying AK-47s. I dove on the other side of the tree and jerked out my .38. I had loaded my pistol with five rounds, leaving a space between the first four and the last. I had decided long ago to commit suicide before allowing myself to be captured. I told my family before I left for Viet Nam that if they heard I was shot down but didn't hear anything further, they would know I was dead. I didn't want to experience what I'd heard some of the POWs in Korea had been through.

I fired. In the excitement I went bang! bang! bang! bang! . . . click . . . bang!

I said, "Oh, shit. That was my last bullet." I hit two of the seven men.

I started to run down a path, grabbed my radio and accidentally broke off the antenna. A grenade exploded. Fragments stung my legs.

A North Vietnamese ran at me on the path. He held an AK-47 with a fixed bayonet. I pushed at the bayonet with my forearm, deflecting it slightly. It just missed my jugular vein as it ripped a two-inch gash into my neck. The blade felt as if it was coming out my nose. I was dazed. The Vietnamese swung the rifle butt around. He slammed me on the left side of the head.

When I came to I felt no pain. Thirty NVA stood around me. They had stripped me of everything but my white shorts. Then they took those off and conducted a very thorough body search. None of them spoke English. One removed my Seiko, a twenty-one-dollar Sportsman. He pointed at my gold wedding band. I said, "No." He tried to pull it off. I flexed my finger. He got my survival knife and returned with a big grin. It was best, I decided, to give him the ring.

A short Vietnamese slapped me in the face, and pulled me over to two men lying on the ground. One of them had a bullet in the chest. He was still alive but appeared to be dying. The other I had shot through the stomach and he was dead. I was taken to a sapling, and my arms and feet were bound around it with nylon cord. Someone put a green T-shirt over my face as a blindfold. I was certain they were going to shoot me.

A whistle sounded. A tall, distinguished-looking Vietnamese arrived. He talked to the short guy who had been slapping me around. The short one pointed to the two men I had shot and pointed to me, jabbering away. The tall man said, "No." Lying on the ground near the tall Vietnamese, whom I assumed to be an officer, was my flying suit with its lieutenant colonel's insignia. I think that's what saved me. It was their day to take a quota of one prisoner. I later found I was only the second or third American pilot to be taken alive in Laos. The tall Vietnamese cut me loose and returned my shorts. I put them on. They led me back up the path several hundred meters.

We entered a base camp. I saw about seven hundred North Vietnamese troops in clean green uniforms, tennis-shoe boots, carrying new AKs. They looked like fresh reinforcements heading for Khe Sanh. Several soldiers slapped at me as I walked by. Their officers kept them away. I stayed there twenty minutes and was given tea and cigarettes. I figured out my position. I was due south of Highway 9, about twelve miles inside the Laos border, and maybe thirty miles southwest of Khe Sanh. I had bailed out in the middle of a major North Vietnamese bivouac.

My arms were tied behind my back duck-wing fashion. I was marched up the trail by three armed guards. After thirty minutes the pain in my arms was so intense that I didn't think I could go farther. I was bleeding heavily from the bayonet wound in my throat. The calves of both legs were peppered with shrapnel wounds. At a fork in the trail we turned right. Commo wire led in all directions. The North Vietnamese had a prepared battlefield—wires, trenches, machine-gun nests, phones. Morale seemed high. I wondered why we didn't have intelligence information about the extent of their operations. Maybe we did, but I wasn't aware of it.

My wounds coagulated after a while. I was encrusted with blood. We walked two hours till we reached a camp with bunkers and hootches dug half underground. The camp was surrounded by barbed wire and a bamboo fence. It was a first-aid station. As I walked past several hootches I looked down and saw wounded Vietnamese soldiers in hammocks. My guards left me at a small wood shack marked with a red-and-white cross. They returned a few minutes later with a medic. He was very kind. He carried an ounce bottle of iodine in the center of a roll of white adhesive tape. He got a basin of water and washed my legs, which were badly scarred by jungle thorns and grenade shrapnel. He cleaned the wounds and taped my legs, and examined the base of my chin where the bayonet had entered. He indicated by sign language that he had no surgical thread or needle for stitches. I nodded. Then he taped my chin very tightly and motioned for me to sleep. Apparently he did a good job. I was only left with a one-inch scar after it healed. The guards had brought along my survival kit and parachute. One made me a pillow from the gear, another brought me some rice, vegetables, and a meat I didn't recognize. I was surprised by my treatment, especially since I'd killed two of their people.

I woke around dusk. A group of Vietnamese appeared at my hootch door. I recognized two of them. One wore my wedding band, the other my watch. It was the slapper. The short Vietnamese hit me in the stomach. The others gathered round and took turns punching and slapping me. They jabbered back and forth and laughed, beat me at their leisure for two hours, then grew tired of the game and went to bed, leaving a guard outside holding a rope tied around my neck.

That night I made the personal code I was to try to live by for the next five years. The shock of my capture hit me full force. The men had beat me, I realized, to a point where I would have spilled my guts had there been someone present to interrogate me. Fortunately, they hadn't asked a single question. For the first time I understood the meaning of my breaking point. I believed the formal Code of Conduct had no real specifics in it, personal values assigned to the individual, values you had to live up to yourself. I knew I had to have something specific and strong to satisfy my own needs.

I sensed that night I was going to Hanoi. I remembered all the things I'd heard about the Korean POWs, how some had gotten into trouble. I made up my mind not to let myself get in that kind of situation. I would die first before I incriminated or blamed any other American or caused camp secrets to be disclosed. My personal code made that night consisted of two main points: (1) I would resist till I could resist no longer; and (2) I would accept death before I would lose my honor.

At 7:00 the next morning the Vietnamese who had beat me got up and left without a word. I never saw them again. I stayed at the aid station the following days. I was given four meals a day and the medic attended my wounds.

An officer came the night of March 25. He knew one word in English: "Name?"

I said, "Guy, Theodore W." I also told him my rank, serial number, and date of birth. He didn't understand. I asked for something to write on. He produced a spiral notebook. I wrote the information, hoping he might later be killed or captured and my name found by U.S. forces.

Three guards came for me at daybreak. They brought me a khaki uniform. My flying suit had been returned to me earlier, so I refused to wear the khaki. I had intentions of trying to escape. I didn't want to be caught in anything without my rank. The guards gave in and let me wear the flying suit. We started to leave camp. My feet were badly swollen. I was without boots. I stopped, pointed at my feet, told them I couldn't walk. One of them ran back and returned with a pair of sneakers. I wear a size eight and these must have been sixes. The guards giggled as they helped me pull them on.

We walked a path for two hours and hit a road, Highway 9. After a short wait a jeep with four soldiers came along. They laid me on the back-seat floor under my parachute and other gear. I discreetly searched for my pistol but it was missing. It began to rain. We drove westward until we reached Tchepone. We crossed a river ferry and stopped at a house. I slept in a hole that night under guard. Next morning I was marched into a village near Tchepone. It was filled with people, mostly young. I was taken to a hut in the village's center and told to sleep. I lay down on a bamboo bed and dozed off. I dreamed people were looking at me. I awoke with a start and discovered a dozen gathered round the bed staring silently.

Outside someone shouted in English for me to come out. I walked out the hut and saw an NVA photographer, who wore a pith helmet and a camouflaged scarf and was covered with an assortment of movie and still cameras. He explained that I was a criminal of war and he wanted to film my capture. I was given my flight boots and helmet to wear and moved to a nearby hill, where I was ordered to walk down slowly with hands up. A short fellow walked behind nudging the tip of his bayonet into my neck and looking mean. The middle finger of my upraised left hand was extended in American code. As I neared the camera I grinned. The photographer was upset. I was supposed to look sad. I had to repeat the scene. This time I looked solemn. Then a young girl came up, and she captured me. After that everybody took turns, including a twelve-year-old boy.

That night at 7:00 I started moving north. I always traveled at night usually by jeep or truck with two escorts, an officer and an enlisted man, who were changed every twenty-four hours. I had the hell bombed out of me by U.S. planes. It wasn't doing much good. But they really bombed us. I crossed into North Viet Nam on March 31, the night President Johnson stopped the bombing above the twentieth parallel. My treatment by the Vietnamese became worse the farther north we went. I saw many signs of the bombing. I think we did a good job of wiping out the bridges. However, we never had any trouble getting across rivers. Makeshift pontoon bridges or ferries were always available.

We reached Vinh city at dawn on April 2. I had walked the whole night and was without sleep for a week. I was taken to a large bamboo building in a village on Vinh's outskirts and placed in a cell, shackled with leg irons and handcuffs. I had barely lain down when a guard roused me. We walked across the village to a small one-room building. A Vietnamese who looked to be about twenty-one was waiting. He asked my name, rank, serial number, and place of birth. I gave him the rest but refused to tell my place of birth because under regulations I was supposed to disclose only my date of birth. He asked if I was married. I said no. He saw the white circle left by my wedding band.

He said, "You lie. You are a criminal of war! An imperialist pig! You will be tried for genocide!"

I lost my temper. "Untie me and I'll show you who's an imperialist pig!"

I kicked him on the leg. He shouted something. Two guards rushed from behind a screened partition. They grabbed me, tied a rope around my hands behind my back, threw the rope over a wooden rafter, and started pulling me up. The rafter broke. I fell and dislocated my shoulder. They beat me with empty rice sacks and kicked me in the stomach. That was the start of my hernia, and two of my teeth were knocked out.

When I awoke I was back in my cell in leg irons locked with U bolts. My wrists were bound together behind my back. I was tied to the bed. That night I was taken to a jeep and made to lie on the back-seat floor. We drove all night, reaching Hanoi early next morning. I could see as we arrived that it was a massive, dingy prison. I knew it could only be the Hanoi Hilton.

12

Tom Davis

The Viet Cong appointed Harker and me as squad leaders to replace Watkins and Strictland. I would have been happier without the job, but it wasn't something that could be refused. We returned to the compound, got everybody together, and said, "For whatever reasons, Harker and I are now it. You know what we have to do to survive. From now on we work as a team."

Harker. Davis was the strongest and his influence was naturally larger in some areas. He was a different personality from Watkins, less assertive and certainly more understanding. Dr. Kushner slowly built up his strength and did more work; and his influence grew proportionately. When problems came up, a meeting was called. Kushner summarized the choices open to us and laid out an ideal solution. All the POWs voted on the question. There was no longer a "camp commander" in the sense that Watkins, whether he wanted to or not, had been. In early 1970, for the first time, we spoke about the 1968 split between the two squads and its repercussions. It popped out one day as we sat around talking; and we began to work it out of our system. This became, I think, a limiting factor that kept anyone else from trying to take over. No one wanted to be talked about the way Watkins was after he left.

Anton. I withheld my vote on all questions in the group meetings. A lot of them couldn't understand. But I knew that some who criticized me for not voting were the same ones who had criticized me for having an opinion when I hadn't gone for manioc. I had an opinion on everything—I always do—but I kept it to myself. I was looking, quite frankly, for the easy way out. I didn't want any hassle from a couple of guys who always tried to find something to hold over my head.

Daly. I believe Harker felt very let down after he wasn't allowed to go home with Watkins and Strictland. He changed after that. He began to do things nobody else dared to do. He talked to Mr. Hom like a dog. Hom would stand there and take it as if Harker was his superior. Mr. Hom would be so mad he'd start foaming at the mouth. Everybody would get scared while Harker was laying it on, thinking he was going to get into trouble. How Harker got by with it, we never knew.

Anton. Mr. Hom didn't speak much about his background. He said what all VC said: that his father had been imprisoned for years and his mother had been tortured and killed by the French or by the Americans. Maybe it was true in some cases, but everyone said the same thing, and we just couldn't believe there were no exceptions. Hom thought us to be his inferiors, no doubt about that. Whenever he got flustered he used American swear words like "fuck" or "shit." It was funny to us because he stamped his foot petulantly when he swore.

McMillan. Anton was lying in bed after siesta time one afternoon and Mr. Hom came in and yelled, "Anton, Anton, get up!"

Ol' Bones jumped up on the bed. His shorts were loose and they fell to his knees. He was standing there with his weapon in Mr. Hom's face.

Hom said, "Oh, very nasty! Very nasty!" He made Anton stand at attention outside the hootch several hours.

The Vietnamese were real prudish, they didn't like nudity. They even took baths with their shorts on.

Harker. The pressures on us from the VC eased somewhat. A second translator arrived, his name was Trieu, or pronounced with our accent, "Mr. Chew." He was a friendly young guy who had tended water buffalo as a child and was referred to with snickers as "Buffalo Boy" by the other Vietnamese in camp. We liked him much better than we did Mr. Hom, and looked forward to the increasingly frequent occasions when Hom was away on errands for the Front.

Mr. Chew's arrival was overshadowed by more significant events. A growing number of North Vietnamese soldiers were passing through our area. Native South Vietnamese guerrillas seemed to be dwindling. There were signs that their military and political organization was under a severe strain. A new edict passed down from NLF headquarters commanded the camp staff and guards to grow eight months of their yearly rice supply. Henceforth the Front would provide them with only a four months' ration through regular logistics channels.

This new tightening of the belt caused changes. A skeleton crew was left on duty around the camp and every spare Vietnamese was sent to the fields to work. When things had gone relatively well we had seen nothing but a spirit of cooperation among the VC. They were *"Anh-Em,"* brothers in war. Often we heard one say, "I bought a chicken, killed it, and now everyone shall eat communally." The moment things got tough the façade began to crumble. Competition became the revolutionary spirit, backbiting was its flag. The guards split from the camp staff. They set up their own kitchen, grew their own food, and told the staff to fend for themselves.

Davis. Not only did Hannah stick it to us, she was doing to the same to the guards. She was supposed to issue them a sweet-condensed-milk ration when they were ill. Instead, she stole the extra milk and gave it to her baby boy. What he was doing in camp, or who the father was, we didn't know. And she herself was eating better than anyone else. When the guards broke away and formed an independent group, all the camp staff, including Rat-face the camp commander and the women, had to go to the fields to work.

Anton. The camp staff wanted us to work their private fields.

The guards objected. They became incensed when the staff tried to take some of us to work without first getting the guard commander's permission. The camp commander and a guard once argued thirty minutes about whether we could be taken from the compound. We pulled for the guards.

McMillan. Denny was known as one of the evilest guys in camp. He took pity on no one. When he got extra food he kept it for himself. Nobody confronted him with this till early 1970 when he became seriously sick. Then we told him all about it. We were saying things to make him angry with us, to make him want to hang on and live.

I told him one thing. I brought up the time his squad cut us on food and split away. He was one of the main guys who did it. I said, "Do you think what you did in 1968 was right, Denny? Now you're sick and can't work, can't eat or nothing, but I'm gonna do all I can to help you."

Many days I took him to the water line and gave him a bath and washed his clothes. Each time I reminded him, I said, "I ain't gonna turn my back on you like you did us."

He admitted he was wrong and apologized.

Davis. Denny was a tough street kid. He grew up in Detroit and ran around with a fast crowd. He told us a wino had once bought him and his friends some liquor and later Denny pushed him out of the moving car.

I said, "Why'd you do that, Denny?"

He said, "The sonofabitch wasn't no good anyway."

Denny's father had to scuffle when he was young; he didn't have much education, but he had worked his way up to a good position with General Motors, and Denny admired him. Denny was a very competitive guy. He always tried to do his share of the work.

I got along fine with him. Kushner and Harker and a lot of others didn't like him. Denny used to do an imitation of a Russian and I'd sit there and cackle. It made Harker so mad.

"Why do you laugh at his jokes?" he'd say with disgust.

I carried him back and forth to the latrine. Some POWs couldn't understand that either. They'd say, "Why don't you make him walk?"

"Are you crazy?" I'd say. "He can't walk." I could never hold a grudge against anyone.

Denny asked me one day, "Why don't the VC let me go? They see I'm dying."

Daly. From past experiences, it seemed when a man was about to die, all the other POWs told him what they thought of him. We did this believing it might help them, might make them angry, make them want to live if for no other reason than to seek revenge when they got better. When Denny asked us that night to tell him what we thought, Kushner started it off and everybody followed. We told him what a rotten bastard we thought he was. I feel bad now about the things we said against the dying. We thought we were trying to help. But, really, it just made things worse.

Harker. It began with someone saying, "Denny, the can's right outside. All you have to do.is get off the bed, go to the doorway, turn right, and feel with your hand and you'll find the can. Just sit on it. Try to crap in the can."

"I don't think I can make it."

"Come on, Denny. You've got to try. You'll save us a lot of trouble."

In the darkness a voice at the other end of the bed yelled, "Get off the bed, Denny! Get off the bed!"

"I'm slowly getting off."

"Denny, you've been rotten. You don't deserve this treatment. The bucket's outside. Try to make it."

"Well, I don't want to cause you guys any trouble."

"You know, you weren't very nice to Williams when he was down. Remember how you used to call him an old goat? Remember how you used to complain about sick guys with dysentery? Now look at you. The day extra peppers were thrown to us over the fence by the Vietnamese POWs you picked them up and didn't offer to share with anybody. Remember?"

"Yeah, I guess I was a little rotten. When I go be sure to tell my parents."

All the while we knew he had crapped on himself before he ever said a word. So we got up and stripped off his clothes and somebody wiped him like a baby while the rest of us held him up. Another POW took his pants to the water line to wash them.

The man is dying and his mind has decayed. You find yourself going crazy with him. We should have confronted him with our gripes when he was well. But we didn't. At the end it was something that just happened, something we got off our chests. You don't want the man to die. Who wants anyone to die? We were just telling him the truth.

Davis. We noticed one day that Mr. Hom had two blue welts on the side of his jaw. We asked what had happened. He said, "I fell from a rock." Quy, the ARVN POW, told us differently. Quy was working in the fields when he saw Hom and two guards with a pig that belonged to another VC camp farther down the hill. The VC had built houses out by the fields where the ARVN POWs were kept overnight when they were working. They wouldn't take us—I guess they figured we'd try to escape. Anyway, Hom and the guards killed the pig, gorged themselves with meat, and buried the rest of it.

The VC from the other camp discovered what had happened. A group of them approached Hom. Hom went for his weapon. They told him to put it down. As he did they started kicking and slapping him around. Later Hom was working in a field with some Vietnamese POWs when someone took a couple of shots in their direction. A ricochet hit one of the ARVN POWs. They brought him back to camp. He had a hole in his head. His brains were hanging out. The medic guy who replaced the girl ran to examine him. Kushner went over but they wouldn't let him help. The Vietnamese are proud or stupid, take your choice. Kushner was fully qualified, trained for years, yet they let a medic who didn't know his ass work on a seriously wounded man like that. The medic tried to make a tracheotomy. He accidentally cut through the ARVN's windpipe and killed him. Dr. Kushner looked at the medic and said, "You dumb sonofabitch," and walked away.

Anton. More and more airplanes were working our area. They gave me a case of nervous diarrhea.

Davis. We worried ourselves to sleep at night, contracting involuntarily like worms when a jet flew over. We never knew when the B-52s were coming. Harker and I were out near the fields one day getting ready to pull manioc when we looked up and saw smoke and dust geysers marching directly at us—boom! boom! boom! We dived into a dry creek bed. The raid stopped short. Below us was a neat bomb path. It cut through a montagnard village. We began to pick manioc. A spotter plane flew over. We jumped into the bushes. When we made it back to camp our nerves were shot to hell.

Harker. It was hard to believe what was happening. We had finally become accustomed to the jungle and learned to survive. Canned goods had been added to our food ration. We were receiving a small supply of mackerel on a regular basis, some Chinese noodles, and occasionally Maine sardines straight from the U.S. Color was returning to our anemic-dull eyes and our general health seemed to be improving. And with all this, it looked as though we were to be killed by our own bombs. The end, we were sure, would be written some night by an unseen B-52 or by an artillery shell. Howitzers were firing nearby, so close they sounded as if they were going off right in our camp. Several rounds exploded twenty-five meters away, showering the area with hot, jagged shrapnel.

The Vietnamese were as shaky as we were. A spotter plane buzzed their rice field and the pilot tossed out a purple smoke grenade. Our camp commander, the North Vietnamese who always talked of fearlessly fighting the imperialist aggressor, made a frantic dash across the field, ripping his pants as he stumbled and fell over logs, and jumped into a creek. A few days later two bird-dog FACs flew over and the guards herded us out of camp through the woods. We thought the spotter planes were going to call in an artillery mission. Anton was renowned for crapping at moments like this. He was chugging up the trail and it started oozing down his leg. Someone, I think it was Ike McMillan, said, "Look at Anton. He's shittin' and gittin'!" The guards got upset and made him return to change his pants.

Apparently a major North Vietnamese base camp was located not far away. Jets made low-level runs over our camp and dropped their loads just over the hill. I was returning from the water hole when a Phantom came screaming over and I hit the ground. The guards laughed at me—nervously.

Later as we sat on the bed playing cards one came over and Anton said, "Drop it, dammit, go ahead." All of a sudden we heard a ba-room! Anton was knocked down in the rush as we ran for the bomb shelter.

The VC moved us farther away, to a temporary camp, in late summer. The advantage of the new camp was its location next to a large overhanging rock, which served as our bomb shelter. The rock was open on three sides and a close hit would have finished us. Moreover, it didn't help us at night when we slept in the hootch, and we weren't overly excited about being in the new camp. In the fall we returned to the old camp for several months and then moved back to the temporary one as the bombing came closer.

Mr. Hom was reassigned to the Front's office of enemy agitation. He was replaced by a new interpreter from North Viet Nam. We were not unhappy to see Hom go, and he took his leave without ceremony. The new translator was married to a schoolteacher who was looking after his elderly parents while he was at war. He told us about life in North Viet Nam; and from bits and pieces of news coaxed from him we thought something important was in the air. Adding our improved treatment by the VC to the relentless bombing, we deduced that the war was coming to an end. Our hopes were crushed at Christmas by the camp commander, who told us he could offer no prediction as to when it would be over. He said, "I've been optimistic the past two years, but now I just can't say."

Before New Year's the VC said, "We have some good news.

What do you think it is?" They liked to play guessing games with us, were almost childish this way.

I later heard that at war's end the NVA in Hanoi came to get a pilot held in solitary confinement for four years, and said, "If you had one request what would it be?"

The pilot said, "I guess to write a letter home."

The NVA said, "No, what would you really like to do?" The pilot couldn't think of anything else. The North Vietnamese said, "How would you like to go home?"

We hadn't quite given up hope as the pilot had. That was the first thing we thought about. The VC replied, "No, you're not going home. It's something even better."

We were to be transferred to Hanoi.

The other POWs were euphoric, happy to be getting away at last from the poor diet, the hard work, and the bombs. I suppose I was the only one a bit depressed. The Vietnamese had done us no favors the past three years. I could not believe they were going to do us one now. I thought they were sending us north to make us into good communists.

As 1971 opened we made preparations to leave. The translator taught us the correct way to tie and roll a hammock. We wove baskets from vines. Kushner and Anton and the weaker ones were made to train for the trip by walking up and down a hill. Our food ration was increased. There were twelve of us now. The last prisoner, a young marine named Jose Anzaldua, had joined us the previous February. Jose had attended Vietnamese language school at Monterey. His intelligence and companionship (which was lit by occasional flashes of hot temper) were welcomed as much as his strong back.

Davis. "You are leaving tomorrow," the VC would tell us. And then we'd wait. This went on for weeks.

They bought a pig from the montagnards and said we would take the meat with us on the trip. But one day they came in from the fields, had an impromptu celebration, and ate our pig. They gave us a little of the meat and shrugged, "You're going to North Viet Nam anyway."

Before we left we were forced to work extremely hard gathering a big supply of firewood for the VC. I was sure they would miss us.

It occurred to us that the blacks had survived best in the jungle. None of us had died. Only the white guys seemed to get edema. They lost more weight and were always weaker than we were. We kept our muscle definition and our bodies got harder. If a white guy gained weight he seemed to get flabby—except for Pfister, who kept good definition. Dr. Kushner theorized that it went back to our ancestors being able to sustain life under harsh conditions. I think it also had something to do with the way we were raised. I was used to hard work; so were Watkins and McMillan. Daly, the weakest black, was from the city. The whites who did best, like Harker, Strictland, and Pfister, were from rural or semirural backgrounds. Grissett, who was off a Texas farm, was a good humper till he gave up. Anton and Fred, on the other hand, were city boys; and Kushner had spent most of his life in a classroom.

Anton. On February 2 a group of helicopters began circling our camp. They turned in a tightening spiral, coming lower, six troop carrying ships, several Cobra gunships, and a medevac, which was painted white and marked with a red cross. When they reached five hundred feet directly above us a guard ran to the compound and forced us into a bomb shelter. I was pressed to the rear. We could hear a tiny light-observation helicopter, a bubble-top LOH, moving back and forth across the camp.

A guard stuck his head into the shelter and ordered us out. I thought a U.S. rescue team had landed and the Vietnamese wanted to get us out of the area. I tried to hide in the shelter. The guard counted the POWs as they scrambled out. He called for me. I said, "No." He aimed his rifle at me. As I came out I saw the LOH following the other POWs as they ran up the path into the woods. No shots were fired. The helicopter pilot had thrown a .ed-smoke grenade into the pigpen. A guard braced his rifle against a tree, started to shoot at the LOH. Another guard slapped the weapon down before he could fire.

Harker. We saw a black American in a chopper pointing an M-60 machine gun our way. We hoped they were coming in after us but, at the same time, dreaded the gun battle we knew would take place. We expected the VC guards who had seen years of action to be calm and collected. They were anything but—waving rifles around, scaring us all. A VC major who had stopped in camp a few days came running up the trail so fast that he ran out of his Ho Chi Minh sandals. Someone said, "The major didn't stop to fight the imperialists." A guard saw us talking and ran over in a frenzy, threatening to shoot us.

Anton. The helicopters left after about ten minutes. We could hear them firing rockets and machine guns in the distance and hear the return fire of the North Vietnamese. We couldn't understand why they hadn't landed at our camp. They had seen us, we were sure. Perhaps they didn't want to risk getting us killed in a fire fight. For whatever, it was something that puzzled us, and still does. That night we slept in the jungle and returned to the camp next morning. B-52s hit the surrounding area. It sounded like a thousand railroad boxcars slamming together.

There's no describing the terror of a B-52 raid, with the earth shaking under your feet and the shock of explosions hitting you like waves washing over a drowning man. The body reacts instantly, instinctively, without clear direction from the brain, running, stumbling, falling, trying to get away. Ike McMillan and I were once in an open field picking bamboo shoots to eat when the eight-engined bombers started dropping nearby. We ran to hide but there was no place. So we tried, like something out of Laurel and Hardy, to hide behind each other; finally found a single two-inch-wide tree and quivered behind it. We fell to the ground laughing at each other after the raid stopped.

Harker. The first group of us left for North Viet Nam two days after the aborted helicopter raid. The second group, which consisted of the four blacks, Jose Anzaldua, and John Peter Johnson, followed ten days later. We weren't sure why or by what criteria the VC divided us into two groups. Perhaps they didn't want to lose us all in one bombing attack. The second group with the blacks and Jose, who was Mexican-American, and John Peter Johnson, who claimed vaguely to have Indian blood, appeared to be divided along racial lines. The VC were always conscious of such arrangements for propaganda purposes. Or maybe the division was made with most of the weak men in the first group so that if any fell out along the way they could be picked up by the second group.

The VC issued us a sleeping hammock and a plastic ground sheet, and gave each of us a can of condensed milk, a can of mackerel, and a ten-day supply of rice. Our backpacks were bulgar wheat sacks with straps sewn on. Our rice was carried in small black bags inside the packs. We had to decide what to take and what to leave behind. We had been prisoners so long that our meager possessions were cherished like gold and jewels. Still, we didn't want to weight ourselves down for the long journey. The VC told us we would be given new clothing in Hanoi. We couldn't take them at their word, they'd lied to us too often, and so we reluctantly left our mosquito nets behind and took our two pairs of black pajamas.

To our growing supplies the VC added some dehydrated milk cans filled with chunks of pig fat, dry nuoc mam, and sesame seeds. Our water jug was a two-gallon oil can. One man carried it in the morning, another in the afternoon.

The VC said, "You will stop at Liberation camps the first ten days. Afterward you will reach the socialist camps and not have to worry about food." The Liberation camps belonged to the Viet Cong; the socialist camps to the North Vietnamese. The difference between the two, we were to find, was more than incidental. The Liberation camps were way stations made up of crude lean-tos, with a place to do our own cooking and not much more. The socialist camps were highly organized transit stations on the Ho Chi Minh trail.

The four Vietnamese POWs saw us off with tears. We had grown very fond of them, had become as close to being brothers as Vietnamese and Americans could ever get, and we departed with a certain sadness, hoping, but far from convinced, that they would survive. We heard later that Captain Nghia and Lieutenant Quy were freed after the Paris cease-fire. Quy was the longest-held ARVN officer to survive up to that point.

We left on a rainy morning, heading up the first of many "long steeps," as the Vietnamese called them, we were to cross. There were six of us, and we had six guards and an interpreter, Mr. Thien. All of us had something to look forward to in the north, and we struck up a strange relationship. We became a happy, almost intimate, traveling group, soldiers on holiday. One guard, who had heard of our tough go in the jungle, took it upon himself to demand extra food for us at rest stops. *"Anh an com nua?"* he'd say. "Do you want more?" The first day we followed a muddy trail pock-marked by artillery craters to the top of a hill, stopped for lunch, and then continued down and hit an open valley. The valley was a checkerboard of green rice paddies. It was dotted with Vietnamese hamlets. For three years we had seen nothing but montagnards and it was odd to discover Vietnamese civilians so close. The valley appeared to be a major VC rice-growing area. Everybody seemed to know each other, "comrades" all. Men smiled broadly as they passed us, pushing Dien Bien Phu bicycles, the frame of each one slung with five hundred pounds of war supplies.

By the fifth day our exuberance had disappeared with our energy. The long steeps were taking their due. My legs felt as if someone was pushing red-hot knitting needles through them; my head had gone through successive stages of fatigue, vertigo, and numbness. We knew before we moved out the fifth morning that it would be a hard day, for the VC gave us extra rice for breakfast. We started our climb and passed through a wooded area that had been B-52ed. It looked so ugly and violent—large trees had been cut down like splinters.

Four of us got to the NVA-run transit station in late afternoon. Kushner and Anton straggled in after dark. Kushner was almost unconscious on his feet. I thought for a moment he was dying. It scared me, I nearly cried, I'd never seen him this way.

We had built a fire in the hootch, and I helped him get his gear off as he slumped down by it. I picked leeches from him and rubbed his hands to encourage circulation. He said quietly, "I just don't know whether it's worth it."

Hopes of returning to his wife and family had always pulled

him out of low points before and I reminded him how much he loved them, and they him. He said, "Yes, I want to get back to my family." I relaxed a little.

Anton showed up about ten o'clock in not much better shape. He said a guard set up a place for him by the trail, where he rested and drank a whole can of condensed milk to muster up energy to make it to camp.

Anton. First someone had to relieve me of some of my rice because my pack was too heavy. After four days my ankles were swollen terribly. By the fifth day I could hardly walk. The area we were in was routinely hit by B-52s. Harker and the rest wanted to get away as soon as possible. Naturally they were upset with me and assumed I was loafing. They never yelled at me, but they told me I wasn't trying hard enough; and it was obvious they believed I was holding them back.

The camp where they waited for me had a small hospital. I told them I couldn't go further. Long had turned his ankle on the slippery trail and couldn't walk either. Three guards stayed behind with us. The other four POWs went ahead with three guards. We rested at the hospital twelve days. Davis and the second group picked us up.

Harker. We continued to move over the mountains of South Viet Nam's central highlands. One day we reached a rest camp and at 5:00 that afternoon we were told to get our gear ready; the VC said we were going to take a ride. I didn't think I'd heard correctly. We walked across an open field. In a far woodline were two Russian-made blue trucks with wooden siding. We had picked up a few Vietnamese along the trail and were traveling informally as a party with three girls and two men, medics returning north. We clambered aboard and jerkily drove off to the sound of grinding gears.

Being on the truck was our first step back into civilization and we burst into song as we rode the bumpy roads, singing over and over "Where Have All the Flowers Gone?" until Mr. Thien finally made us stop. The road was muddy and so uncertain in spots that it had been corduroyed with trees. We halted frequently at checkpoints, the drivers had whispered conversations with sentries, and we continued on. We saw a bulldozer repairing a bombed-out stretch of road and mechanics working on stalled trucks. They seemed as organized as the U.S. Army.

We reached our way station at 2:00 the next morning. On the bottom of the dishes we used was scratched the word "Kon Tum." We were in the center of South Viet Nam near the Laotian border. We had actually traveled southward, away from North Viet Nam, to reach this major intersection of the Ho Chi Minh trail. I wondered how many thousands of North Vietnamese soldiers had passed through our station, how many would ever return.

We remained at the way station the next day and then crossed into Laos. The boundary between the two countries was marked by a small stream. We had been on the move in South Viet Nam two weeks.

Davis. We found Anton and Long at the hospital. A Viet Cong from our old jungle camp was also there. He was a funny guy, the laziest VC we ever saw, always stealing or trading for food to bring to our camp. And now seeing Anton and Long there he tried to con them out of their manioc, but the guards caught him. He was supposed to be hospitalized with malaria. He was better; but when it came time to return to his unit or to do work around the hospital he suddenly suffered a new attack and started shaking violently with fever.

We took a truck on the last hop to Kon Tum, then crossed the Laotian border. Near the border we passed through an area of incredible desolation. Trees were twisted and uprooted, craters covered every square inch of soil, bomb holes on top of bomb holes. There was no way anything could have survived the attack. Fuel-storage bunkers were dug on the roadside. A Catepillar was working down from this stretch. The U.S. had bombed the road that day and the machine was repairing it the same night. The process would be repeated the next day. The Vietnamese had tenacity—you had to hand them that.

Anton. After we hit the Ho Chi Minh trail in Laos we were always with a large group of travelers, usually two to three hundred a day. They treated us without hostility, in some cases quite warmly, as fellow travelers. They were young and old, men and women, kids and babies, civilians and wounded soldiers. Some civilians said they were going to North Viet Nam to escape life under the Saigon government; a few said they were going north to school. We saw an eight-year-old boy with one eye, a pretty eighteen-year-old girl with an arm missing, and others with a gruesome assortment of war wounds. They had been hit, they said, during bombing raids on their villages.

Harker. As we moved into Laos the terrain changed. We crossed flat land with eight-foot-high elephant grass on both sides of the trail, which was usually no more than two or three feet wide, traveled single file, always in the daytime, and in the open. When jets glinted high overhead no one paid them any attention. Farther on, the trail was camouflaged by triple-canopy jungle, which muted the sun. The filtered light made us feel like we were walking during a very overcast day.

Each of the forty days it took us to hike across Laos was practically the same. We walked all day and stopped in late afternoon at a way station. The stations were measured out along the trail, each one usually a full day's walk from the next, though sometimes we were able to cover two in a day and other times walked only a few hours before stopping to rest the remainder of the day and night. A typical station had twelve or so medium-sized thatched-roof hootches and a main kitchen situated in a well-camouflaged area fifty or seventy-five meters at its widest point. The stations were always located near a mountain stream or creek.

The hootches were often lowered half underground as security against air attacks. So you stepped down about five feet into the hootch, which was unfurnished, and slung your sleeping hammock. One side of the hootch wall opened into an A-frame bomb shelter dug completely underground and reinforced with thick logs. If the bombing was close we spent an uneasy night in the stuffy shelter; if not, we slept comfortably in our hammocks. Most travelers were tired after a hard day of walking and they ate quietly and went to their hootches. Later we heard singing or someone strumming a guitar in the night.

The kitchen was a large open shed. The cooking pots were of the size found in army or college mess halls, so large that shovel-type stirring utensils were used. The stove was made of baked clay. Its chimney was tunneled underground so that the smoke seeped up and was dispersed at intervals. Mealtime was signaled by someone blowing on a whistle. As POWs we usually had priority and two of us took turns picking up the food. Sometimes the guards got it for us. They told the other travelers that we were "progressive" Americans, and we were accepted without question. There was always enough rice and once a day we received a vegetable, chopped cabbage or something that looked like broccoli, and a meat, occasionally braised pork from the People's Republic of China. It was excellent.

Daly. Halfway through Laos I became constipated. It has always been a problem for me. The North Vietnamese told me no laxatives were available. I felt so bloated I didn't want to eat. Yet if I didn't eat I got so weak I could hardly walk. I was miserable. I thought I'd die before I reached the north. It finally gave way after fifteen days.

Harker. Each group of travelers carried an authorized travel card, a pass, that had to be presented to the way-station commander. He then made hootch assignments. Occasionally the hootches were full and we had to sleep outside in the cold. Lists of names were kept and head counts were made to insure that no unauthorized persons used the trail and that no one lagged behind. The way stations were linked by field telephones. Each station commander knew how many transients to expect that evening and how much food to prepare. We stopped at about thirty stations during the journey.

At daybreak everybody rose, accommodated nature, ate breakfast, filled canteens, and prepared to resume the march as the sun burned away the night fog. Vietnamese travelers were required to attend a morning formation before starting out. All gathered round in a small meeting area. The station commander made a roll call and gave them a little pep talk combined with a briefing on what to expect that day, whether air strikes were likely, and, if so, what evasive action to take. We were more or less on our own and not compelled to attend the briefing sessions, but once when we did we listened for thirty minutes as a travel-group leader criticized the station commander because the camp wasn't, in his opinion, up to usual standards. Jose Anzaldua overheard another Vietnamese complaining vigorously to his group leader that they weren't getting as much rice as they'd been promised.

Seeing the same travelers day after day bred a certain familiarity. The three girls still traveled in our party; two were very attractive, with long black hair and finely chiseled faces. I went to wash up one evening. I was tired and sweaty, and unknown to me they were farther downstream shampooing their hair. They shouted that I was stirring up mud. Mr. Thien told me to go elsewhere to bathe. I lost my temper and yelled at the girls, "I'll be glad as hell when I don't have to live with you!" I returned to my hootch and sulked in my hammock.

Mr. Thien sometimes called meetings in the evenings. He tried, usually with not much success, to turn them into subtle criticism sessions, and he told me that night, "Harker, you very impolite to girls today." I apologized. Mr. Thien was too pleasant-natured to pursue it further.

For security reasons we were under strict orders not to talk to outsiders. The rule was almost impossible to keep because everyone we saw asked our name, age, marital status, and what province in the States we were from. These were stock questions that the Vietnamese, Viet Cong or otherwise, asked all Americans they encountered. Mr. Thien frequently gave us stern warnings against talking. He barely got one warning out of his mouth when he called us over to introduce us to a complete stranger who had struck up his acquaintance. He was proud to be escorting American POWs and naturally anxious to show others the large responsibility the Front had chosen to place in his hands. We later learned that U.S. intelligence knew when we left South Viet Nam and when we reached Hanoi, though all our specific names were not known.

The Saigon government launched Operation Lam Son 719, the first—and last—massive invasion of Laos, as we started up the Ho Chi Minh trail. A way-station commander told the assembled Vietnamese at a morning briefing, "They have just put a battalion of puppet ranger troops in this area. We have run them out, but if you see any stragglers shoot them." We saw no ARVN soldiers fighting, but we did see whole companies of captured troops, many of them badly wounded. It was an unfortunate military operation. The ARVN were beaten, and they soon retreated back into South Viet Nam.

Mr. Thien told us before we left South Viet Nam, "Will be like Fourth of July in Laos. We shoot at very many aircraft." We were skeptical but it turned out to be an accurate description. The sky was lit nightly with fiery tracers and exploding puffballs of flak. Literally hundreds of antiaircraft positions were firing around us in the distance. Spooky, the propeller-driven C-47 armed with fast-firing miniguns, arrived punctually each night to battle it out with the North Vietnamese. We saw no jets shot down. The Vietnamese appeared to be poor shots. But the nightly duels seemed not to bother them at all.

Each day on the trail we passed battalion after battalion of fresh North Vietnamese troops heading south. They walked single file, strung out for long distances, carrying new AKs, SKSs, B-40 rockets, heavy machine guns with wheels, and mortar tubes. They humped along quietly, it was hot and always a little hazy, and we sometimes got past without their recognizing us.

Anton. The soldiers were a problem throughout the journey. Especially the younger ones going into battle for the first time. Often they stared at us and then burst into tears of frustration because their officers had told them not to bother us. They obeyed orders pretty well, lucky for us. But most of us were hit one time or another by rifle butts or hiking sticks. If they couldn't hit us, they tried to push us off the narrow trail into the jungle bushes.

Sometimes they swung at us with walking sticks and swore

loudly. By this time we knew all the favorite Vietnamese words, and when one hit me with a stick I said, *"Do May,"*—mother-fucker.

He turned around and popped his rifle at me as if he was going to shoot.

I said, "Go ahead. It's not loaded anyway."

My guard ran up and grabbed him, then pushed me down the path. He said if I fought back or said anything again I could expect no help from him. After this we moved with travelers who usually got between us and the soldiers if anything happened.

Not all of them were unfriendly. Some gave us candy and cigarettes. Others smiled and ignored us. Once we turned a corner and came face to face with a file of three hundred uniformed women, medics and cooks, led by female officers armed with machine pistols. They saw us, screamed *"Meey,"* Americans, and ran away into the woods.

Davis. My group had no trouble keeping up because Daly was out in front setting the pace. One day the guards told us to go ahead to the way station without waiting for him. Later he strag-gled in madder than hell. He had given a guard a ration of jive and the guard had tried to push him off a cliff. Back in the jungle camp he'd always had a tendency to talk back to the Vietnamese. We warned him to be quiet. He'd say, "I tell you, this sonofabitch ain't gonna tell me what to do." Whap! He shut up then because the VC had finally smacked him. That's why I was surprised by what Daly later did in Hanoi.

Anton. John Peter Johnson got sick and my legs gave out again, so we fell behind the others and stayed in a hospital a month. Two guards were left with us. The hospital was still under con-struction and not yet officially open. It was a large complex with fifty hootches as wards and a spacious retangular-shaped build-ing designed to serve as an operating room. The operating room was made of prefab thatched material. In many way stations we had seen prefab parts of hootches scattered outside the camp area. Should the station be wiped out in a bombing attack, a new one could be constructed from the prefab materials in about four hours. Some stations had been destroyed and new camps built nearby.

A doctor at the hospital took an interest in us. He was kind and seemed medically competent. He didn't have much medicine, but he gave us some cortisone, a little penicillin, and lots of vitamins. He wanted to play chess. We tried to make a board but settled on checkers instead. We played for hours as the nurses watched. Our guards permitted us free run of the hospital and the way stations where we stopped. When we walked around the camps Vietnamese travelers often invited us into their hootches to watch them play cards. Pointing and emphatic grunts substituted for language. After a month we got ready to leave. A guard fell ill and we stayed on three more weeks till he recovered.

The time spent in the hospital with John Peter Johnson was not exactly lively. We probably exchanged no more than several dozen words. That was JPJ's style. Although generally well liked by everyone, he was considered the strangest POW in our entire group. He was habitually silent and seemingly detached from everything around him. He had a dry chuckle, a kind of inward laugh, which we were most likely to hear at unfunny moments.

We had listened to a NLF radio broadcast, in our jungle camp back in South Viet Nam, by a young marine that began, "My name is John Peter Johnson. I was in the Third Marine Division at Da Nang. I crossed over to the side of the Liberation Forces."

A few weeks later a new prisoner showed up. He was first placed with the ARVN POWs, then later moved in with us. After he joined us we heard a repeat of the earlier broadcast. "My name is John Peter Johnson . . ."

We said, "That's you, John."

He said, "No, it's not me." He continued to deny it, though later he softened this by saying he had suspected he was bugged while under his initial interrogation. He certainly did nothing to indicate to us he was a crossover, and we supposed it to be just another case of POW confusion shortly after capture.

JPJ was blandly good-looking, stocky, almost fat, but weak. He had several stories about his capture. He said his company was

about to stand-to for a major inspection and he wasn't ready, so
his company first sergeant told him to make himself scarce till the
inspection was over. He went to China Beach and lay down, and
the VC materialized from the bushes and took him away. We
thought the story possibly had another unstated variation, that
perhaps he had been AWOL at the time. We never knew.

When we did get him to talk he reminisced about his days as
a machine gunner on Guantanamo Bay and his love of tropical
fish. His favorite story concerned his drill sergeant in basic training, who had been killed, JPJ said, by someone who taped a
grenade to the inside of his car door.

"What happened, John?"

"He just fucked with the wrong dude," he'd reply, and give us
that dry chuckle. Some POWs thought JPJ was the wrong dude.
I doubted the whole story. He had some T-shirts stenciled with
the name Elbert. He told us they belonged to a guy in his unit
who was killed in action. We were suspicious from the beginning.
But only after we got to Hanoi, after already having lived with
him several years, did we discover that John Peter Johnson was
really Fred Elbert of New York.

Harker. We passed Highway 9, which cut across Laos into Khe
Sanh. That night a parachute flare fell on our hootch. We walked
the following few days till we came to a hillside from where we
could see a dirt road winding through a series of steep mountains. We hit the dusty road and came upon travelers who were
waiting for nightfall, hidden under the camouflage of trees on
both sides of the road. Mr. Thien said, "We are now in North Viet
Nam." A shout of joy went up from the Vietnamese. Actually I
think he was a little confused—he meant North Viet Nam lay just
over the mountains.

We heard a dull rumble like thunder in the distance. The
rumble grew louder. As the last bit of twilight disappeared a
seemingly endless line of trucks began to roll pass, duece and a
half's with blackout lights, some new, others old, cabs with
pointed noses, all of them axle-heavy with supplies, heading
south.

Above the rumble of trucks could suddenly be heard a sharper, more piercing noise. The trucks killed their lights and stopped. We took cover in a roadside bunker. Antiaircraft positions in the distance opened up; guns near the trucks remained silent. The jets made passes, dropped bombs, went away. Trucks began to move. We waited for a north-bound vehicle. Mr. Thien said, "Okay, let's go!" We headed down the road. A jet made a run on our area, flak guns boomed, and we tumbled into another bunker. Everything around us came to a standstill. When it was quiet once more we were told to get into a truck.

There were ARVN POWs from the Laos invasion, ourselves, and the guards crammed into the truck's rear—maybe twenty or more men. It stopped only several times that night—at camouflaged checkpoints, and we took the opportunity to urinate over the sides. Vo Luc, a guard who was soon to be married, sat next to me. During the trip through Laos he had been very inquisitive about our past sexual experiences. We could see he was anxiously trying to prepare himself. On the truck ride he got sick and had to throw up. I didn't know whether it was from car sickness or because he was approaching his moment of truth.

As day broke we finished the mountains and hit level ground. Off to the sides, in the paddies, we could see mist-shrouded silhouettes of SAM missiles. North Viet Nam. The countryside was quiet. No planes were in the air. Vietnamese civilians clustered at bus stops waiting to be picked up. It looked like the beginning of a normal workday any place in the world. I felt a warm tingling in my spine. The jungle was gone forever.

At 9:00 we left the main road and stopped at some rural hootches. The guards ordered us to be quiet. They said, "The people here want to beat you but we won't let them." We washed up, ate, and got some sleep. We were put in irons for the first time since our capture, cuffed by twos with ancient French shackles. Next day we resumed the truck journey to Vinh. We were blindfolded but I managed to pull mine down.

Mr. Thien smiled broadly and said, "We're going thirty-five kilometers an hour!"

"In America we can go a hundred thirty-five an hour," we retorted. We could never resist trying to one-up them with tales of our money and possessions in the States. This didn't bother Mr. Thien, however. He was serenely enjoying riding as fast as he had, or was ever likely to, in his lifetime.

In a village near Vinh's outskirts we were met by a man with an ugly throat scar. He was a veteran reassigned as escort officer for POWs passing through. He took us to a private home. He said, "We were heavily bombed here in 1967. Fifty persons died, including some of the family of the man at whose house you will rest. His home is his prize possession but he has generously agreed to let you use it." The man didn't look too happy to see us. The first thing he did was to remove a large picture of Ho Chi Minh from the wall, as though Ho would be debased by our presence.

At 10:00 that night we were taken to Vinh's train station and put in a boxcar with seventy ARVN POWs. We persuaded the North Vietnamese to remove our shackles. Vo Luc came to tell us good-by. Mr. Thien was conspicuously absent. I was a little hurt, though I realized it was a very Vietnamese reminder that the shared journey was over. We had a rough, rocky night ride over a narrow-gauge track; the chuffing train seemed ready to jump the rails at any moment. We reached Hanoi at 5:00 in the afternoon the next day, April 1, 1971. Our car, after much indecisive shifting back and forth, was stopped below the station. Long-haired girls handed out rice balls to POWs as the door was unlocked and we tumbled out.

A uniformed North Vietnamese prodded us into a green International Scout-type vehicle with a canvas top. We were blindfolded and told not to talk. We could hear sounds of the city all around us, sounds more stirring than music. We drove for five minutes. The vehicle stopped. Iron gates scraped open. We moved again, backed up sharply, stopped. We were ordered out. Blindfolds were removed. In front of us was a long warehouse-looking building made of stucco and with a tin roof. One room of the warehouse stood open. We were pushed inside. The door was locked behind us. Wooden planks lay flat on the pitted concrete floor, which was puddled with water from a recent scrubbing. Someone, with customary optimism, said, "This must be where they're going to keep us overnight." In a few minutes a guard returned. He brought us bread and soup. Bread!

13

Ted Guy

The Hanoi Hilton's interrogation chamber was two-tone green, baseboards were dark and walls olive, and the room was twelve by sixteen feet. A long veneer table covered with blue cloth was at one end. A high-intensity lamp was placed on the table. The interrogator sat in a chair behind, the POW in front on a low stool, with the effect of making one look up over the table at the Vietnamese.

"So you have been through air force survival school in the States," the pudgy, uniformed Vietnamese said as he took his seat. "Don't worry. We too are survival experts. We can break you."

I refused to speak. The Vietnamese ordered me to my knees and left me there two hours. After a few minutes the pain was killing. I was in bad shape from the beating I'd received in Vinh. My dislocated left shoulder sat well forward from the rest of my body. When Pudgy sensed I could take no more of the kneeling he made me stand in a corner another two hours. I looked down and saw that someone had scratched into the baseboards, "Keep the faith, baby." Knowing other Americans must be around made me feel much better, but I realized my refusal to speak was getting me nowhere, and I decided to switch tactics.

I told him I was ready to talk. An intelligence officer, a civilian, walked in and Pudgy left. He knew I was from Cam Ranh Bay. He began to quiz me about the base. He asked how many pilots were in my squadron. We had twenty-two but I told him fourteen. He asked their names. I gave him fictitious ones. This went on two hours. He asked a question, I answered with a lie. He sat looking at me impassively, nodding his head as I spoke. He did not take notes.

He stood and left the room. He returned in a few minutes carrying a brown leather-bound book; it resembled a scrapbook, about two inches thick. He opened the book and leafed through it. The pages were cheap, tissue-thin paper covered with the delicate handwritten script of the Vietnamese. He briskly began to read out information about my squadron: how many planes we had; what missions we flew; what time we took off and returned; where we lived and ate; and the name of the squadron operations officer, Theodore W. Guy.

I was startled by the detail. I sat glumly thinking about the lies I'd just told. He looked at me and sneered, "So you see, Colonel!" There was no doubt in my mind that the information had come from VC agents in Cam Ranh.

Later when they asked for information, the North Vietnamese always added, "We don't care if you lie. We'll go south for it." I don't know how comprehensive it was, but they did seem to have a great deal of intelligence on many subjects, particularly information on our B-52 bases.

I changed then to a tactic of telling half truths. In order to protect myself for future interrogations, and I was asked the same questions over and over again the next five years, I developed a system of adding or subtracting a set number from true answers, or reversing digits. It was imperative to have a simple system of deception that could be easily remembered.

The intelligence officer interrogated me the remainder of the day. At the end he said, "We know you are still lying."

He rose to leave and told me to bow. This was the manner by which the Vietnamese saluted superiors. "I will not bow," I said.

He looked at me and said quietly, "We will teach you."

He left and a guard entered. Two glass doors opened outward from the interrogation room. The guard placed a chair five feet from the door, ordered me to sit, and tied a rope around my neck, fastening the other end to a door knob. The guard stood behind me with a fair-sized stick. Someone outside pulled open the door. I was jerked forward. Simultaneously the guard hit me in the back of the head.

After I was jerked and hit a hundred times the intelligence officer returned. I said, "I have learned to bow."

He made no reply. The rope was removed from my neck.

That night I was put in a jeep and taken to the Plantation Gardens. I was given a cup and a spoon and a bedroll, which was a thin bamboo mat. The jeep pulled up outside cell number 5. The building looked like a warehouse. The translator told me to keep my room neat; he locked the door and went away. The cell was lit by a dim, unshaded bulb which burned twenty-four hours a day. It was ten feet wide and twelve feet long, bare, except for wooden planks that served as a bed. The floor was concrete, square yellow tiles covered the ceiling, and the wall was divided by several barred windows that had French-style louvered shutters locked tight. I lay on the planks and immediately fell asleep.

At 5:30 the wake-up gong sounded, someone beating a section of rail with a steel rod, at first slow, then with increasing tempo. "Bong . . . bong . . . bong . . . bong bong bong bongbongbong . . . bonggg!"

I got up and straightened my gear. A turnkey opened my cell, gave me water, and allowed me to put my defecation bucket outside for collection. I was issued two blankets, a mosquito net, two pairs of black pajamas, two pairs of shorts, some sandals, and a toothbrush, which was replaced semiannually. Toothpaste was rationed out every two months and a brownish bar of strong lye soap every forty-five days. I was given three Truong Son cigarettes daily. The guards stuck a light through the four-by-four-inch peephole in the door, which could be raised and lowered only from the outside, at wake-up, 11:00 in the morning, and 8:00 in the evening.

Twice a week I was taken from my cell and escorted to the shower room at the other end of the warehouse. Running water was collected in a large cistern. One bathed by filling a bucket and pouring it over oneself, Asian fashion. The water was cold, especially in winter, and the break from the monotony of the cell, I found, was more interesting than the shower. For the first two weeks the North Vietnamese removed all laundry from the clothesline near the shower before taking me from my cell. They thought this way I would not know other Americans were nearby.

Lunch, a bowl of soup and a French loaf, was served at 11:00. Half an hour later a gong announced naptime; another woke us at 2:00 P.M., and the long wait began for the evening meal and then the bedtime gong at 9:00. It was against regulations to lie down except during naptime and at night. The guards frequently and unexpectedly raised the peephole to check on me. I was made to sit at attention on the bed for long stretches if caught lying down at an unauthorized time. Other than this, I was completely alone and unbothered.

I became sick with dysentery shortly after reaching Hanoi. I was wracked by continuous bowel-bursting pains. I thought I was dying. The North Vietnamese refused to give me medicine; I wasn't told why. One night when I was at my weakest point a guard opened the peephole, pushed through a half loaf of bread, put his fingers to his lips and whispered "Shhh!" I was too hungry to wonder why he'd taken such a risk, and I ate it gratefully.

As my intestines slowly mended, I realized my troubles had just begun. The walls started closing in. Boredom and inactivity could prove as deadly as a bullet, I knew, for I had always been extremely active; and so I began to devise a mental and physical discipline to keep me going, at least till I could better take stock of my situation and decide what I was up against. I went through the alphabet and tried to remember all the boys' names that began with each letter, then did the same with girls. I tried to recall every detail I could about people I'd known with those names.

My dad, who was a professional musician, taught me to play the piano, accordian, and organ when I was a kid. He had started out in the 1920s with the big bands, had the Dorsey brothers with him awhile, later played piano for Paul Whiteman, and was an accompanist for Fanny Brice. In 1939 he switched to the Hammond organ and stuck with that till he retired in '65. I began with songs like "Always," "Because of You," and "Dearly Beloved," trying to recall the precise tunes and lyrics of numbers we used to play together. I'd whistle softly or hum. I kept up the exercise my entire imprisonment. It took me two years to get "C'est si bon" down perfectly.

Next I worked backward into my life. It was the first time I'd explored my childhood, the first time I'd really had time—prison at least gave me that. I thought of every mistake I'd ever made, why I'd made it, and resolved never to do the same again. I began probing my decision to become a professional military officer. I guess I've always liked the idea of military life. I can't remember when I didn't. I grew up during World War II and that perhaps explains a great deal. I've always liked authority and regimentation, liked the color and ceremony of uniforms, and thought a man could have no higher ideal than to serve his country.

At the end of World War II, I began military school. I was attending a large high school in Elmhurst, not studying particularly hard, and failed Spanish my sophomore year. My parents knew of my interests in military things—I'd been in both Cub Scouts and Boy Scouts—and I think they felt a military school might put me on the right track. They suggested it but left the decision up to me. We sent away for catalogues from various schools. After looking them over we settled on Kemper Military School in Missouri, a well-established institution that offered the equivalent of a junior-college degree. It turned out to be an excellent choice; my younger brother followed me four years later.

I was on the rifle team at Kemper and graduated in the upper quarter of my class. At the end of four years I applied for a competitive appointment to West Point. My real interest was flying, an interest that dated back to 1939 when I was given a ride in a Piper Cub for my tenth birthday. I saw West Point as a ladder to the cockpit. I was notified that I was the first alternate for the appointment. This meant I would have to wait another year. I checked around and found the air force had a flying program which required only the equivalent of two years of college. So I went down and signed up in April, 1949, and took my flight physical.

By summer I still didn't know whether I had been accepted. I wrote air-force headquarters and told them I would join the Naval Aviation Cadet Program if I didn't hear something soon. I got a quick letter back telling me to report for training in August, 1949. I graduated number two out of three hundred fifty cadets in flying grades and was first sergeant of my training company. I was commissioned a second lieutenant in September, 1950.

The Korean War started the summer I graduated, and all of us in my class were made command-training instructors. I volunteered for jumbos, helicopters, recces, fighters—every aircraft we had in Korea at the time—in an attempt to get into the war. But instructors were critically needed in the States, and it was not until October, 1952, that I finally got there. I flew 101 missions as a F-84 fighter pilot, saw a lot of MIGs but never had the chance to shoot one down. We did mostly air-to-ground work, bombing targets north of the thirty-eighth parallel and flying close support for ground troops. For this I won two Distinguished Flying Crosses and six air medals.

After the war I went to Luke Air Force Base as a gunnery instructor. In 1958 I was transferred to Canada as an exchange officer with the Royal Canadian Air Force. At the end of that tour I was reassigned to the Air Command and Staff College, where I graduated in June, 1961. I was very fortunate to be selected for Command and Staff College. I was one of the first captains to go; most of the others were majors. After several years as ops officer of a training squadron, I was assigned to Randolph AFB in Texas, where I wrote syllabuses to teach young men to fly, and later became chief of standardization and evaluation.

Besides playing mental games and reconstructing my life, I undertook an intensive exercise program. On Monday, Wednesday, and Friday I walked nine miles in a circle around my cell. Tuesday, Thursday, and Saturday it was six miles. When I walked around the room a hundred times, I stopped and did a hundred pushups. After the second hundred times of walking, I tried to do forty one-arm pushups. I built up two and a half inches on my chest.

My outside entertainment came from the Liar's Box, a vibrating radio speaker inside an eight-inch-square green box, which was placed in each cell just out of reach above the door. Along with frequent interrogations, the radio was the primary means by which the North Vietnamese tried to influence us at the camps in Hanoi. (The secondary means was by infrequent indoctrination classes and by propaganda reading material.) The radio material was of two types. The first was programs fed directly from the Voice of Viet Nam, Hanoi's official radio station, usually read by a man and a woman (whom we called Hanoi Hannah) and sometimes accompanied by music. The second was selectively edited news programs and propaganda which were tape recorded in the radio rooms of the particular camp and then run through a record-player-type amplifier into our rooms. The intracamp tapes, most disturbingly, I found, were being read by Americans.

The two chief pressure points of the North Vietnamese, I quickly learned, were centered on taping and writing. They constantly tried, by a variety of methods, to get POWs to make antiwar and propaganda tapes. They especially wanted tapes that could be broadcast and distributed world-wide by the Voice of Viet Nam. I considered the making of this sort of tape to be a far graver offense than that of a POW reading propaganda over the intracamp system, though I was very much opposed to both activities. The North Vietnamese, too, constantly pressured us to write or sign antiwar appeals and letters. They were intent on using us as instruments in their highly coordinated propaganda campaign around the world.

At the time we were getting up to five hours of radio programs each day, beginning at 6:00 A.M. with the Voice of Viet Nam. Over the intracamp system, with Americans reading, we heard the four-thousand-year history of Viet Nam. We heard reports from the Soviet Union and articles taken from *Nhan Dan,* North Viet Nam's official newspaper, particularly those which told of so-called American atrocities. About an hour each day we heard what bad criminals of war we were and how we would enjoy better privileges if we corrected our ways.

We immediately learned about anyone in the States, from government officials to entertainers, who said anything against the war. We liked the popular music Hanoi Hannah played. If she said the U.S. had bombed hell out of them and killed many people, we knew of course that we were making advances on the battlefield. You had to listen between the lines, to pick up the overtones.

I enjoyed the radio even though I thought I was hearing a big bunch of b.s. It passed the time. I think that's one of the reasons the NVA drastically cut down the programming time a few months later—we were taking it as entertainment. It gave the guys with roomies something to talk about. The North Vietnamese didn't want us to talk about anything. They wanted us to sit around feeling sorry for ourselves.

Before going to Viet Nam I had read Bernard Fall's *Street without Joy,* but nothing else except the usual news reports. I didn't consider myself very knowledgeable about the country. Listening to the radio was often like sitting in a history class. I enjoyed the part where the Vietnamese fought against the Chinese. Even though they preached Mao's doctrine, there was no love lost between North Vietnamese and Chinese, you could see that. We heard very often about the battle of Dien Bien Phu. The North Vietnamese did a fantastic job there, all historians recognize that; and in certain ways I came to admire them quite a bit.

I didn't know the South Vietnamese. A lot of them worked at the Cam Ranh base when I was there. They did common-labor-type jobs, mowed the grass, and so forth. The base had a large community-relations program. We taught them to drive automobiles and taxis and to operate machines. We had a very expensive civic-action program in Cam Ranh city to construct an orphanage. We also built them a merry-go-round, a latrine, and fixed up their school.

I had no personal contact with the South Vietnamese, however. None whatsoever. I was working sixteen to eighteen hours a day. I suppose I felt about them the same way as I had about the South Koreans. They were an undeveloped nation who needed our help. This was the point. I had done a lot of reading on communism. I thought we were right being in South Viet Nam. I felt very strongly that as long as anyone wanted to be free, regardless of their race, creed, or color, the United States ought to help them.

I had been in solitary confinement only a few weeks when I received a note by covert means. It said, "Welcome to the Plantation Gardens. You are in our smallest suite. There are more of us here and we are all praying for you. To beat these guys you must have faith in us, have faith in your country, and keep your spirits high." The note went on to give me the tap code. It was signed, "The Rogues."

Receiving the note was a tremendous morale booster, as was the description of the tap code, by which I was able to establish communications with other prisoners. The tap code was very old —someone said it had appeared long ago in the Boy Scout manual—and it was brought to Hanoi by a navy commander. The first line of code was *A-B-C-D-E*. To spell out a word containing one of these letters, you made a tap on the wall, then paused and tapped out the number one for *A*, two for *B*, three for *C*, and so on. The second line was *F-G-H-I-J*. Two taps and a pause, then the number of the letter, one for *F*, two for *G*, etc. *K* was omitted and *C* substituted where necessary. The third line, introduced by three quick taps and a pause, was *L-M-N-O-P*. The fourth and final lines were *Q-R-S-T-U* and *V-W-X-Y-Z*. The method was bulky at best. But we were able to transmit rapidly by devising a shorthand composed of many abbreviations.

We also established commo by setting up message drops. I

dropped my first notes by scratching messages on the bottom of my dinner plate. Four or five POWs were assigned to collect and wash the plates and utensils for the entire camp. The duty usually was rotated among various cells. The guard opened the door and I left my plate outside when I finished eating. Soon a POW came by and collected it, read the message, and someone later answered through the tap code or by several other methods we developed.

Through commo I began to learn more about the camp. The Plantation Gardens had opened fourteen months previously. Before then all POWs apparently were maintained at the Hilton, kept separate from the regular complement of political and criminal Vietnamese inmates. The Hilton was a large—perhaps a city square block in size—former French prison. There was no way to conceal that it was a dismal and drab affair. It was thought that the North Vietnamese wanted a show place, a camp where foreign dignitaries and international reporters could be shown carefully screened POWs in relatively pleasant surroundings for maximum propaganda advantage.

From an aesthetic point of view, the Plantation was an unusual prison. It had been the home of Hanoi's Vietnamese mayor during the French occupation. In the center of the walled compound was a two-story yellowed stucco colonial-style villa, similar to any of the nicer houses in Viet Nam. It served as the camp staff's offices and quarters, and had rooms with tiled floors and fireplaces. We called the villa the Big House; we were more familiar with its interrogation room. Outside was a large bomb shelter, and flowers grew here and there.

On the compound's east side was a long building we codenamed the Warehouse. Judging by the hooks hanging from the walls, that's exactly what it had been during the mayor's time. At the south end were outbuildings, probably formerly servants' quarters, which we named the Gun Shed; at the north end were more outbuildings converted into cells, the Corncrib. On the west was an area called the Movie House, for that's where we were later shown outdoor propaganda movies. A small, worn, pressed-gravel courtyard near the Warehouse had a basketball goal at either end.

I learned of the secret POW organization within the camp and the senior ranking officer's policies. The SRO was a lieutenant colonel like myself—I think he had me by a month on date of rank. In June and July he was beaten by the North Vietnamese in an attempt to extract a confession from him. He was then jailed in a section of the camp where it became impossible to contact him for guidance.

In July, 1968, I decided, as next senior ranking officer, to assume command of the camp. I was prompted partly by what happened the same month when some American prisoners were released and sent home. The day before the release I could see other POWs through a crack in my door as they passed on the way to take showers. They gave me the thumbs-up sign or tried to whisper to me when the guards weren't looking. The announcement that three men were going home brought a stunning change. The other POWs shuffled by my cell with heads hung low, wouldn't even try to look my way. Camp morale was shattered.

I passed the word that I was taking over. The camp policy at the time was that the sick and wounded could go home first if offered release by the North Vietnamese, followed by those who had been captured longest by date of rank. I felt that no one should go home regardless of date of rank or how long held. There was one man at this time who I thought was sick enough to accept release—John McCain, Admiral McCain's son; he was badly wounded.

We were all in it together. We should all go home together. There were only two ways to get out as far as I was concerned: either dead or with heads held high. We would all stay if it took another twenty-five years.

I put out my policies by tap and note. I kept them simple and followed along the lines of the Code of Conduct. "First," I said, "We will back U.S. policies." By this I meant the U.S. would remain in Viet Nam until American interests could be maintained and the South Vietnamese were able to determine their own destiny. "Two, we will resist as much as possible. Three, we will not accept any personal favors or gratuities from the enemy. Four, remember your American heritage, that you are an American and proud to be one. Five, do not write. Six, do not tape. Seven, do not go home early."

Forty-four POWs were in the Plantation, all air force and navy pilot officers, except for an eighteen-year-old navy-enlisted kid who had managed to fall off a ship and get captured. It took nearly three months to pass my new policies through the entire camp. I had vacant rooms on my right and left, so I had to tap through an empty room to get to the next wall. To hear more clearly we placed a tin cup with the open end toward the wall and put an ear to the cup bottom. First we tried thumping on the wall to get the other room's attention when we wanted to transmit. But the NVA caught us at that and we then worked out specific times to send; right after the last morning gong, for example. Some days I spent several hours tapping, till my knuckles were bloodied.

We sent out everything through commo. It became our life line. I learned how to play chess through the wall. We swapped information about our families and kids and told jokes we'd heard. Some jokes got awfully long; you forgot what it was about before the punch line was tapped out. When I first started, I wrote what was coming over on a piece of toilet paper with a toothpaste tube. But this was dangerous because the NVA would hear us tapping and bust into the room and catch us with the paper. We soon learned to remember without writing.

I was trying to boost morale. That was my main idea. I wanted to get everybody thinking about resisting as much as they could. Many prisoners were beat once and thereafter routinely began to comply with the NVA. Once was not enough. My policies were not totally inflexible, however. I modified them to say that if you felt like you were going to be beaten, then go ahead and make the intracamp tapes, the ones being played over the radio to us. But you should absolutely not do anything that could be used on the Voice of Viet Nam. They really had to have a go at you to make tapes for Hanoi Hannah.

A value of the tap code was that we could find out what questions the North Vietnamese were concentrating on at interrogations, prepare our answers to jibe, and stay one jump ahead of them. A POW who was pulled out for questioning returned and told us what he was asked. I then put out my policies regarding the questions. For instance, the NVA asked what we thought of China. I had written a paper for the Command and Staff College in 1961 in which I said I thought we should establish diplomatic relations with Red China but, at the same time, not desert Taiwan. So that became my policy. As camp commander I had to be, in effect, president of the U.S.

In August the North Vietnamese began cracking down. I was called in. The camp political officer was in charge of POWs. We had little contact with the camp commander, who was mainly an administrator.

The political officer, a small and skinny effeminate-looking guy, told me, "We know you are passing out orders. You must stop or you will be punished."

My policy since the Vinh beating was to be polite to them. I said, "No, sir, I won't do it anymore. I'm sorry."

I was returned to my cell. I immediately called up the next room and said, "Press on."

We were setting up a secret organization. Every combat pilot heading for Southeast Asia was required to go through the air force's survival school in Washington State. When I went through the school I was convinced that the only thing I had learned was how to be miserable for three weeks. But when I got to Hanoi I realized that I had absorbed many things—interrogation methods, overt and covert communications, escape techniques—and I began to try to put them into practice.

As 1969 began we had made a good deal of progress. Our communications committee was a cell containing four prisoners. It was their job to make drops and to figure out new ways of communicating. The commo officer coordinated call signs (only code names, of course, were used) and assigned cells different times to transmit. Our morale officer, a physical-education major in college, passed out ideas for exercises to keep people busy and in shape. Our overt committee began to plan a harassment campaign against the NVA. Some POWs sent out to spade flower gardens for the Vietnamese flipped the dirt over their shoulders into the guards' faces. They were sent back to their cells. When we carried our defecation cans to the bathroom, we were supposed to stop, set them down, and bow to any Vietnamese we encountered. Instead, we dropped the cans and spilled the contents all over the ground. They made us clean it up, but they were getting the message.

Perhaps a little too well. In July they found a note I had circulated through the camp. They beat several prisoners and got some information out of them about me. There was another POW release around this time. The navy-enlisted man, who asked for and got my permission to leave, was sent home, as were three more pilots, who accepted release unilaterally. The North Vietnamese continued to interrogate prisoners about our organization during August, and near the end of the month I was called in. They had a prepared list of a hundred crimes they said I'd committed. They knew my commo call sign, which at the time was Fox; they knew all my policies.

I was interrogated for four days. I wasn't bothered September 2, Independence Day. I was recalled the morning of September 3 and ordered to confess to the hundred crimes. I wouldn't. I was taken by three guards and an officer into the torture room, a bare chamber in the northeast corner of the villa. They made me kneel and began to beat me across the back with a rubber hose. At about 9:30 A.M. the camp political officer entered and said something to the others. The guards quit beating me. I was taken back to my cell. They gave me no explanation. Later I was told that Ho Chi Minh had died that morning.

We enjoyed a two-week moratorium while North Viet Nam was in mourning. They left us completely alone. At the end of it I was called back in. They said that because of Ho's death I would not be punished further if I realized my mistakes and promised not to communicate. I said, "Thank you very much. I will not communicate any more."

I was ordered to write a letter of apology to the camp commander. I began, "Dear Camp Commander, I'm sorry for my very bad acts."

On October 15, 1969, our treatment changed for the better. I think it was because President Nixon had come out very strongly in support of the POWs, focusing international attention on the problem. We were given six cigarettes instead of the usual three when the guards made their morning rounds on October 15. Next day we began to get three meals instead of two, with the addition of half a loaf of bread for breakfast. Then we were allowed outside about thirty minutes a day to exercise. We could see each other for the first time. Three rooms at a time were turned out. No one was allowed to talk. The guards kept us apart. From personal descriptions passed through commo I recognized every man.

I was given my first package from home. I almost didn't get it because during interrogations I was asked my wife's address and I had given a fictitious one. The NVA officer said, "This package is not for you because it's from another address."

I thought a minute and said, "Okay, that's me. I lied before. Give me the package." It contained my reading glasses from Cam Ranh, some One-a-Day vitamins, M & M's candies, Lifesavers, and a T-shirt.

Inside my glasses case was a picture of a bird and the number six. I said, "Oh, my God! My wife's mixed up with the peace movement." I thought the bird was a dove and the six meant "in six months the war will be over."

I passed on this info through commo.

Someone replied, "Well, I think the six means oh-six, the numerical listing for a full colonel, and the bird is an eagle, a colonel's insignia."

I said, "No, that can't be it." I was promoted to lieutenant colonel six months below the zone, but I couldn't believe I was being advanced to the rank of full colonel three years ahead of my contemporaries. In fact, I didn't actually believe it until I received confirmation when I returned to the States.

We re-established commo. I was caught once again. On December 10 I was transferred to the Hilton. At this time the NVA moved most of the light and full colonels from the various camps into the Hilton. I think it was because they planned to pull a big propaganda stunt at Christmas—POWs photographed enjoying Noel—and because they knew we all had strong organizations going in the camps and this was the best way to break them up. I was put into solitary confinement in a cell-block with twelve other lieutenant colonels. I was allowed out for exercise each day. Though the Hilton was rat-infested and exceedingly dreary, the food was a little better there than at the Plantation Gardens.

The beatings had generally been stopped by this time. But we were under heavy pressure to write antiwar appeals and to make tapes for the camp radio. One side of my head turned snow white. The white hair eventually fell out and I was half bald till it grew back its normal brown color. By Christmas I felt very low, depressed; the loneliness was becoming harder to face. Nearly two years had passed without my talking to another American. My family did not know I was alive. I thought constantly about my wife and three sons.

Over the radio I heard POWs thanking the camp authorities for permitting them to write home. On Christmas Eve there was a commotion on the cell-block as other prisoners were given roommates. Only three of us were left in solitary confinement in my section of the prison. Shortly after New Year's, 1970, I was told I would be given a roommate and allowed to write my family if I agreed to read over the camp radio. I went back to my cell and thought it over. The North Vietnamese wanted me to read a chapter from *Viet Nam Today,* an English-language publication that was mainly a description of the country. The chapter I was to read began with the climatology of Viet Nam and covered the country's early history.

I felt it was worth the risk to myself to read one chapter. I told them I would do it. I was taken to the small radio room to tape the material. A week later I was called in for another interrogation. I asked the interrogator, a guy we called the Pig, when I could write home. He said, "In the near future. The camp commander is considering."

I knew then that I'd fallen for their lies. I regretted it very deeply. I said, "When he considers favorably I'll consider reading again."

The Pig continued to pressure me. I refused to read. I was put in a cramped sweatbox and kept there three days without food, but I did not give in. The Pig was a North Vietnamese with a fat face, a blunt snout of a nose, and beady eyes. He said his mother had been killed by cluster bomblets. He loved Ho Chi Minh dearly. When he started pressing me, I asked about Ho. He would sit back, relax, and recite the history of Ho. It was the only way I could get him off my back.

On June 10, 1970, I was called before the Hilton's camp commander. He said, "What is this sniff-sniff?" He made sounds with his nose.

I said, "I guess you have a cold."

He said, "No. You communicate."

I had worked out a commo method when I bathed. The bathhouse was closed but without a ceiling. There were usually other POWs outside exercising during the time I was washing. One of them worked his way close to the bathhouse, and I talked to him by sniffing out the tap code. He answered by doing a body code as he exercised. I watched him through a peephole in the door. If the head was touched that meant one tap, the shoulder was two, the chin three, and on. This way I learned the camp policies and recent news, particularly about the space shots.

The camp commander, speaking through an interpreter, said, "We are sending you to a place where you'll never be able to communicate with anybody. You'll never be able to organize any activities. You'll stay there till you die."

That night I was jeeped eighteen miles southwest of Hanoi to a large North Vietnamese training area that was encircled by SAM missile sites. Half a mile from the main training center was a POW camp. There were three small cells on the POW camp's outer perimeter. I was locked in one of them, a cell six by nine feet, extremely hot, and occupied by rats. It had been, I think, an old ammo storage room; scratched into the wall was the date 1939.

I was more than a hundred yards from the main camp, which was surrounded by screens. Through cracks in my cell door I could see legs walking under the screens. I estimated there were thirty people in the camp; I later found the correct number was forty-four; they had all been captured in Laos and South Viet Nam. We were getting only two meals a day, roughly half the food I'd received in Hanoi, and were down to two cigarettes. Half the POWs were kept in solitary or total isolation. I was getting no exercise. I was supposed to sit on my bed at attention at all times, something I did only when I knew guards were looking.

The Vietnamese gave me communist literature to read and quizzed me about what I'd learned. If they gave me something to read, I read it just to have something to do. It was like interrogations—you looked forward to them because you were actually talking to someone. I could never, however, answer the questions they asked. They made me sit at attention for hours on a stool in the middle of the interrogation room until I tumbled off from exhaustion. But I was not really physically touched at this camp.

In late November a U.S. Special Forces rescue team made a surprise helicopter raid on the Son Tay POW camp, which was about ten miles north of us. The raid was unsuccessful, the prisoners had been moved a few weeks earlier to another camp. I, of course, didn't know what was happening. But I heard NVA fighters go up, the sounds of explosions, and SAMs whooshing off in the distance. Next day the Vietnamese put gun emplacements around our camp and hung wire to prevent helicopters from landing. Then at 7:00 Thanksgiving evening guards opened my cell and told me to roll up my clothes and bedding. I thought I was being taken to the main camp to get a roommate. I was put on a bus with the camp's other prisoners, and we were driven to the Plantation Gardens.

The Plantation had been vacant for three months. The POWs

who were with me last time had been consolidated in the Hilton. From the night we arrived till near the end of the war the Plantation was to be used mainly as a prison for Americans captured in Laos and South Viet Nam, many of them enlisted soldiers and marines. No one in the U.S. knew whether most of us were alive or dead. I was placed in solitary in a room next to my old cell. I tried without success to make contact with POWs passing by. The NVA decided to take away the temptation after a month. I was moved to the compound's south end into the Gun Shed. I was the only prisoner in that section, in total isolation.

From my room I had a view of the rest of the camp through faults in the louvered shutters. I was upset by what I saw. I estimated that from 80 to 90 per cent of the nearly fifty POWs were either sympathetic to or actually collaborating with the enemy. Most of them, I think, were doing this out of fear. They were extremely subservient, bowing all the time, saying "sir" to them, and making tapes for the camp radio.

It was easy to separate the prisoners who were forced to tape from those who weren't. Those forced spoke in a monotone, mispronounced words, slurred phrases. The guys not forced read with feeling. It was obvious they believed what they were saying. I could see everyone who entered the radio room. When a tape was played over the box, I correlated the voice with the prisoner I'd seen go in two days earlier.

How could an American be a fighter and then all of a sudden turn his back on his country? I couldn't understand it. I used to tell the POWs through commo, "I may be the first one to turn against this war, to condemn it when we get home. But I'm not just going to listen to what the North Vietnamese tell me to believe. We will go home and read both sides of the story when we're released." By then we'd been captured a long time and didn't know what was happening in the outside world.

I had a tremendous amount of faith in our elected leaders. Maybe it was one of my shortcomings, but the faith was there—and still is.

I began trying to construct another organization. When I

bathed I tapped on the next stall trying to make contact. Nobody knew the tap code. This stemmed from a failure, I thought, on the part of the military. We had POWs captured in late 1972 who didn't know the code, although it had been widely used in Hanoi for years. The reason it was not taught in stateside military survival schools was, I assume, for security reasons. But this was rather foolish. The NVA already had caught us using it many times and knew what it was about. What they didn't understand were the abbreviations, nor did they have enough people who spoke fluent English to monitor us all the time. So nothing should have been classified.

In February, 1971, I was allowed out twice a week for thirty minutes. As I exercised I flailed my arms, trying to attract the other POWs' attention, but the guards caught on and stopped me. I was getting a little discouraged. Then in April, '71, big things began to happen. I was called in by the camp commander on April 18. It was my forty-second birthday. The Vietnamese knew our anniversary dates, and they tried to use them to maximum advantage. I was given my first comb. My hair was long and unkempt.

The NVA said, "We are thinking about giving you a rommate."
I said, "When?"
"Maybe in a week." I didn't know what had caused their change of heart.

The following day I was taking my after-lunch nap when I heard noise outside. Three guards, grinning broadly, flung open my door and escorted Major Artice Elliott inside. Elliott was captured in 1970 near Dak To in South Viet Nam. He was a U.S. Army adviser to ARVN troops. After thirty-seven months in solitary confinement I could hardly get the questions out fast enough. I quizzed him about what had gone on in the States up until he was captured, the changes in fashion, cars, if we actually had a man on the moon, how the war was going in the south, and his opinion of the ARVN.

His opinion of the ARVN wasn't too high. They had run off and left him in battle minutes before he was captured. He thought the

Saigon government would eventually fall. I didn't. I made a bet with him then and there.

Elliott had been transferred from another cell in the Plantation. I asked if he knew who I was. He said, "Yes, we saw you going to the bath and we were quite sure you were an officer." I guess they were able to tell by the way I carried myself. I always tried to walk very straight and tall.

I gave Major Elliott my policies, both official and private. When we were in the room, I told him, he could call me by my first name. Outside he would call me Colonel Guy and I would call him Major Elliott. He was to walk on my right and one step behind me in the proper military manner when we went to our baths and took exercise. I didn't particularly want to do this, but I thought it best so that if any POWs overheard or saw us they would know our ranks and who we were.

I made it clear that I was the camp's senior ranking officer and, as such, in charge. I explained my policies concerning discipline. I was a very firm disciplinarian. I thought we had to have discipline in the camp in order to survive. The decisions I had to make, in my opinion, involved people's lives. This may be a hell of a thing to say, but I felt that in the military you had to act like a machine. You tell someone to do something and he has to react instantly. I told Major Elliott all this the first ten minutes he was in the room. He received it well. He was a military man.

Something else happened in April. Harker and his bunch arrived at the Plantation, followed by another group ten days later. They were allowed outside quite extensively at first. I could see them and I knew by their clothes that they had been held somewhere in the south or Laos. I didn't think too much about their taking extra privileges from the North Vietnamese. They didn't know my policies; they didn't realize that other POWs were not getting outside to exercise that much.

But it was not long before I heard some of their group reading propaganda on the radio. I made up my mind to get in touch with them.

14

John Young

I was taken to a camp in Nghe An, the dirt-poor home province of Ho Chi Minh. I arrived the day after Easter, 1968. The camp was on a wooded hillside not far from a small village. Sixteen Americans were held in one building in cells that looked like chicken coops. There were a few more men, officers, in outbuildings further away. I stayed in a chicken coop only one day and then was moved, along with Brandy, to the camp's hospital section.

We were placed on a wood platform. A hole was cut in the platform and we slid over it when we had to use the bathroom. The North Vietnamese gave me penicillin twice a day. The infection in my leg cleared up. Brandy and I were on permanent exhibition. Any Vietnamese VIPs who came to the camp were brought to our room to see how wounded American POWs were treated. A movie was made of a medic working on me.

Brandy was thirty-one, a career soldier, and in good shape except for his shrapnel wound. He was extremely competent and I was impressed with him at first. We had nothing to do but talk all day. We exhausted the topics of Lang Vei and the special forces and soon began to get cabin fever. He recognized it first and said, "Let's knock it off and just play games." So we made a chess set and a deck of cards. The time passed slowly.

The North Vietnamese asked us to fill out our autobiographies, personal history information on our families and careers. Brandy outranked me, he was a sergeant, and the NVA went to him first. He said, "I'm sorry."

They came to me and I said the same thing.

They looked at Brandy and said, "You are a die-hard."

We consented to do a partial biography. We printed everything, including our names. They wanted us to do it over and write it out. We refused. The translator pulled out a pistol and said, "If you don't do it you won't live to see the sun come up tomorrow." Brandy and I looked at each other. I'd made it this far and maybe I could make it a little longer. I guess Brandy thought the same thing. We wrote it out just the way they wanted.

In August, 1968, we were moved to a camp about eighteen miles southwest of Hanoi. I was to remain here for two years, until the Son Tay raid in November, 1970. The main part of the camp looked like an old French motor pool. The largest building was yellow stucco. It was partitioned into different-size cells— some held twelve men, some ten, four, two, and one. The cells had solid wooden doors with small peepholes cut into them. They were equipped with radio speakers. A group of POWs was assigned to clean and care for a section of the camp; a second group took care of another area. We got outside nearly two hours a day for exercise and were allowed to bathe.

Before this time I couldn't have given anyone a definition of colonialism. I thought it was something that went out with the American Revolution. I certainly didn't realize that France and Britain had colonies in Asia until the 1950s and that France had sucked Viet Nam dry. Neither could I define capitalism. I had my own definition in my mind, I guess. "The American Way of Life." That's the way I put it. When the Vietnamese said something about capitalism, I'd say, "Yeah, that's us."

"We want you to understand our side," the North Vietnamese told me. So I expected everything to be from their perspective and at first I thought it was just lies. While they didn't want me to read Marx, they did give me books on Viet Nam. Six of them were by American authors, including Schlesinger's *Bitter Heritage*. I read a couple of Wilfred Burchett's books, which I enjoyed immensely. His *Mekong Upstream* was very influential. In the States I had heard about Southeast Asia in terms of "the communists." Now I was reading the human story of the people.

Despite my reading and thinking about the war, I felt no particular sympathy for the Vietnamese at this point. I was more or less indifferent. I believed the war was wrong and the U.S. shouldn't be in Viet Nam. But in personal relations with the camp officials I was occasionally rebellious and often insubordinate, especially if I was down in the dumps. In fact I got thrown in solitary confinement for six months starting in October, '68.

I was in a room with two other prisoners. We got a regular ration of cigarettes and saved our butts to make extra smokes. For this we needed rolling paper. The only paper available was the propaganda materials they gave us to read. I ripped up a *Viet Nam Courier* and stuck it inside my pajama shirt. It fell out one day and a guard saw it. He reported us. The camp officials said, "Who tore it? That is against camp regulations." None of us would confess. They tried to cause a split by making one or two of us kneel for long periods while the other was allowed to sit on the bed. In the end we all claimed each other did it, and we all went to solitary.

Our main contact at the camp was a senior lieutenant we called Cheese. His real name, which I learned only a few days before we were repatriated in '73, was Le Van Vuong. He was extremely thin and sickly looking. He wore glasses but he didn't show them to us at first because he was a little shy. His black hair was combed straight back, and he wore sort of baggy military uniforms. He was forty-eight. He had served with an artillery unit at Dien Bien Phu, after the war was a math professor at Hanoi University. His wife was a doctor, and they had two children.

Cheese was interrogating me one day while I was in solitary. I told him the National Liberation Front did nothing but lie. He slapped me so hard that I almost fell out of the chair. I couldn't believe such a fragile man had such physical power.

"What you said is words for death!" he shouted.

"Go ahead, you Communist!" I screamed back. "Kill me!"

Cheese stood in front of me shaking with rage. A guard brought a towel and stuffed it into my mouth. Cheese slapped me again. After giving me a long emotional lecture, he sent me back to my cell.

I finished my time in solitary and was put back in a cell with my old roommates. We began to talk of escaping. We worked the bars loose in our locked window but couldn't get them completely out. There was a small trap door in the ceiling. One prisoner stood on my shoulders and pried loose the door. It opened a little, just enough for us to see that it was covered, like the rest of the roof, with barbed wire, and impossible to penetrate. Some plaster around the trap door fell into our room and the Vietnamese spotted it on their morning rounds. Surprisingly, they didn't say anything. Having escaped punishment for that, I was soon accused of insubordination and thrown back into solitary confinement for another six months.

In July, 1969, a Vietnamese official stopped by my cell. He was from the camp radio station. He said, "There's a drive on in the United States, a movement to end the war. Would you like to send your support to them?"

I said, "Even though I'm opposed to the war, I don't think I should do it." He asked if my decision was final. When I said it was, he left.

I wasn't aware there was an antiwar movement before I went to Viet Nam. I knew there had been demonstrations, but I assumed it was an isolated thing by hippies and radicals. The Vietnamese showed me an antiwar magazine called *Moving Together*. It told of the big protest demonstration scheduled for Washington in November; and I began to realize the depth of the dissent in the States.

This coincided with the thinking I was doing about the war. I was asking myself questions, trying to be as unbiased as I could. I had reached the decision earlier that I was against the war. I was trying to expand my feelings as to why I believed it to be wrong. It instinctively felt wrong to me. I could see no rational explanation for what we were doing in Southeast Asia. "If we're wrong," I said to myself, "Why not admit it? Let's get the hell out of here." Whether a soldier or not, I was an American first, and I decided it was my duty to speak out.

I was also influenced by what I was learning about Ho Chi Minh. Not only through books I read but by listening to the way the guards, Cheese, all the English-speaking Vietnamese talked about him. Even the people who didn't speak English would say to me, *"Ho Chi Minh tot lam. Ho Chi Minh so mot."* It's impossible to find anyone in our country who likes our recent presidents— possibly excepting Kennedy—the way the Vietnamese did Bac Ho. For a man to have gained so much love and respect of his countrymen, Ho Chi Minh, I decided, had to be really and truly working for the people.

From his writings I pictured President Ho as an extremely physical man, with a firm voice and strong manners. I was shocked when I saw him in movies and discovered he was just the opposite, delicate and soft-spoken, as gentle and lovable as a grandfather. On September 2, 1969, Independence Day, I said to myself, "At least he lived this long." I didn't know he was sick or anything, I was just thinking about how old he was getting, how much he had been through in his lifetime, how happy he must be to have brought his country this far. I was hoping to meet him.

Then the next day I knew something had happened. I could see it in the guards' faces. At first they didn't wear their pieces of black cloth around the camp; they didn't want us to know. But I could feel their intense sorrow. On September 17, after two weeks of mourning, they told us. Cheese tried to hold back his emotions as he spoke. But he couldn't. He started crying. I cried too.

Four days later I made an antiwar tape to be broadcast over the Voice of Viet Nam. I asked Cheese to let me make the tape after he told me Ho had passed away, but he refused. The Vietnamese were irritated that I hadn't made the tape in July when they first asked me. An American peace delegation was in Hanoi at the time, and the Vietnamese planned to send the tape back with them for use during the moratorium protest. I had to ask Cheese several times before he finally allowed me to make the tape.

I had made a tape addressed to my family at Christmas, '68. I had also written an antiwar appeal to American GIs. I considered the first tape as just a way of letting my family know I was alive. It was never used. The appeal addressed to the servicemen was a straightforward declaration that I was against the war. But the tape I made after President Ho died marked the beginning of my protest.

I couldn't blame the American people for the war, nor the GIs fighting it, the men flying the jets. I blamed the money-grabbing people who refused to help end it. I began making frequent tapes. I was so strongly opposed that I didn't care what I said. I considered what would happen to me when I returned to the States. I knew I would have to face the consequences, that I would probably wind up in jail, but I was prepared.

Over the next three and a half years I made thirty-three tapes for the North Vietnamese. I wrote several letters to President Nixon, in which I got very heavy. I probably wrote a hundred letters all told, to Congress, to GIs, to people in my home town. One of my letters was published in the *Daily World,* which made me feel a little bad because I knew not many people would accept it coming from a paper like that. Other letters were published around the world, including quite a few in Soviet newspapers. When I wrote letters to American GIs, I explained the war from my standpoint and urged them to follow their own consciences.

I knew other POWs were making tapes. I saw them entering the radio shack. But I didn't know who they were. Everyone was afraid to express opinions in conversations. I could talk to one guy, my roommate, Mike Branch, a young army truck driver from Kentucky, who had been captured while walking a road near Utah Beach in Quang Tri Province. He was a country boy. I found he was as much opposed to the war as I was.

In early 1970 Cheese called me out of the room and told me an American had just tried to kill himself. He was very upset and he asked me, "What should I do?"

I said, "I don't know."

He asked if I would help.

I said yes but repeated that I didn't know what I could do.

The next day the North Vietnamese moved a ping-pong table into camp. That afternoon Cheese came running to my cell and told me to go to the office. The American had tried it again.

When I got to the office I saw a medic bandaging a POW's wrists. I recognized him as B——, a marine who had been a prisoner for nearly four years. He had tried to end it by biting at his wrists. When that didn't work, he removed the top from his defecation can and tried to cut himself with the top's rough edges.

I said, "Hey, man, what are you doing here?"

He said, "They're trying to castrate me!"

"Take it easy," I said. "No one is going to hurt you."

After the medic finished, Cheese took us over to the ping-pong room and told us to play. B—— wasn't enthusiastic but he appeared to be calmer.

Cheese told me privately after the game, "Maybe you come over each day to cheer him up."

I said, "Okay."

B—— was returned to his cell. He lived alone. That night he made another attempt.

First thing next morning Cheese moved B—— in with Mike and me. An interpreter, a medic, a turnkey, and a guard were stationed outside our room. The door was left open and a lantern was placed inside. B—— lay on his bed pretending to sleep. When our attention was diverted he turned on his side and began gnawing at his wrists till they bled. Mike and I took turns watching him. We went three days without sleeping.

The guards locked our door again after several days but left the lantern with us. Mike and I went outside one day to dig a new latrine. We had been gone only ten minutes when we saw a doctor running for our room. This time B—— had managed to cut himself deeply, and it took a long time to stop the bleeding. I was getting a little irritated with him. He felt sorry for himself, I thought, and wanted our sympathy too.

I warned him not to let me catch him doing it again. He just looked at me. He spent most of his time lying on the bed, hardly ever spoke. A few days later Mike saw him gnawing. We were playing cards. Mike got up and went over and pushed his hands away. As Mike returned I saw that B—— was doing it again. I slowly got up and walked over and backhanded him as hard as I could.

"If you want to hurt," I told him, "I'll hurt you."

Mike got shook up. We almost got into a hassle about whether I should have hit him. But B—— didn't try it any more that night.

He made several more attempts in the following days. Cheese decided to move us into a larger room near six enlisted men at the other end of the camp. B—— started it again and I really got pissed off at him. I grabbed him and threw him all over the room. I didn't hit him, I was just pushing him. He tried to defend himself, which was unusual, the first sign that he was taking an interest in himself. I slapped him around. I think at this time Mike understood. We couldn't give him sympathy, for the more he got the deeper he regressed.

Our troubles continued over the course of seven months. He wouldn't put up his mosquito net at night and we had to do it for him. There was something going on all the time. Finally he stopped. Why, I don't know. But he stopped. He came back on the same plane with me. I saw him at the president's dinner at the White House. We talked awhile but neither of us brought up the subject. I still feel guilty about slapping him around, but now I think that maybe I did save his life.

We were isolated from the few officers in the camp. There were no communications in the sense of trying to establish an organization. We talked out the windows to the six men near us. We talked about the war, about women, about the guards masturbating (we could see them through holes in our doors), about what we were going to do when we got out, about how much money we were making. Money, of course, was on everybody's minds. I talked about it too, but not very much; I really didn't expect to get anything when I got out.

In November, 1970, we began a project the Vietnamese called "beautifying the camp." Sections of us worked at cutting down the brush near the compound and putting in flower and vegetable gardens. We made a turkey coop, and we began to look forward to Christmas. One night in late November I heard jets for the first time. I could hear missiles going up. Next morning guards moved into camp in full battle gear. As soon as I saw that I assumed the U.S. had raided a POW camp. I was opposed to the Son Tay operation. I knew that if our camp was raided and I left my cell the Vietnamese would shoot me. And if I refused to go the Americans would probably shoot me. Either way I was going to lose.

On Thanksgiving evening we were bused to the Plantation. The situation there was completely different from our old camp. It was much more congested; I'd say the entire compound was about 150 meters by 100 meters. Eight of us were placed in one room. We divided ourselves into four two-man teams and split up the housekeeping chores. We had to sweep every morning, dish out our food, empty the defecation cans, and wash dishes.

We started feeling each other out about Viet Nam. Not everyone was opposed to the war. One or two were against it but didn't feel it was proper for POWs to say anything. I wasn't sure about a young, solidly built marine corporal named Al Riate. He vowed he would do everything he could to resist the Vietnamese. He was captured in early '67 and had already made three escape attempts. He and Bob Chenoweth, a helicopter door gunner, were the two key personalities in the room. Chenoweth had made tapes and written letters. Another marine, Larry Kavanaugh, was leaning in opposition to the war. Larry was about five foot six, slight, but very nice looking, with a swarthy complexion and raven-black hair. He always walked straight and with a little swagger. You could tell he was a marine.

As we talked about the war we got into some pretty good

arguments. Each person tried to argue down another who had an opposing viewpoint. Then we said, "We're not getting anyplace like this," so we stopped. We realized that no one was really arguing in support of the war—the debates centered around why the U.S. had gotten into Viet Nam in the first place. We couldn't figure it out. We tried to decide who was getting something out of it. The big oil companies and the giant corporations with military contracts were obviously making billions of dollars. That was the only reason we could see for the war continuing.

The Vietnamese influenced our thinking very little, mainly through the material they gave us to read. I asked them who was making money out of the war and they told me, "You figure it out." I asked them why Congress didn't do something to stop the fighting. They wouldn't reply. They said, "We just want you to understand the war and what is happening in Viet Nam."

We read about Ho Chi Minh and the Vietnamese Workers Party but had no books on Marxism at this time. Chenoweth, though he knew little about communism, was more widely read than anyone else, and he took the lead in our discussions. I guess some of us resented Chenoweth at first. He was a scholarly looking guy with glasses, and his only personal quirk was that he sometimes acted like he knew everything. Nobody wanted to admit it but he did know a lot more than we did.

It wasn't long before we decided to do things to protest against the war together. Everyone was coming around to that feeling, except three guys who thought we were getting too heavy. They wanted out. We told them we understood. We talked to Cheese and asked if the three could be removed from our room. They were transferred to another cell around Christmas time. That left Chenoweth, Riate, Kavanaugh, Mike Branch, and myself.

We saw a lot of Le Van Vuong. He asked us one day, "Why do you call me Cheese?"

We said, "Because in America the man in charge is called the head cheese."

He smiled broadly.

We came to like him very much. It was just that he really

believed so hard, so much, in what he was doing. And I think he tried to be as fair as he could with us. I learned to look at him as a friend. He was sort of like an uncle. He taught us patience and understanding.

The five of us grew closer. We talked about our families and our backgrounds, the things we had done before entering the service. I was probably from a more middle-class environment than anyone except Chenoweth. Riate and Branch were extremely poor. Riate was half Indian and half Filipino. He never really had a father—his dad died shortly after he was born—and he had trouble with his mother and stuff like that. He was an aggressive guy but he'd been on his own since he could walk, and I could understand. Larry Kavanaugh was a Chicano; his Irish grandfather had married a Spanish girl. Both he and Riate felt that they were sort of outcasts, minorities. I think they had something of an inferiority complex—not from us, but from what had happened to them in the States. We tried to explain that our room was not the States, that here we were all on an equal basis. Branch was a Catholic and pretty religious. I didn't claim to be anything and neither did Chenoweth.

I think I was more active than anyone in the room at this time. I wrote my own antiwar appeals and signed them, then volunteered them to the North Vietnamese. I kept the appeals in simple language, expressing my own viewpoint. Most of the time the North Vietnamese told me it was too strong. They said, "Your government will use this against you to punish you. Do not write strong. Suppress your feelings. Do not condemn."

We made a few tapes in early '71 and started seeing movies regularly. We usually watched the films outside near the guards' volleyball court. Two or three were run at a sitting once or twice a week. Many of them were Soviet-made films on Shakespeare, circuses, the Soviet space program, documentaries on the war, but nothing political.

We did not hide what we were doing. By this time we had seen Colonel Guy through a crack in our door as he passed by, but we didn't know who he was. Nor had we noticed any hostility from other POWs in camp. We had not, that is, until '71. It was after our morning meal. Our room had the duty of washing dishes. We were walking along the row of cells picking them up. Air Force Capt. Edward Leonard and his men were shaving in the wash area. They were thirty-five meters from us.

Suddenly Captain Leonard walked toward us, snapped to attention, and yelled, "Kavanaugh, you and your men are ordered to stop all communications and collaborations with the enemy!"

Someone yelled back, "Fuck you!"

I don't know who said it. To this day I honestly don't. I remember Riate saying that he would protest the war till the day he died. He told Leonard that. Someone else made a comment, and we moved away. Three guards rushed up and pulled Leonard to his cell. To us his act was asinine. He could have gotten killed and gotten us killed too. The guards didn't speak English, they didn't know what he was saying; for all they knew he was telling us to jump them and take their weapons.

His action surprised us in another way. We had no hint that anyone was down on us for expressing our feelings. We knew there would be some opposition, but we didn't figure anything like this would happen. We left the dishes and went to our room to talk it over. Leonard was an officer and perhaps he felt he had to do his duty—if that's why he did it. But we basically thought he was trying to earn medals at our expense.

It changed nothing. We continued what we were doing. We did ask the camp authorities not to punish him though. We tried to explain that he was an officer and felt it was something he had to do. They told us they were not punishing him for having an opinion, but because he broke the camp's rules. They put him in solitary. I think they later moved him down to Colonel Guy's section of the camp.

From that moment on the North Vietnamese kept us out of sight of the other POWs as much as possible. I don't think they wanted any trouble in the camp, any dissension. They knew there was opposition to us, and, in some ways, I think they tried to discourage what we were doing. Of course, there were times when the others couldn't help but see us, like when we took our baths and they were out exercising.

Harker and his group had come in during this period. We saw them the day after they arrived. They were terribly thin and sick-looking. We wondered: Who the hell were these guys, where were they from? Cheese told us the group had been in the jungle several years, that some of them had died, and that they were depressed and feeling bad. Then we heard Kushner reading over the radio. His protest was more or less from the American point of view. He was worried about what the war was doing to the U.S., how it was hurting our country. It was a strictly patriotic point of view. We felt we were patriots too, but at the same time we felt sorry for the Vietnamese because they had suffered. We felt guilty about what had happened to them. I think Kushner lacked this kind of feeling.

We asked Cheese if we could move near the group. We made the request but it may have also been a scheme by the North Vietnamese to put us close to them. I don't know. Actually it wasn't our intention to try to get them to come over to our side. We just wanted to talk to them, to find out their experiences, and to cheer them up. The POWs at our end, I guess, were saying they didn't want us around. They called us the "PCs." It stood for "Peace Committee." Some used it to mean "Pro-Communist."

15

David Harker

In the jungle I was always worried that I might wake up one morning, my eyes dim with that distant light I'd seen in other eyes before they went out. I made myself work, stay busy, take cold baths, fearing that if I stopped for a day it would happen to me too. When we reached Hanoi perhaps I let up too soon, for I fell deathly ill the first week with a high-fever malaria which several of my group had picked up on the trail. For a while I managed to get outside to sit on top of the bomb shelters in the yard. But I quickly reached a point where I couldn't drag myself out of bed. I was vomiting at midnight when a doctor arrived. He started shooting me with sugar in the veins, using a 50-cc syringe.

The malaria and dysentery eased. Then one night my respiration shot up, my heart pounded in my chest, I gasped for breath. I had to get out of the cell. I banged on the door and screamed for the turnkey. Two men pulled me back. "They aren't going to let you out," said Kushner, "take it easy." I was frantic, ready to kill to get outside, away from the suffocating cell. The other prisoners walked me around and finally coaxed me into lying down. I was shaky for two days.

We began to adjust after several weeks. Our appetites increased. The Vietnamese gave us a little extra food. We put on some weight and began to do daily exercises. Lunch was usually soup and bread. The soup seemed to have two six-month seasons, divided between pumpkin and cabbage. Once a day we got a side dish of fried vegetables or a little canned meat. The food was hardly anything to sing about but it was certainly much better than we'd had in the jungle. Five shower stalls were at the other end of the compound and we were allowed to take a bath sometimes every day.

It wasn't long till we were called to a classroom for indoctrination, a lecture on Vietnamese history. It was nothing we hadn't heard a hundred times before. The course lasted a week, six sleepy hours a day. We listened to the professor, wondering if he'd ever studied English or Spanish or French history, if he knew anything besides the Trung sisters and Nguyen Hue.

At the course's conclusion the North Vietnamese brought us an appeal to sign. I was very reluctant. I put them off several times, but wound up signing like everyone else. On July 4 we were called over to the villa. We sat around with the Vietnamese for an hour drinking tea. When we returned to our cells we discovered that no one else had been allowed outside that day. The North Vietnamese thought we were progressive, based on the fact, I suppose, that we had written antiwar stuff in the jungle. Our records were brought with us to Hanoi.

We were operating from attitudes formed in the jungle, formed when we had little choice. And at first Kushner taped for the intracamp radio and Pfister typed news material. But as we regained our strength we started thinking about opposing the North Vietnamese. We were out of touch with the rest of the camp. We knew nothing about what the senior officer's policies might be or even if there was such a thing. Meanwhile, the North Vietnamese took advantage of our confusion to move the Peace Committee next to our two cells.

Guy. From talking to my roommate, Major Elliott, I found that the army did not put a great emphasis on training soldiers in resistance methods. A course in escape and evasion techniques was taught during infantry training but it was nothing like the survival school that air-force personnel had to attend. I realized that we had a problem in the camp, because the majority of the POWs were army. I appointed Elliott as my deputy and we started working out methods to communicate with other cells.

In May, 1971, two new POWs were moved into the cell next door to us, a warrant officer and a captain, both wounded, who had been captured at the DMZ. We established contact almost immediately by yelling out the door and passing notes in our defecation cans. The two-liter cans were painted black, had a handle and a top that never fit, and around the can's base was a metal ring that held the bottom half an inch off the floor to keep it from rusting out. We sometimes put notes inside the ring and occasionally just dropped them on the excrement where they were picked up.

The warrant officer and captain were eventually moved out to the other end of the compound and we lost contact with them. Our real breakthrough came in July when all POWs captured in Laos were moved back to the Plantation. Four pilots were put in our section, two of them next door. They were very die-hard gung-ho fellows. The North Vietnamese made a big mistake the next morning when they allowed the pilots to use the bathhouse on the other end of the camp. The pilots immediately got in touch with the Corncrib, which was about a hundred fifty meters north of us. Then more pilots were transferred to the Gun Shed.

We set up overt and covert committees. I appointed an awards-and-decorations officer to keep track of heroic acts and achievements of POWs so when we got back we could recommend them for medals, which we did. It took from May, when we first started, to October to get communications through the whole camp. We had to go through individual cells and many people were still afraid of what would happen if they were caught; some of them wouldn't answer.

But over the months we were able to establish commo with everybody except the Peace Committee and the new group from the south, which we code-named the "Dirty Dozen" because their number suggested the movie of the same name. We frequently saw them exercising in the yard. A pilot in the cell next to me yelled to them, "Resist!" The Dirty Dozen—or at least the six who were out that day—turned and looked toward our cells. Nobody said anything. Everybody was scared, scared to death. Next day the North Vietnamese plugged up our louvered windows so we couldn't see out.

I didn't try to hide what I'd done earlier. I told them through commo that I had made a tape. I said, "Yes, they got me to that point in 1970 when I was very low and under a lot of mental pressure. I thought I could get word out to my family if I made a tape. The promise was broken so I quit. I expect everybody in this camp has a different breaking point, depending on how long you've been captured and your mental attitude on any given day. Some days you will be called in for interrogation and won't be able to resist at all. Okay, make the damn tape. But don't do it every day. Next time make them take you to that point or further. As far as writing, if you can write your family, go ahead, but don't sell your soul to do it."

There was still some reluctance in the camp and I made another policy decision. We had a typical GI cross section—guys who were AWOL when they were captured, a couple of deserters, some who had openly collaborated with the enemy. My new policy, which I put out via note, said: "I fully realize everybody can make mistakes. But no one should make the same mistake twice. I cannot grant amnesty to anybody for what they have done in the past. However, if on receipt of this note you follow my policies and directives from this time onward, I will do everything I can, I will even go to the president of the United States, to get you relieved from any acts committed before this date."

In one week there was an amazing change in camp. I could see it through the cracks in my door the Vietnamese weren't able to plug. A lot of men were taping and writing. I told them to taper off gradually so as not to arouse the suspicions of the North Vietnamese. The next day seven of the nine POWs who were taping quit. They were in different buildings for the most part. Others stopped bowing and some started giving the Vietnamese the finger. I sat in my cell practically quivering. Even I would bow in certain situations. But some prisoners walked past the camp commander, looked him straight in the eye, and wouldn't lower their heads.

The North Vietnamese, of course, immediately realized we had established commo. The first thing they did was stop us from using the bathhouse at the other end. They built a new bathhouse in our section and screened in our area with black tar-paper fences. We had contingency plans for such a move; new drop points had already been set up.

On October 7 the NVA found a note. The camp commander called me in for interrogation. He knew all my policies. He said, "We will not punish you if you admit you are wrong."

I said, "Okay, I admit I am wrong."

"And you will not do it again?"

"I will not do it again."

McMillan. Me and Jose Anzaldua were sweeping out our cell. Five prisoners had moved into the room next door. We swept over toward their cell. The door was open. The big thing was to ask people where they were from back in the world, you know. So we asked these guys their home towns, real quietlike, because we weren't supposed to be talking to them. Riate was from L.A.; Chenoweth was from Oregon; and Kavanaugh was from Denver.

These guys had a debate going on. One dude says to the others, "If my kid was a Communist I'd respect his opinion."

Me and Jose popped up and said, "Not us. We're imperialists."

They got the face at us then and didn't make any reply.

Kushner and Harker and four others were in the cell next to us. We went back and called them up and said, "Hey, something funny's going on next door."

A few days later Cheese came by and told us there was a Peace Committee in camp and asked if we wanted to join it. He showed us a magazine they had put together and said, "They have many extra privileges. They can write home and receive letters. They get beer and candy."

We said, "Naw, man, we don't want no part of this Peace Committee. The Peace Committee is gonna get burnt."

Cheese said, "Ya, ya. Peace Committee very good."

I saw Cheese often because I was having a little trouble with the guards. At night we kicked up a lot of noise in our room. The guards would beat on our door and tell us to be quiet but we usually ignored them. They would be patrolling the compound singing their war songs, and we'd start howling like dogs at the moon. "Yiiii." It really made them mad. Next day someone would be jerked out and taken to Cheese's office.

Cheese would say, "Lon, you very stupid." (Lon was my Vietnamese name—every POW had one.) "The guard tell the chickens to go to bed. Go to bed! He tell the pigs. Go to bed! But he tell you to go to bed and you not go. You stupid, Lon. You crazy. I think I punish you."

I said, "Look, man, I won't do it no more. I'm sorry." Of course, soon as I got back to the cell I started it again. Cheese had it in his mind that he could influence me to join the Peace Committee. That's why he didn't treat me rougher. If it had been Harker or those guys he would've put them in shackles in a minute.

Cheese was as thin as a toothpick. He must have been the oldest first lieutenant in the North Vietnamese Army. I think he had bugs or something because he was all the time scratching.

After we rapped a lot he asked me one day why I was always happy.

I said, "I'm just like that, you know. All you are doing by keeping me here is making me rich. My money is piling up in the States. When I get back I will really be a capitalist then."

"Black man, you being treated like a slave in America. Why do not you protest against the war? You away from your family. Yet and still you do not think about them. You think about money."

"Yeah, I love money, man. You said I've been a slave all my life, right?"

"Yes. You slave. You slave now."

"Okay. I want to stay here a long time so when I go back I won't be a slave. Dig?"

He didn't say anything. He just stared at me. I knew I was messing up his mind.

One morning Ol' Cheese walked out of the villa and when he got in front of our cell he started mumbling to himself and began to pace back and forth with his hands behind his back. He turned and went toward the villa, then reversed himself and headed for our room again. He did this for about five minutes. We said, "This dude is crazy, man. We better leave him alone because he might have us executed."

Daly. My attitude began to change when I got to Hanoi. In South Viet Nam we had nothing to read except some outdated propaganda newspapers and a *Life* clipping about My Lai. But as soon as we got to Hanoi we were given a series called *Viet Nam Studies.* I think everybody in our group thought the war was wrong. But to say why it was wrong, other than on moral grounds, we couldn't. We had no facts to really get our teeth into. As I read the *Viet Nam Studies* I picked out things right away that I knew to be the truth. The more I read, the more doubts I had about U.S. involvement. It sounded very logical that we should be against the war.

After the history course they began to call us out one by one for interrogation. Each of us went to Cheese's office. Cheese seemed to concentrate on my cell, which had the four blacks, Jose Anzaldua, and Long. He wasn't as interested in Harker's room. I don't know whether I should use the term reactionary, but that's the best way to describe Harker. He had turned worse and worse against the Vietnamese.

Anyway, Cheese started off the session by asking about my health. I suffered a lot when I got to Hanoi. Compared to the other guys, I looked healthy because I hadn't lost much weight, so they were given the vitamin shots and I got very little. Cheese would have a newspaper article on the war from the States and he'd show it to me and we'd discuss it. Then he asked me how

I felt about the war and I told him. He wanted me to write about the things I'd seen and disliked when I was soldier in South Viet Nam. (These sessions were stretched out over several months; he worked slowly.) We talked about why the Americans acted as they did in Viet Nam. At the end he asked if I did not want to do something to help end the killing.

The North Vietnamese also explained about colonialism. They told us about the British empire and pointed out the difference between the British method and the American method, which they called neocolonialism. "Much different," Cheese said. The British installed their own government in foreign countries, but the Americans supported independence and just put puppets in key positions of power, as in South Viet Nam. "A puppet can't act on his own," he said. "Must have someone to pull the strings." This made good sense to me. I remembered how when I was first captured I had seen men, women, and children carrying supplies for the Viet Cong. Trails and trails full of them. They certainly weren't supporting the Saigon government.

Every prisoner who went to the Big House came back with the same story, no matter how long he was gone. "Oh, the North Vietnamese just gave me the usual news about how they are winning the war," everyone would say.

One day Cheese came to the cell and gave Jose some paper to write an antiwar letter. He returned after a while to pick it up. Cheese looked at the letter and scratched his head. He said, "I do not understand. When you come to my office you write very good letters. But now you write in your room—ah, I think very poor."

We laughed. After Cheese left we teased Jose. He and I got into a fight about it. I knew goodness well you didn't go to Cheese's office just for him to tell you how the NVA were winning the war and then return with the oranges and candy he had given you. But everybody tried to pretend that was the way it worked. Cheese asked us if we would like to join the Peace Committee. We agreed more or less because we didn't want to oppose him. He had us write a letter to the camp commander asking permission to join. We wrote it but I don't think the other prisoners in the room were sincere, and nothing came of it.

In early fall, '71, we heard about Colonel Guy for the first time. We discussed what could happen if we returned to the States and Colonel Guy turned us in. It wasn't that we were doing anything, but we heard through commo what the camp thought about the Peace Committee and some guys in my room were afraid we might be lumped together with them. Everybody got real shaky and decided to send a note to Guy to let him know we weren't turning into communists. Someone wrote at the end of the note, "Better dead than red."

Harker. We had been isolated from military discipline so long that news of Colonel Guy being our camp commander was very startling. I wasn't exactly a military lover, but it made me feel sort of gung ho to know that someone was passing out orders, that we had an organization and were joined together. Colonel Guy ordered us not to make tapes for the radio after New Year's, '72. He said he would try to cover for anybody who had done anything before that date. I thought his policy was fair enough.

We had already begun to resist before we got word from him. Kushner had stopped doing the radio and stopped writing unless forced. Although he never wrote anything about the war he didn't actually believe to be true, he got tired of the North Vietnamese using him. On July 4 they had given him a pair of glasses his wife had sent to Hanoi, but they wouldn't give him the letter she had written, and he was sure there was one, so he wasn't at all happy with them. In November they tried to make him write an antiwar letter to a radical peace group in the States. He refused. Next morning at 7:00 A.M. the guards opened our door and said, "Kushner and Anton, take your beds and move to another room!" We were astounded by the bluntness of it all. Gus tried to give them a hand but a guard pushed him away. Taking them from our room was like pulling our teeth. We felt the absence for weeks. If anything, it hardened our opposition to the Vietnamese.

Davis. I caught a glimpse of Colonel Guy in the yard. He was sort of short, maybe five foot eight, thin, with a lantern jaw and brown hair neatly combed and parted. He looked clean and lean. You always think of guys in the air force as soft. Colonel Guy was more like an officer in the marines or army. A real tough nut.

McMillan. All the POWs called Colonel Guy hard-core. And he was, he really was. I liked him though. If it wasn't for him a lot more prisoners would've joined the Peace Committee. The thing that got me was his policy about not going home. Quite a few peace delegations from the States were coming to Hanoi and Colonel Guy told us not to accept probation. I said to myself, "Man, you're crazy. If these people call me and tell me I can go home—I'm going home." Colonel Guy might have been dedicated, but there are limits to any normal man's dedication.

Anton. Kushner and I sent a reply through commo that we respected his opinion but not his judgment and if offered unconditional release we would take it. Out of eighty-two prisoners in the Plantation at that time, we were the only two to tell him this. The rest ostensibly agreed with his policy but behind his back many said they'd be gone if the North Vietnamese offered to free them.

Guy sent us another message: "I remind you this is an order, not a request."

We didn't reply.

When we learned Colonel Guy was our camp commander we felt that—it's hard to say how we felt. For four years we had had to make our own decisions and both of us sort of rebelled against someone telling us what to do through commo which was passed on and distorted by fifteen different people. And to be honest, the Vietnamese had us a little hung up, because they were talking to us about a release. They told us, "Maybe you will be released." We said, no, it can't be. Yet we had a feeling that maybe it was. They played us very cleverly.

One day a guard opened our door and asked if we wanted some ice cream. We found out two weeks later that we and the Peace Committee were the only ones in camp who got it. And, of course, everybody watched our end of the camp, several prisoners did nothing but look out cracks in their doors all day long. They saw the ice cream going into our cell and, oh, wow!

We received a message saying, "I don't know what you're doing but whatever it is, stop it."

We said to ourselves, "And who the hell are you?"

Actually we weren't doing that much, although the day we were removed from Harker's room and placed in a cell by ourselves, the North Vietnamese had begun to work on us. We hadn't been in the new cell two minutes when a fat, happy little Vietnamese came by and asked if we needed more blankets or anything, just like room service. We called him Mao, Chairman Mao. He told us he'd like to learn English better and asked us to write a selection of American slang. Then he asked us to write some poetry. Just before Christmas he asked if we'd like to write a letter home. There was just one catch. If we wanted to write our families, he said, we first had to show our appreciation by writing a letter to the American people about our opposition to the war.

When we reached Hanoi we heard a lot about the antiwar movement. It seemed that it was more or less a hippie thing. Not that we disliked hippies, but we thought for that reason it wouldn't be effective in ending the war. As time passed we realized the movement was more than a small radical protest, that a large percentage of Americans were definitely part of it, though we were never really able to grasp the atmosphere of the thing, it was a period of history that remains lost to us.

I was confused by people like Senators Mansfield, Church, and even George McGovern. We heard edited versions of their remarks over the camp radio. I really respected Mansfield. If he was against the war, how could opposing it be so bad? So both of us wrote a few times. We occasionally wondered if what we were doing would ruin our careers. We never thought that we'd be court-martialed for it. Later, when we got roommates, pilots shot down in mid-'72, they told us that according to Pentagon policy any antiwar appeals that could be justified wouldn't be held against POWs.

In January the North Vietnamese gave us an article from the *New York Times*, a Christmas story written by Kushner's wife Valerie, who was active in an organization of POW wives who were against the war. After reading it Kushner wanted very badly to write his wife. The North Vietnamese said, "You write something for us and we'll let you write home."

I was touched by the article too. I wrote an appeal to Senator Mansfield, told him I supported what he was doing, and asked that he please urge Congress to increase the pressure on Nixon.

I Cannot Rejoice*
by Valerie M. Kushner

1962—We were such newlyweds we counted Christmas Day as our four-month anniversary. My husband had just begun medical school. We didn't buy a tree (saving money) until at ten that night. We made much of trimming, then admitted that we missed our big family celebrations. The sleet turned to snow. By early morning we were on our way to our parents' house.

1963—So wonderful. Our daughter born on Christmas Day. A month earlier, Jack Kennedy had died. Feeling my child stir within me that November afternoon, I feared for her.

1964—A glory brought to us by our child. From now on birthday cake became the dessert for our Christmas dinner.

1965—Our daughter at 2 still played with the boxes more than the toys. I became a full-time wife and mother. In a few months my husband would finish school, and enter his profession.

1966—We swam on Christmas Day. My husband was doing an internship at Tripler Army Hospital in Honolulu. My husband made his rounds that morning at the hospital—so many wounded men. The next month he volunteered for duty in Vietnam.

1967—Explain to a child on her fourth what missing in action means. She reminds me: "Daddy said he won't be home when I get four, but he promised to be back when I get five." I was carrying our second child.

1968—The waiting. Gratitude for sure knowledge that he was

alive, constant fear for his survival. Our son at nine months could not walk. I said to the children, "Maybe next year we will be together again."

1969—An airplane flying to Paris, 96 children and 45 wives and mothers sent by Ross Perot to plead for our men. The North Vietnamese told us to tell our children that their fathers were criminals.

1970—Beginnings of disillusionment. Public concern ineffective. Congress apathetic. The Sontay raid brought me to a low point. Some troops were being withdrawn, but my husband was not home. His agony was being used to prolong the war.

1971—I have been married for ten Christmases. This is the fifth year of our separation. The words choke me. Our Christmas child does not make any predictions for her ninth birthday. Withdrawn. Winding down. Vietnamization. Meaningless phrases. Must have an end to this war. I see no end. I cannot rejoice in the birth of the son of God. My son has no father.

This Christmas Day we celebrate the birth of a son to Mary. This Christmas Day some other mother's son will die in Vietnam. That death takes away all that was taught by Christ's birth.

We were given a number of books to read, though they weren't passed around to everyone. *War and Peace,* Shakespeare, a series of French classics. The Vietnamese didn't offer us any books on communism, but we noticed they had several in their offices and we asked to read them. It was the first time I'd read the *Communist Manifesto.* The book that influenced me the most, however, was *The United States in Vietnam,* by George McTurnam Kahin and John Wilson Lewis, two American academics. I was surprised the Vietnamese let me read the book because it was a balanced account of U.S. actions in Viet Nam until 1968 and included such things as charts showing Viet Cong atrocities in the south. Here was something we knew was not propaganda. The truth of it was overwhelming.

The Vietnamese were extremely aware of what the American press was writing about the war. They had their own library and read all the major stateside newspapers and news magazines.

One guard told us he looked at *Playboy* every month. "Very dirty," he said.

"Why do you read it if it's dirty?" we asked.

"Oh, I just have to see," he said.

Although we could get away with such conversations with the guards, we didn't dare try it with Skinny, who was our main source of information. Skinny was a lieutenant and apparently one of Hanoi's bright young men who held a top position. He spoke the most fluent English of any Vietnamese we saw (and better than a lot of Americans) and dealt with all POWs in Hanoi. He usually escorted visiting foreign dignitaries around, we saw him in a film with Jane Fonda; and his wife, a doctor who spoke four languages, was a member of the American-Vietnamese Friendship Committee.

Skinny argued the North Vietnamese line but did it in a down-to-earth manner, almost like an American intellectual. He quoted congressmen and senators who were against the war. He always had the latest *Time* in his black attaché case. He gave us a copy once and let us take it to our room. The issue had a picture of Jackie Kennedy in a see-through blouse. That caused the biggest debate on the cell-block for months. Should Jackie wear a see-through? A lot of POWs were absolutely indignant.

The spurts of activity notwithstanding, most of the time we did nothing. Nothing. We were completely and utterly bored. Had we been specifically sentenced to ten years in jail, at least then we would've known how long we had to wait. But for us the end could come tomorrow—or never. The uncertainty was agonizing.

After our release someone from my group told a reporter that Hanoi, compared to our jungle camp, was like a Holiday Inn. The statement angered pilots who were held much longer in North Viet Nam. But in a physical sense it was true, Hanoi was much easier for us, nobody starved, nobody had to work themselves to death.

Yet there was no adequate way to compare the two. Confinement in a small cell held its own special terrors. You underwent a constant fight to keep your sanity. Some of the pressures could be worked off by dealing with the guards about little things, like cigarettes. We got six cigarettes a day. (I didn't smoke but I got them too.) Sometimes it was difficult to get the guards to bring a light and the smokers really got upset about this.

The pressures of closed-in living caused a lot of spats, arguments petty in retrospect but major at the time. Kushner and I were by ourselves from November till April, '72. We got along fine at first. But I wasn't the type to give in to his arguments, not when I thought they were wrong, and he believed he was never wrong. In the jungle, arguments could be avoided by simply getting up and walking away. But in a small cell there was no place to go. So we lost the closeness we'd once had. He said things to me I could never forget. Some of it had to do with what had happened in the jungle. He thought I hadn't tried hard enough. In April, after we got four new roommates, we went two weeks with out speaking to each other.

Harker. I saw the Peace Committee for the first time one day when we were allowed outside to play basketball. Their door was open and covered by a curtain. The ball accidentally went inside on a rebound. I went to get it and we talked several minutes while they stood behind the curtain. I saw peanuts and candy and Birley's lemonade on their table.

I asked who the prisoners were in the cell further down.

Someone, I think it was Chenoweth, said, "They're just hardcore reactionary officers."

I said, "What the hell. What's reactionary?"

The PC said, "Well, they won't give in. All they think about is their pay."

I was startled to hear them making excuses for why other Americans were kept in solitary confinement and punished for no apparent reason.

Jose Anzaldua's room, which was next to the PCs, was talking to them. Jose's attitude was let's strike up an acquaintance and not worry about the political side of it. I couldn't do it. The Vietnamese had beat them, had let their own people die, and now were using them against their country. I couldn't see it. It wasn't simply a matter of being for or against the war. We were all against it.

Cheese told us that Jose's room was going to have a special Christmas ceremony with the Peace Committee and asked if we wanted to join them. We said no.

Daly. We were thinking about two things when we agreed to have Christmas with the Peace Committee. First, we saw the big preparations being made and we figured the NVA might be planning to release someone. We knew that if anybody was released it would probably be the PCs. The North Vietnamese seemed to like us too, and we didn't want to make them angry by refusing to join the PCs for Christmas. Maybe we would also be freed. And second, Jose said, "Perhaps by talking to the PCs we can get them to stop what they are doing." But when we met, the PCs did most of the talking and we did the listening.

Young. We honestly wanted the group from the south to enjoy themselves for a change. I suppose at the same time the North Vietnamese were sort of using us, for they took pictures of us playing cards and talking together. A few days before Christmas the guards began to leave our cell door open from 9:00 A.M. till 6:00 P.M. We could play basketball if we wished, but that got old fast, and we usually just sat outside in the sun reading. We were given extra candy, beer, cigarettes, a thermos jug, a goldfish bowl with twelve goldfish. The extra stuff was Cheese's idea. We weren't opposing the war because of the benefits we were getting, but a lot of POWs took it that way and the whole camp turned against us.

A room was set aside for us in the villa. We decorated it with Christmas scenes copied from old French cards. On Christmas Eve we went over and Jose's room joined us. Harker's room refused to come. We were sorry but there was nothing we could do. Jose's room, we found, was opposed to the war. But they didn't have the nerve to go out on a limb as we did.

One of the blacks said, "Look, we're getting money when we get back, more than we'll ever have at one time in our lifetimes. We don't want to jeopardize it."

That was the major thing keeping the younger enlisted men and many of the officers from speaking out. True, they feared military recriminations when they returned home. But their biggest worry was for all the back pay they were going to get.

We toasted Christmas with wine. Riate and Chenoweth and myself made talks about the war. Jose read a beautiful poem. Then Davis or McMillan began the Lord's Prayer. We tried to join in. The moment was too emotional. Everyone started to cry. We returned to our cells. On Christmas Day we ate in the villa. Vietnamese cooks brought out turkey with all the trimmings. Jose's room broke down again, this time with joy and disbelief. It pleased us to see that they were so happy.

Daly. I joined the Peace Committee on December 28. I had listened to their talks at Christmas and I was impressed. They sounded very sincere. I was tired of the hypocrisy in my room. One minute the men with me would be speaking about how the Viet Cong had helped us in certain situations in the jungle, and then the next minute they were cursing and wishing that Nixon would bomb hell out of Viet Nam.

Still, I wasn't totally convinced what the Peace Committee was doing was right. I thought perhaps if I joined I could talk to them about religion. I found it impossible to speak about religion to the group I'd lived with in the jungle. Even before I was captured I'd learned what I had to do to get along with other soldiers—joke and cuss like they did, which was something I'd never done in my life. Once I did this, though, it became difficult for me to talk about my religion because they laughed at me and reminded me of things I'd said earlier when I was just trying to be one of the gang.

The Peace Committee didn't know me. I thought I could get a fresh start with them. However, it didn't turn out that way. The first week after I joined I had a big argument with one of them about the Bible. Then I had to make an agreement that I wouldn't speak about religion any more, because it caused dissension in the room.

Davis. Daly said, "I think I'll be able to save these guys."

I asked him about his mother and sister, what would happen to them.

He said, "They'll be all right. I'm not sweating going to jail."
I think he wanted to get out of our room. Ike McMillan and Jose
teased him a lot. After he left he wouldn't look at us when we saw
him outside.

Harker. Fred Elbert, whom we'd known as John Peter Johnson
in the jungle, started making regular nightly visits to the villa
after New Year's. He told us he was writing his autobiography,
which he'd never done before. Soon we realized he was actually
going over to talk to the PCs. One day we went to take a bath and
the guard ordered him to remain in the room. We washed our
clothes and returned to the cell. Elbert and his bedding had
disappeared.

16

Ted Guy

By Christmas, 1971, I knew that the North Vietnamese had broken our commo system once again. And I knew that they knew we knew. Before midnight on Christmas Eve I was taken to the villa to the room decorated by the Peace Committee. Christmas ceremonies were traditional in Hanoi. Usually every prisoner was allowed out for a few minutes to see the Christmas tree and to receive a small bag of fruit or candy. Earlier in the day music of the season was played over the camp radio. While I was in the villa the Vietnamese photographed me as I pointed to a picture drawn by the PCs. I suddenly got the feeling that something was up. It was nothing I could put my finger on but it came from the way the camp officials watched me with interest.

I returned to my cell and talked to the colonel and the captain next door. As more prisoners arrived the tap code became obsolete; we could easier talk through the walls using our cups as telephone receivers. I told them of my premonitions. The colonel said, "No, you're imagining things. The war's almost over. You're off the hook." The following days passed uneventfully. I began to think that I was indeed imagining things.

Then at 7:30 A.M. on January 22, the guards opened my cell door. I was taken to a filthy room in the villa. Cigarette butts and globs of spit littered the floor, the smell of urine drifted out of the corners. There was a small stool in front of a table. Behind it in a chair sat the Snake, an effeminate, thin-faced Vietnamese with long hair and a two-inch long nail on the smallest finger of his left hand. He made no motion for me to sit and I remained standing at attention.

"What is your name, rank, and serial number?" he asked.

"You know that," I said.

"Name, rank, serial number?" he shouted.

I told him.

"Who's the Hawk?"

"It's me. You know my commo code name was changed from Fox to Hawk."

"What orders have you given?"

I refused to answer.

Two guards came in and forced me to my knees. They stripped me of my clothes and began to beat me with a whip made from an auto fan belt fastened to an eighteen-inch piece of bamboo. I squirmed as they beat me. They tied my elbows behind my back and then my wrists and feet. I was still able to squirm around. This time they put me face down on the floor, placed an iron bar across my neck, and a guard stood on either side of the bar.

They beat me on my buttocks and legs. They were careful not to hit me where scars might show. The lashes drew large blood blisters. The beating lasted until 4:00 P.M. on the first day. I was urinating, defecating blood, and throwing up on the floor. They stopped and made me kneel for the next eighteen hours. Two guards and an officer were left in the room with me. I was slapped or kicked awake when I dozed off.

I was beaten for the next five days, given nothing to eat or drink and not allowed to sleep. After every heavy beating a doctor was brought in to examine with a stethoscope. As he checked me over he either nodded his head yes to permit them to continue, or said no to stop them for a few hours. Interrogations came between beatings. The Vietnamese wanted to know our organization and methods of communications. They particularly wanted our plans for escape should the Plantation be bombed by U.S. planes. Although the 1972 spring offensive was three months away, they apparently believed the U.S. would resume the bombing in retaliation.

I told them stuff I was certain they already knew.

They said, "We know Major Elliott is your deputy and Sergeant so-and-so runs the enlisted men."

And I said, "Yes, that is correct." I was groggy and exhausted, but able to hold my own until the morning of January 28. They told me then that they were going to beat the other prisoners until I agreed to cooperate. I heard tables being moved around in the next room. Someone screamed and began thrashing around on the floor. A guard from my room went out carrying a whip. I heard him laugh and call out "Cau, Cau!"—Major Elliott's Vietnamese name.

I told the Snake that I wanted to see the camp commander. He came and I told him I would do anything he wanted if he stopped beating the other Americans. The noise in the next room died away. The camp commander told me I first had to write an apology. I was made to write in the initial version that I was sorry for what I'd done, that I agreed to cooperate, that I would write and make tape recordings. I was then ordered to a write a new version; in this one I was made to beg for forgiveness. In the third and final version I was forced to say that I agreed to do anything the North Vietnamese asked. Part of this letter was read over the camp radio to the other POWs.

The camp commander said, "Now you will write a letter to the antiwar groups in America." I tried to resist but he warned me that other POWs would be beaten again if I didn't. I sat down and wrote a letter to the Vietnam Veterans against the War. In the letter I used typical communist jargon. "I, Colonel Theodore W. Guy, represent the POWs in North Viet Nam and we would like to express our solidarity with the Vietnam Veterans against the War. We are wrong being in Viet Nam. We should leave the Vietnamese alone."

This version was rejected. They told me I had to write about the atrocities that had supposedly taken place, and I refused. I wrote five more unacceptable versions. Finally they handed me a letter composed by them. The camp commander said, "You write this." I copied the letter, which was later published. It was quite evident that it was written under pressure.

On January 29 I was given my first food. I was taken to the radio room that night and ordered to make a tape for the camp radio by reading from the *Daily World,* an English-language communist newspaper. After finishing the tape I was taken to a room in the villa and kept until the next night when I repeated the process. On February 2, I was told I could shave and take a bath. I was returned to my cell. Elliot was gone. He had been moved next door.

I called the next room and asked, "How's Elliott?"

Elliott himself replied, "I'm just great."

"Well, you sonofabitch, didn't they beat you?"

"No," he said. "I'm fine."

The North Vietnamese had fabricated the beating and I'd fallen for it.

When I went to take a shower I saw a guard I knew well. I liked the kid, he was always nice to me. I stripped off my clothes and turned around and said, "Here's what communism will do to you." The kid started crying. He got sick to his stomach and threw up, then turned and ran away. He disappeared for two weeks. When I saw him again he had been beaten.

I felt I had tarnished my honor somewhat. I was depressed. When I think back on it, I don't believe I could have gone any further. I'm not ashamed. The North Vietnamese wanted to know the names of my escape committees, wanted me to incriminate other people, and this I did not do. I wrote two appeals to the Vietnam Vets against the War and an "I'm sorry" letter. I'd written a few "I'm sorry" letters before, only this one they showed to some of the weaker POWs in the camp, trying to get them not to resist.

I had thought they were going to beat the other prisoners. I have to admit, though, that if they had asked me earlier to write the antiwar letters I probably would have done so without further prodding. I guess a certain portion of my consent to cooperate stemmed from personal fear—I can't deny that. But I couldn't give the names of others POWs as they wanted. That went back to my original code. It was a question of honor. There was just no way that I could have talked. We never lost commo with the rest of the camp. While I recovered the colonel next door carried on.

McMillan. They beat that man so bad it was a shame. He was covered with bruises. He lost so much weight that he looked like he'd aged fifteen years. And it was all because of the Peace Committee. The PCs told the NVA that commo came down from the most ranking officer in camp. Boom! Quite naturally they were going to go to Colonel Guy.

We later heard him on the radio. He said, "I'm . . . Colonel . . . Theodore . . . Wilson . . . Guy . . ." His voice sounded hollow and distant, like a Catholic priest's. He advised us to go along with North Vietnamese policies.

His code name had once been Hawk and then it was changed to Moses, and I said to myself when I heard his voice, "No, that can't be Moses." But it was, and we immediately knew that they had forced him to make the radio.

Young. In October, '71, King Rayford joined us. There was too much tension in the cell he was in and he wanted out. It was more or less a racial problem, plus the fact he was against the war. His room had been all white except for one other colored guy who was an Uncle Tom. From Rayford we learned about Colonel Guy and the commo system for the first time. He told us the kind of messages that were being passed around, ranging from information on promotion and pay raises to news about *Playboy*'s decision to show muffs. We were interested at the moment, we peppered Rayford with questions, but we really thought it was asinine to risk people's lives by passing such worthless information around camp. Later when Daly and Elbert joined us we learned more, but it was the same stuff. A lot of POWs blamed us for Colonel Guy's getting caught. Everything that happened they automatically blamed us. The Vietnamese knew what was going on. But I don't think we ever mentioned to Cheese that the Americans had established commo, because we weren't out to get the Americans.

Harker. After New Year's the Peace Committee was given an extra cell, which they converted into a reading room. Their doors were left open all day and some of them were usually sitting around outside in the courtyard. We asked the Vietnamese to make the PCs close their doors while we took our exercise. We simply didn't want to associate with them. Naturally the NVA refused. They wanted us to fraternize, hoping that others would join. By this time everyone thought the PCs had approached the point of no return. We heard John Young on the radio accusing a special-forces sergeant who was captured with him at Lang Vei of having executed fifteen Viet Cong prisoners during an operation in South Viet Nam. The sergeant sat in a cell at the other end of the camp.

Young. The Vietnamese gave us books on communism and socialism, and in the spring of 1972 there was a big change in my political thinking. It affected the whole room. Even though working conditions had improved since the *Communist Manifesto* was written, it was clear that it could be applied to the United States today. Sections of the *Manifesto* were difficult for us to understand, particularly the part about the surplus value of labor, but we thought it pretty well laid out the situation. That along with books by Mao Tse-tung, Ho Chi Minh, Le Duan, Truong Chinh, Marx, and Engels influenced our thinking.

The Vietnamese gave us the books reluctantly. I don't think they wanted to confuse us. At the same time, they knew we would probably get in trouble when we returned to the States for our antiwar views, and I don't think they wanted to add an additional burden to our backs in having to defend our new-found political beliefs. They refused to answer our questions in the beginning, but as we got deeper into our studies they said they would try to help us. As a matter of practice, though, we usually wound up answering questions we had ourselves. They seemed enormous at the time. We sat in the villa for hours discussing them. One of our biggest questions was why hadn't the socialist movement taken hold in the United States. Certainly the the time had been ripe for a socialist revolution during the depression; why hadn't the socialists and communists grasped the opportunity? We came to the conclusion that the socialist elements had had poor leadership, a deficiency that still exists today.

I considered myself a Marxist. I tried to act the way I believed a socialist should act. I think the majority of us felt this way, although some weren't ready to accept it because of a conflict between their religious beliefs and communism. I'm speaking of Daly, who was a Jehovah's Witness, and Mike Branch, who was a Catholic, and to some extent Larry Kavanaugh, also a Catholic.

There was something else that spring. We saw a film on the Winter Soldier investigation, an inquiry sponsored by peace groups and conducted in Detroit and Canada. Soldiers who had served in Viet Nam gave public testimony. I cried but at the same time I cheered because they had the nerve to tell the American people what was actually being done in Viet Nam in their name. All of us in the room except Branch, who was a truck driver, had participated in the things the Winter Soldiers described—burning villages, spraying areas with machine-gun fire, killing kids. Chenoweth, who was a crew chief on a helicopter, talked about it too, how he used to throw a red smoke out and watch the jets come in on it. He was ashamed. We all were.

Before hearing about the Winter Soldiers we had felt isolated. We knew other POWs were protesting the war, but we didn't know whether they were sincere or were just looking for the easy way out. It boosted our morale to know that we weren't alone any more. We added more feeling to our appeals. Earlier we had been restrained, wondering if people would believe us or whether they would think we'd been forced to protest by the North Vietnamese. Now we began to write without powdering it up.

It was during this time that I made a fifteen-minute tape that was broadcast to the camp. I talked about the things I'd seen and done when I was with the special forces in Da Nang. I described the time when my Nung security guards caught two Vietnamese fishermen on the Da Nang beach. They were brought to our headquarters and I checked their I.D. cards, which seemed to be in order. I asked an American major if the fishermen should be released. He said to let the Vietnamese take care of it. That afternoon my translator told me the guards were beating the fishermen. I went to investigate and found them locked in a conex container, an airless six-by-six-foot metal box. They were in bad shape. I returned their I.D.s and told them to leave fast.

I talked about things I'd done that personally shamed me. Soldiers I met when I reached Da Nang occasionally played a "game" by driving in a jeep by Vietnamese women on the road-side and leaning out to snatch their purses, then ransacking them for souvenirs and tossing them away farther down the road. I did this three or four times until I saw the destruction we'd caused around Da Nang. I also talked about incidents that had been told to me by others, such as the special-forces soldier who recounted how he had cut off the hand of a Vietnamese girl, a VC suspect, to get the gold bracelet she was wearing. I had no reason to believe he was lying, for I had seen the VC ears wrapped in tin foil and waxed paper that some Americans carried.

And I spoke about the special-forces sergeant who told me he had killed fifteen VC prisoners, one by one, as they knelt with hands tied behind their backs. He said it had occurred when he was on an operation deep in the jungle and his patrol couldn't take prisoners along. I don't know whether it was true or not—I have no proof—and he later denied the story. When I prepared my statement for broadcast I left his name out.

The North Vietnamese looked it over and asked why I didn't name him.

I said, "I don't want to get him in trouble."

They said, "But we already know who it is."

I don't know how they knew.

I did what I did to wake people up as to what was actually going on Viet Nam, not to hurt Brandy. I didn't want to hurt him, I really didn't. He was a nice guy, although I disagreed with his views on a lot of things. I wanted him to have the courage to admit what he'd done, maybe to feel ashamed, but more importantly, to bring it out so it wouldn't happen again. I realized I'd made a mistake when I heard the tape played over the radio. The other POWs, I knew, would feel I was ratting on Brandy to get him in trouble. Truthfully, the people in my room didn't agree with what I'd done either. It reflected on everyone in the room and turned the other POWs in the camp, if they weren't already, completely against us.

Daly. I disliked John Young from the first minute I joined the Peace Committee. He seemed to force himself to believe things. He was the type who was ready to give his life for the communist cause, totally convinced that it was right, yet didn't know what it was all about. In a way he was like the professional military officers who were ready to die for South Viet Nam without understanding anything about the country beyond a few weak clichés.

Harker. The North Vietnamese apparently anticipated the bombing resumption because we'd had air-raid drills the previous several Sunday mornings. Our camp was not far from Hanoi's main railhead to the south and we'd seen them moving tanks and supplies for six months. We were not aware, of course, that preparations were being made for the 1972 spring offensive, in which the North Vietnamese tried, for the first time in the war, to overrun South Viet Nam by launching a massive, conventional tank-and-artillery attack. President Nixon responded by bombing and blockading North Viet Nam's harbors.

On April 16, 1972, when we heard the sirens we assumed it was another air-raid practice. Then we heard the smooth "whoof! whoof!" sounds of SAM missiles being launched from pads. And the explosions of bombs. The doors and windows of our cell began to rattle as if blown by invisible gusts of wind. "Wa-whoom . . . Wa-whoom . . . Wa-whoom." Cheese came running to our room. He was in battle dress and his eyes were barely visible under his too large helmet. He ordered us to sit on one bed;

perhaps they thought it was another Son Tay raid. The flak guns of Hanoi were going off in a staccato roar. I felt like I was back in the war.

McMillan. We were told through commo by Colonel Guy that all POW camps in Hanoi had been pinpointed by the U.S. Air Force. I'd already seen examples of "pinpoint" bombing. We had an old saying, that a B-52 was like a man's organ: it would strike anywhere.

Anton. "The camp is bound to be hit," I kept saying to myself. I couldn't get it out of my mind. "We're going to be killed by our own planes."

Some of my roommates were ridiculously brave about it. When the siren was sounded they ran to the door and looked out, screaming, "I saw one! I saw one!" Another pilot and I were huddled under our beds shaking. I couldn't stop until long after the planes were gone. The Vietnamese had given us sawhorses to elevate our plank beds; the beds wouldn't have stopped a bomb, of course, but they may have saved us from falling plaster.

As a gunship pilot I was always scared but I had liked what I was doing. The challenge of flying in combat gave me a rationale for controlling my fear. But I felt the bombing of North Viet Nam was useless, that I was going to be killed for nothing. The Vietnamese always said they fought so long with so little because they had a cause. I believed that. But I was without one and I completely lost the ability to control my terror. I didn't care what the other pilots in my room thought about me. I thought some of them were silly not to have any concern at all. We had some who would calmly lie on their beds and say "Wow! That was close" as the bombs fell around us.

In the early days of the bombing I thought seriously about joining the Peace Committee. I figured they would have a bomb shelter in their room. I debated with myself the price I'd have to pay to get to that shelter. I didn't agree with what the PCs were doing. I felt that they were trying to get extra privileges. I had read some of the things they wrote and it seemed to me they were confused more than anything else. I wasn't really anxious to join their activities, and I finally gave up the idea. Had I mentioned it to the North Vietnamese, I'm sure they would have moved me in with them in a minute.

Daly. The bombing was horrible. It got to everybody in the room. We were doing what we could to end the war. Yet everybody agreed that writing antiwar appeals wasn't doing much good. We had to help the Vietnamese, to get out and work in a hospital or something. While the air raid on April 16 was still going on, Riate sat down and wrote a letter to the North Vietnamese. It was standard procedure to let others in the room read what you wrote and to give them the choice of signing it. Someone asked to read Riate's statement after he finished, and said, "Oh. Can I sign?"

I thought I understood everyone in the room. But when the letter reached me for my signature I was shocked. Everybody else had signed. I didn't feel I had much of a choice, particularly since I'd said that I wanted to do what I could to help the Vietnamese; so I signed too. The letter was a request to join the North Vietnamese Army.

Young. Two months earlier the North Vietnamese had allowed us to visit Hanoi under escort. We were taken on a tour of the National Historical Museum and to a Vietnamese circus. Other POWs were taken on similar tours, although I think we were the only ones who got to see the circus. It was hilarious, we really enjoyed ourselves. And as the bombs fell we could tell that they were hitting near the circus and the Hanoi Technical College, in populated areas. We watched many planes go down. It really hurt me to see Americans dying. Yet at the same time I knew the plane would no longer kill Vietnamese; and I was happy.

The day after the bombing started Cheese told us another POW wanted to speak to us about joining our room. We went over to the Big House where he was waiting. Cheese brought us a beer and we all sat down. We said, "Okay, you wanted to talk to us. Talk."

He said, "I'd like to come down and live with you. I'm opposed to the war and I don't like living in the room I'm in."

We said, "It's not up to us. You'll have to ask the camp authorities."

He joined us several days later, followed by three more prisoners. Of the four new men, we believed only one to be sincere in his beliefs. We distrusted the motives of the others, thought they were interested in joining us only in order to get extra privileges. From the beginning the four got the impression that the eight of us planned to remain in North Viet Nam after the war was over.

In fact we had thought quite a bit about staying on in Hanoi to continue our studies. None of us wanted to return to a society that bred such hate and dissension. And I must admit a certain fear of what faced us in the States had begun to accumulate. We also talked about the possibility of going to Sweden or someplace else. We read up on the twenty-one Americans who chose to remain in China after the Korean War and found that it was a bad experience. All of them eventually returned home. We figured everyone would say we'd been brainwashed too. This we discussed at length. Were we brainwashed? We didn't think so because we did everything of our own free will—no one forced us.

Harker. We overheard one of the PCs telling Cheese, "Those poor people in the circus are being bombed now, and I just wish there was something I could do to stop the U.S. imperialists." Things were quickly coming to a head between us. Even Gus, our flower child, was against them. The morning after the bombing started Cheese moved Davis, McMillan, Anzaldua, Long, and Lewis into our room, making eight of us. We talked about it and decided not to go outside for any reason while the PCs' doors were open.

Several days later the North Vietnamese passed down the word that every cell had to be whitewashed. The walls were of dull stucco and had become dingy with all the sweeping. We mixed the whitewash outside and sent Jose Anzaldua and two others across the courtyard to get some water. They saw the PCs lounging around outside, so they turned and came back to our cell. The guard ordered them to get the water. They refused. He locked our door and left.

We knew they would be coming. We wondered what was to happen to us.

The guards threw open the door and took Jose Anzaldua to the villa. They beat him in the kidneys and places that would never show and put him in solitary confinement for a week. That day we washed the camp dishes as was required of us. But when we finished we decided that we had to do something, we couldn't just let Jose take the blame for our decision. So the following day we refused to do the dishes while the PCs were outside.

Cheese came to the cell and said, "Hat, put your long shirt on."

The rest of the room said, "No, we're all guilty and we'll all go."

Cheese said, "No, only Hat."

I was taken to the villa. The Snake was waiting.

He said, "Hat, get on your knees and put your hands over your head."

I got on the tile floor.

He said, "Why did you refuse to do the dishes?"

"Because we don't want to associate with the Peace Committee," I answered.

He got excited and told me I had broken the camp rules and must apologize.

"There's nothing to apologize for," I said. "I don't want to go against the camp rules but if it means going out with those people, then yes."

Cheese slapped me across the face three times with his bony hand. I could feel my face swelling. "You are a criminal of war," he said. "You must condemn Nixon for killing innocent people." He put paper and pen in front of me. I'd seen the same hard-set faces many times before, and I realized it was futile to resist. I wrote several versions of the appeal, none of which they were satisfied with, but they seemed to think that I was trying, so they sent me back to the cell to complete it.

Everyone was quiet when I walked in. My cold food was waiting. They saw my swollen face. Explanations weren't necessary. We talked about what we should do. We decided to continue to wash the dishes because under camp rules that was a POW responsibility. But we would refuse to take our daily thirty minutes of exercise if it was offered. The PCs knew what was going on and they tried to humiliate us. The other cells neatly stacked their dishes outside and put their spoons together. The PCs left theirs scattered over the courtyard, and they watched us as we collected them like servants.

Our policy became one of ignoring them. The bombing distracted our attention and we had little chance for further confrontations. We were not allowed outside much for exercise anyway because the guards, who were tense and edgy, often overslept. During air raids we had to return immediately to our cells, even if we happened to be lathered up for a bath. Our bread ration was cut and we were given noodles as a substitute. The Vietnamese said the air force had bombed the bread factory.

We lapsed into a kind of nervous boredom. Before the bombing we had seen movies fairly regularly, at first propaganda films, then an assortment of Russian-made movies which were very entertaining. But those stopped and we had only the radio. The Pentagon Papers were read to us. We could see that brilliant men like Bundy and McNamara and Rostow had misjudged so much. We liked the part of the Papers that dealt with Lansdale and his bunch. It was like listening to a soap opera.

Anton. Our small cells were sweatbox hot, everyone kept a heat rash in summer. We sometimes lay our beds on the floor and our arms outside the mosquito netting just to get the coolness of the cement. The guards' bathhouse was behind us and it was a breeding ground for millions of mosquitoes. There were other problems too. With the better diet our long-forgotten interest in sex revived.

We joked about masturbation, about so and so getting under his blanket at noon every day or someone taking an extra long time in the shower room. The Vietnamese opened the shower-room door and caught a couple of people and tried to embarrass them. And we caught a couple of guards doing the same thing. The Vietnamese had a rigid attitude about sex. They told us that in the pilots' camps, "All of them very bad. Masturbation and homosexuals." I imagine they told the pilots the same thing about us. I certainly never saw any evidence of homosexuality. It was difficult for it to happen because the cells usually contained more than two guys. Maybe one or two wanted to do something, but where would they do it? The others weren't about to go along. Most of us learned after we got to Hanoi that one homosexual approach had been made and rebuffed in our group while we were in the jungle.

Daly. Before the North Vietnamese moved the four new men into our room they asked us how we were getting along as a group. We told them we had unity. They said, "Are you sure? Unity is when you stick together and nobody can divide you." It was just a matter of days before we began to have trouble. One of the new men was intelligent and well read, and there was almost a split between the guys who listened to him and guys who followed Chenoweth. Another of the new men was the nervous sort who had been in fights with his former cell mates because he continually walked around the room all day.

Young. It was a schism between old and new. We knew they weren't really sincere. They still called the Vietnamese gooks, whereas we didn't, and there were many little things like this that irritated us. The top blew off one day when Riate was in the shower room washing his clothes. One of the new guys was taking a bucket shower and he splashed water on Riate. Riate asked him to stop. He did it again. Riate quietly left and hung his clothes on the line and waited for the new guy to finish. When he stepped outside he nailed him.

We gathered round them. They were wrestling on the ground, with Riate on top. I tried to break it up. I respected Riate but there was, I must say, a little tension between us. He wasn't my favorite guy. I was really trying to break up the fight, though, I wasn't on anybody's side; but when I started pulling Riate off, Larry Kavanaugh jumped on me. Kavanaugh identified with Riate because both were from similar backgrounds, and Riate had the dominant personality. I punched Kavanaugh three times, gave him a bloody nose. I felt bad about it and apologized. He was angry but later on he understood, I think, what I was trying to do.

Daly. Riate screamed the fight was because of racism, although I think the new guy was just playing around. He was an easygoing person for such a big fellow. Kavanaugh joined in with Riate and they began hollering that they hated all white people. They considered themselves to be brown-skinned minorities. Riate even spoke against the Vietnamese, accused them of trying to brainwash him. He later apologized and said he didn't mean it.

I was surprised by Riate's actions but not so much by Larry Kavanaugh's. His views and all, you know, were sometimes a little weird. And another thing, he was often hard to get along with. Everyone in the Peace Committee knew it. We kept our room spic and span but Kavanaugh went overboard with it. No matter how long it took me to clean the room, Larry would come right behind me and do it again. This annoyed me a lot. When Kavanaugh talked about returning to the States, he imagined something that wasn't here when he left—a paradise. He talked about how he would be happy the rest of his life with his wife and his little girl, how they would move someplace off by themselves and not bother with anybody else. He talked about it all the time.

Harker. In October, U.S. planes accidentally hit the French delegation building and the bombing stopped the next day. Four nights later we heard trucks pulling into the compound, leaving, then returning after several hours. Word was passed through commo that small groups of POWs were being taken to visit various spots in Hanoi. Colonel Guy said we could go if asked but told us not to write anything for the Vietnamese on our return. They took my cell out one Sunday night. We were given black suits, ties, and boots to wear. The guards were in civvies and carried their weapons inconspicuously in small satchels. The end of the war must be near, we knew, if they were allowing us out without blindfolds.

We were trucked to the door of the war museum. We got out

and went directly inside and sat down at this tremendous wood table, sat in chairs, not benches, and were served tea. We thought we were really living. The museum was full of displays of what the Vietnamese called war crimes. There was a blown-up picture of an American patrol with a line of decapitated heads in front of them. I wondered if the picture was trick photography. I just couldn't believe Americans were collecting heads. A POW in my group whispered that he recognized one of the Americans in the picture.

We were shown a short American-made movie on the battlefield of the future. We heard Gen. William Westmoreland saying, "In the war of the future we will seek out the enemy and destroy him instantaneously." The cool voice of the narrator told about the coming electronic battlefield which would have enemy-spotting sensors in the form of little bushes, twigs, and human feces. It gave me the shivers.

On the way back to the Plantation we passed the Lake of the Redeemed Sword and saw other landmarks. Hanoi was a lovely and quiet city but crowded with refugees. It was about 11:00 P.M. and we could see people with little kerosene lamps unrolling bamboo mats on the sidewalk where they slept at night.

Girls on bikes rode gracefully down the street. The guards pointed at them and said, "*Dep,* huh? *Dep.*"

We said, "Yes, okay." They certainly looked all right to us.

Later I made another trip to the Bach Mai hospital and a nearby housing complex. Both had been bombed.

When I returned the camp commander asked me to write.

I said, "No, I think it was an accident."

He said, "Did you see any military positions?"

I had to admit I hadn't, but I still refused to write. It was odd how their attitude had changed. They were asking us to write and when we said no they didn't push us. A ping-pong table was put in a convenient spot in the camp, and we began to have ping-pong and chess playoffs between different cells.

Everything was becoming easier for us. The Vietnamese called our room to the villa and asked for a show of hands of those who supported Nixon and those who supported McGovern. Everyone voted for Nixon. Actually we thought McGovern had a good chance and some were pulling for him, but we weren't going to give the North Vietnamese the pleasure of knowing that.

Nine of us were walking to the bathhouse one day in two files and we passed a translator without bowing. He halted us, made us do a left face and stand at attention, and asked, "Why didn't you salute me? Very arrogant. Very arrogant. You must salute or I'll have you punished." But whenever he saw us coming again, he avoided us.

Davis. Their propaganda got to us at times. They played up the demonstrations back in the States. They showed us polls concerning McGovern and the antiwar sentiment. We said, "Damn, if McGovern is that popular maybe we do need to get out of Viet Nam." After a while you don't really take the war into consideration, whether it is right or wrong. You just want to get home.

Harker. In late October we learned that Henry Kissinger was meeting with Le Duc Tho. We were once more put on the roller coaster that had sapped our emotional energies so many times before. We heard that a cease-fire was about to be signed—and then that the talks had been broken off.

A week before Christmas the bombing started again. This time it was B-52s. We heard the SAMs whooshing off and saw a flash of orange as they exploded. The ground rumbled, our cells shook, the doors went "whump whump whump." I had confidence in dear old Uncle Sam and aerial reconnaissance. Every day a high flying SR-71 came down the middle of North Viet Nam and broke the sound barrier over Hanoi. Or an unmanned drone suddenly materialized at treetop level under the radar screen. We could hear the whirr of the drone and then the startled booming of the flak guns. Still, I was very happy to see the picks and shovels the Vietnamese brought us on December 20. We dug a five-by-fifteen-foot bomb shelter in our cell and slept in it at night. We finished the bomb shelter in one day through thick cement, and would have dug deep enough to strike oil if they had let us.

17

David Harker

A temporary cease-fire was announced but we had one bombing raid on Christmas Eve. There was no Christmas tree in the villa. The Vietnamese brought us a small package of candy and fruit and a cup of coffee. On Christmas morning we were given a sweet roll and later a turkey meal. We were allowed out to watch a ping-pong match between two POWs who had made it through the elimination playoffs. Two days after Christmas we were told to get our gear together. Our spirits hit rock bottom. We thought we were being moved to China.

The trucks arrived and all one hundred eight prisoners were herded aboard. We backed up, turned around, traveled two blocks north, four east, and in ten minutes we were there. We got out. It was a big prison. The walls were much higher than at the Plantation Gardens and broken glass was embedded in the cement. We passed through a gateway which had racks of parked bicycles to the side. The prison was massive and divided into various cell blocks, but as we walked through it we heard no sounds and saw no one. It could have been deserted for all we could tell.

We were put into a section of the Hilton that American pilots almost a decade before had named Little Vegas. The walls had been knocked out to make larger cells. There were eighteen of us in my cell, a mixture of enlisted men and officers. The wooden plank beds were positioned by twos eighteen inches apart and mounted on concrete pedestals. There was an open cement hole at one end which served as our latrine, and the cell next to us had a bucket bathhouse that we could use at any time. Vietnamese POWs had once occupied our cells, perhaps twenty years before during the First Indochina War, and they had left their names scratched on the walls, unknown and forgotten Huynhs and Nguyens.

The ventilation was much better at the Hilton, at least in our cell; windows were open and we could see the sky and didn't feel so closed in. That night the B-52s came over. We watched as one went down in flames. There were no parachutes.

I awoke one night in late January and went to the latrine. The guards outside were listening to their transistors. The girlish singsong voice of the announcer echoed in the courtyard and I thought I heard the words *"Het chien tranh."*

I woke up Jose Anzaldua and told him to listen. He strained for a few minutes to make out the words and said, "The peace agreements are to be signed January 27."

We heard the guards yelling to each other, *"Het! Het! Het!"* We passed the word along through commo. If we had heard the news the previous October when Kissinger was meeting with Le Duc Tho, I'm sure we would have shouted for joy. But our hopes had been shattered so many times that we were silent, each of us thinking it couldn't be true.

Anton. Around noon we were called out for an announcement. We were just sitting down to eat and we were a little irritated that they chose that moment to tell us. We knew what they were going to say anyway. Everyone assembled in the courtyard. Colonel Guy was there; it was the first time we'd seen him legally though we'd caught glimpses of him from afar. He looked thin but in pretty good shape. The North Vietnamese camp commander said because of his "lenient policy" he had decided to tell us a day earlier than was actually required that the peace agreements had been signed. There was no cheering. We wanted to ask questions but he refused to answer them.

I was the first one back in my cell and I shooed away the pigeons that were drawn to our meal while we were outside. I told some of the men when they returned that the pigeons had been in their food and they got upset.

Harker. So it was really over. I thought about the jungle, the men who wouldn't be going home, the twelve of us who had survived. So many things had happened, so much we wanted to forget. We knew each other better than our wives would ever know us. We were beyond the simple emotions of love or hate, forever joined by the most intimate exposures of our deepest selves, made brothers by that drive to survive when all seems lost. As I stood thinking about how very few men have ever known each other this way, Ike McMillan slipped up behind me and whispered, "Harker, you can have my one twelfth of the sunshine now."

Daly. While we were at the Hilton waiting to go home, everyone was allowed outside at the same time to exercise and certain officers began to try to talk to members of the Peace Committee. Colonel Guy told King Rayford that if he cooperated Guy would keep him out of trouble when we got back.

Rayford said, "I'll tell the truth when I get back."

According to Rayford, Colonel Guy replied, "I didn't ask you that. I asked if you would cooperate."

Rayford and one of the four new men in the Peace Committee had an argument in front of Colonel Guy during this time. That's how Guy found out that we'd volunteered to join the North Vietnamese Army. The new man claimed to have seen the letter, which was a lie. He learned about it from me the night of Riate's fight outside the bathhouse. Riate was screaming against the Vietnamese and I asked him how he could say those things after he had written the letter requesting to join their army. A lot of people got angry with me when I mentioned the letter. We later denied it had been written because there was no proof, just the hearsay evidence of the new man.

There was also a camp rumor that we had asked for Vietnamese citizenship. That was wrong. We put in for political asylum, not in Viet Nam, but in Sweden. A representative from the Swedish embassy in Hanoi came to the camp and told us the Swedish government couldn't accept us. The representative said that if our request had come before the peace agreements were signed, the situation might have been different. But under the circumstances, he said, people might suspect Sweden of helping North Viet Nam keep certain prisoners of war from returning home.

We applied for political asylum for one reason. We knew we would have to confront the other prisoners in the camp at a court-martial if we went back. That didn't bother us; their evidence would be entirely hearsay. But we had had trouble within the Peace Committee itself, and if they could get one of the men who lived with us—just one—to testify against us, then that was it. Everyone's argument was this: "Why go back? In prison for five years to return to prison again. That's stupid."

We argued with the camp authorities for weeks. They brought many Vietnamese officials to convince us that nothing could happen to us. Even Skinny, who was at the release ceremony, spent a lot of time talking to us. The North Vietnamese said, "You are at the first step in becoming revolutionaries. If you are interested in helping the American people, you must return to your country. You cannot learn revolution from another country about your own country because every country is different. If you do not return home now you may never be able to go back. This is your best chance."

Then the North Vietnamese began to tell us all the problems the Nixon administration faced. "The Nixon administration cannot afford to prosecute a single prisoner," they said. "We guarantee you."

We argued that they could not guarantee us because they couldn't predict what the Pentagon might do. We said, "Who is to say that the U.S. will do what it says it will do? If the government always abided by agreements it pledged to honor, such as the nineteen fifty-four Geneva accords, we would have never been here in the first place."

Finally the North Vietnamese told us—and I wasn't suppose to

repeat this—there was only one way we could remain in North
Viet Nam, and that was by taking individual acts after we went
through the release ceremony. They said that if we refused then
to get on the plane, the U.S. could not use this for propaganda
to say Hanoi had broken the peace agreements. They told us,
"There will be foreign newsmen from all over the world at the
airport. The U.S. would look very foolish to try to force you to
return." We thought for a while this was what we would do. But
the North Vietnamese added, "We know you will make the right
decision and not miss your great opportunity." That meant, we
knew, they hoped we would choose to return home. They were
very worried that our actions might affect the agreements they
had signed.

At any rate, I don't think I could have lived the rest of my life
in North Viet Nam. Their customs and attitudes were too different from what I was used to. And besides, we knew the war was
not over. "This is not the end," the North Vietnamese told us.
"This is just a step."

Harker. We were released in staggered groups. From February
to March 27, when my group was freed, seemed like a long time,
another five years. We were given current reading material for
the first time, articles from the *Stars and Stripes, Sports Illustrated,*
and a few books including George Orwell's *1984.* A song-and-
dance emsemble was brought to camp for an outdoor perform-
ance. The group's theme was war, but the women were lovely and
so it was a festive occasion. Our favorite number was the Highway
9 song, a sad ballad about unending war along the forlorn stretch
of road that cuts through Laos into South Viet Nam. We ap-
plauded for an encore.

The North Vietnamese measured us for a set of freedom
clothes. We tried on dark pants and shirts and gray windbreakers.
The clothes were then put back into a small travel bag which also
contained some toothpaste and soap. We needed the soap and
asked if we could take it to our cells but we were told no, we
would get it the day we were released.

Our departure was delayed for five days. The camp commander told us the U.S. had broken the agreements. Then we were told that everything was set for the next day. We thought they would come for us by 9:00 A.M. but we sweated out the whole morning and nothing happened. Around noon we heard boot steps on the concrete outside. We thought it had to be the camp commander because he had begun to dress nicely in a proper uniform instead of wearing his usual plastic sandals around camp. The door opened and in walked a delegation of Canadians from the International Control Commission. A Canadian sergeant started passing out Winston cigarettes but the NVA later made us give them back. The sergeant said, "You guys take it easy. You'll be out of here in a few minutes."

Young. Our group was not the same after Riate's fight until we got to the Hilton. After the peace agreements were signed and the war was over, the four new men wanted to get out of our room and break off relations with us, just as we'd expected. When they left the eight of us came back together again. It's difficult to say exactly when we decided to return to the States. The North Vietnamese said the decision was up to us. One of the translators, who said he was speaking only for himself, urged us to remain in Hanoi; so did many of the guards. They believed the U.S. would not respect our rights and beliefs and would claim we had aided the enemy.

We talked about it and decided that many Americans would say we had been brainwashed if we didn't return. They would say that we had been after the extra privileges, that we didn't have the courage to face up to it. They would say we didn't really believe in what we were doing. We decided we were just not going to let that happen because we did believe.

Colonel Guy came to our section shortly before we left. This was the first time we'd actually had a conversation with him. We weren't military, we were antimilitary in our attitude, but we had agreed among ourselves to show him respect. We saluted and addressed him as sir. He read to us from a piece of paper: "On the day we depart you will wear the zipper of your jacket half way up. You will carry your handbag in your left hand. You will have your gig line straight. You will not receive any packages once you leave the camp, no flowers, or anything else. If the Vietnamese try to take pictures, you will turn your back and try to cause a disturbance."

We listened. We didn't agree or disagree. As it turned out, there were no incidents at the release ceremony. Our impression was that he wasn't much of a leader. An officer who really believed in what he was doing and believed that we were wrong would have pointed these things out to us. "You will be prosecuted when you come back because I'm going to bring charges against you." He never mentioned it, not one thing.

Nobody did really except for what Brandy said to me and he didn't say a lot. We knew, of course, that some prisoners had made threats against our lives. Brandy just said, "I'm going to see what I can do to get you punished." He said it matter-of-factly, very civilly.

I said, "You know you did it."

He said, "You had no right to say anything like that. You jeopardized my life."

Guy. The PCs returned in my group. I haven't figured this out, why the North Vietnamese sent them home with me. I told them before we left how we would wear our uniforms, that we would go out as a military group, and they would do exactly what I told them to do. I said we'd march like a military outfit, we'd get on the airplane like a military outfit, and when we got off we would salute the flag. Nothing would be said about what went on in the camps until we were debriefed by our own intelligence officials. They didn't argue. They all said, "Yes, sir."

Why? Because there were about a hundred men behind me who were ready to kill them if I told them to. I'm not being overly dramatic. The PCs were kept alive because I wouldn't let the others kill them, and I'll tell you that. Some wanted to kill them for a long time. And there were ways we could have gotten to them.

Daly. Before we left the Vietnamese asked if we had any special requests. We told them we'd like to have a lot of Vietnamese food and to go to the theater to see an army play we'd seen once before. They said okay, and brought us different Vietnamese dishes our last four days. We had a good-by party. We had reached the point where everyone felt—at least everyone said they did and I did too—everyone felt like the Vietnamese were brothers and sisters to us. It's hard to explain. Jane Fonda once described her feelings when she met the Vietnamese and it was the same with us. We cried at the party, we couldn't help it. They told us not to show our emotions when we were released because it might be held against us.

Anton. The Canadian and Indian delegations from the International Control Commission came to check our cells about 11:00 A.M. Everybody climbed up and hung on the bars to look at them as they walked past. The Vietnamese got pretty uptight because they couldn't do anything about it. The team members opened my cell and looked around. We stood at attention. Then they left and the Vietnamese took us out to a big courtyard, in front of the cells where the pilots had been kept, and lined us up on a big plastic sheet. They gave us the small bag with our new clothes, two packs of cigarettes, soap, and toothpaste.

They watched us as we changed into our new clothes. They were worried that we might try to smuggle out notes and stuff. Why I don't know, since the names of all POWs held already had been released. Then the guards marched us outside to the buses. Several hundred Vietnamese civilians were gathered to see us off. Some of them looked angry but most waved to us and smiled. We made about a forty-five-minute drive through the city to the airport. I was surprised there was no damage right outside the Hilton gates because the bombing had sounded like it was almost hitting our walls. For the first half hour we saw little destruction. But within fifteen minutes of the airport there was nothing but rubble. The big train station and all the buildings around it were bombed and burned out. I'm sure some civilian areas had been hit by accident. But there were no signs that the air force had purposely carpet-bombed nonmilitary targets. There was no destruction within five minutes of the airport, and I was happy to see our gateway to freedom hadn't been hit.

We pulled up at the airport and saw a Western girl with blonde hair. She was a reporter, from UPI I think. She wasn't really good-looking but she wore a very sexy miniskirt, the first we'd ever seen. We knew then that everything was going to be okay.

We went inside the Hanoi terminal, a small dinky room, and the Vietnamese gave us a bottle of *Bier Hanoi* and a pork submarine-type sandwich made with a French loaf. We waited and nothing happened and we began to worry again. Then we heard the airplane. A C-141 came down to about two hundred feet and made a run down the middle of the runway, turned in a tight circle and landed. A second was right behind him, and a third circled overhead.

We waited thirty minutes while the U.S. military people debarked and got set up. We were getting nervous again. We asked the Vietnamese what the holdup was. They said, "There's some discussion about the list. Maybe you'll have to go back to camp." As they told us that, the driver pulled up five feet and we were ordered off the bus. It was their last attempt to needle us.

Harker. The big bird was sitting there, wings swept back, low to the ground. Our hearts caught in our throats. It seemed so unreal. We were sleepwalking.

I could feel the change in the men around me. Discipline was returning. We're all conscious now that we're military men and we try to act like American soldiers. We get in line in the order our names are to be called. My name is announced and I walk up and give a salute for the first time in five years. A one-star U.S. general receives me, he's a blur before my eyes. I shake his hand and he says, "Glad to have you back."

I say, "Glad to be back, sir."

I walk to the plane. Two nurses are waiting, smiling. They hug me. The smells almost knock me out. Perfume. America.

Davis. There were *Penthouse* magazines on the plane. Wow! Nurses were on board and everyone was pumping them with questions. We sat there drinking orange juice and waiting to take off. Everybody fell quiet until the wheels lifted up and then people went wild. I looked out the window and saw the land it had taken me months to cross disappearing so incredibly fast. The plane's navigator, who was from Alabama, discovered I was from Eufaula and he invited me to the flight deck. I sat in a daze looking out at the sun shimmering off the warm blue sea as we headed for Clark Air Force Base in the Philippines.

Harker. When we landed at Clark the military reception team told us the flag was to the left and we could salute if we wanted to. The ranking officer in our group had prepared a little speech. We got off as our names were called. It seemed unreal to think people would be there to welcome us back. But I could hear the cheering and clapping after each man's name was called and it sent chills up and down my spine. It was a renewing of the old patriotism, the American spirit. I walked down the ramp and I really felt proud to salute the flag again. The American people were the greatest in the world.

Davis. I thought when we reached the Philippines that we would be scooted very hush-hush-like to the hospital and then be shipped back to the States. We knew how unpopular the war was at home and we thought the only people we would see would be military personnel. It really changed things when we found civilians waiting to greet us in the Philippines and in the States. I didn't consider myself or any of the POWs as heroes, although some had performed extraordinary acts of courage. We were just men doing a job who had been trapped by circumstance. But we really needed the reception we got. For five years we had felt so worthless, so insignificant. And as people greeted us with POW bracelets and cheers it really made us feel good, as if we had done a service for our country after all.

Anton. Each of us was assigned a special escort, a military sponsor to help us through the re-entry process. My sponsor met me when I stepped off the plane and handed me an envelope. It contained a letter from my parents and some recent family pictures. "I'm happy to tell you," he said, "that nothing drastic has changed with your family since you've been gone." He gave me my back-pay vouchers and told me I had sixty-two thousand dollars waiting for me.

Although we seldom discussed money in the jungle, it became a big morale factor in North Viet Nam when we learned through commo about pay raises and promotions. Some prisoners refused to talk about it. Kushner would say, "I don't give a damn about my back pay."

Harker didn't talk about it either. But the others would say, "You'll care when you get home." The debate in North Viet Nam was mainly about whether we would get extra money above and beyond our regular pay. It turned out we got a five dollar a day bonus for "inhumane treatment" and didn't have to pay income taxes on the total amount.

The whole time I was captured I thought something terrible might have happened at home, that my parents had been killed in a plane crash or an auto accident. I was very relieved to find everybody was okay and that my brother was married and had a little boy.

I made a phone call home and the first thing my mother said was, "Where did you get that southern accent?"

"It's a long story," I told her.

My Dad got on the line and he said, "You've heard only Hanoi's side. You've got to see our side now." The air force had passed on to him some of the things I'd signed while I was a prisoner.

Kushner and I were put in a hospital room together. I found a stack of old *Time*s and *Newsweek*s in the dayroom outside. I thumbed through them and couldn't help but shouting, "Look at this! Look at this!" I thought I would find that everything the Vietnamese had told us was a lie. But it wasn't. The antiwar movement was bigger than I'd thought, most Americans wanted to get out of Viet Nam. The realization hit me that I was right in being against the war.

Harker. My first dinner was steak and eggs. I'd dreamed about it for years and it tasted good, but I didn't have the appetite of my imagination. Some guys really consumed the food. There were so many things to do and to think about that it became a secondary consideration for me. I phoned my family in the States. They sounded strange, their voices a different pitch and tone from what I'd remembered. But their love was the same bright light. I asked my father to contact the admissions office at Virginia Tech and tell them I was coming back. I knew at last what I wanted out of life.

Daly. From the minute we landed in the Philippines the members of the Peace Committee received completely different treatment from the other prisoners. The eight of us had two escorts apiece.

That night a doctor stopped me in the hospital corridor and asked why I appeared so calm. I acted like I didn't know what he was talking about. He stuttered around and said, "We received, uh, word in our briefings that, uh, you know, you are special prisoners."

The next morning the doctor who examined me said, "Everybody here sympathizes with you. I hope everything turns out all right."

Guy. I sent out messages with the earliest groups released saying how I thought the PCs should be handled. I believed they might try to skip the country when they got to the Philippines. But they were taken care of very well, guarded closely. I myself was kept under security wraps and not allowed to talk to anyone. In fact I was scheduled for a press conference the night after I reached the Philippines and it was canceled by the secretary of defense five minutes before I was to go on.

Harker. I landed at Andrews Air Force Base outside of Washington and went to Valley Forge hospital by chopper. My family was waiting. I felt queasy because I knew it would be an emotional occasion. The trip seemed like it would never end. We landed and drove to the hospital. The press was there to cram microphones in my face. After a few questions the colonel in charge of my group said curtly, "That's all," and he took me down the hallway to my room. My parents and my four brothers and two sisters and their families enveloped me. The long hair of my older brother was shocking—I just didn't expect it. My younger brother also had hair down to his shoulders and a full beard. There were changes in the whole family. I didn't recognize them. I felt like a stranger. We sat down. Everyone started talking at the same time. We spoke of home, the births, marriages, and deaths that had happened since I was gone. I mentioned briefly that I'd been held in the jungle for three years and then moved to North Viet Nam. After an hour things began to skid into place.

Davis. My hometown had a Sgt. Thomas Davis Day when I got back. Gov. George Wallace and Sen. John Sparkman came for the ceremony. Wallace's wife Cornelia is a nice-looking woman, really sharp. The town's mayor was sitting between me and her and we had a conversation going across him. Every now and then the governor would lean over to ask me a question, but I spent most of my time talking to her. I had no qualms about participating in the ceremony with Wallace. After I met him he seemed like a better guy than I thought he was. He said in his speech that "This day should be remembered because we are working for freedom for all regardless of race, creed, or color." I did a double take.

There did seem to be harmony in the community. I was surprised to see lots of black people in key positions. White schoolteachers were teaching black kids and black schoolteachers were teaching white kids. It may have been all phony, but it certainly looked good from my point of view.

My mother really enjoyed the ceremonies. I was invited to speak at many places and she flew around the country with me. Her sisters have been joking her ever since. "Oh, you have forgotten us now since your son came back," they say. Mother protests happily that this just isn't true.

Anton. I was required, like very other POW, to see an army psychiatrist once a month when I got back. He gave me a box of questions to answer, which took up six or seven hours of my time. The questions were completely idiotic. "Do you feel like there is a spider crawling on your head?" "Do you ever feel like you would like to be a girl?" Maybe not idiotic for someone who has problems, but for me they were idiotic and I finally stopped going.

My feelings of guilt for what had happened in the jungle were brought up by the psychiatrist and he probed deeply into that, of course. But it was something I had already begun to work out for myself. There were times in the jungle when I thought very ill of myself. I saw the others working when I couldn't and I felt rotten. I thought I was truly sick even though they sometimes convinced me that maybe I wasn't.

Before I was captured I tried to fool myself about my weaknesses. I've become more able to look at myself now. And I no longer feel guilty. I respect the men who were in the jungle with me. I don't resent their anger, their bad words and thoughts. I know what they were going through. At the end of the war I told each man that I wanted to thank him because I knew that I'd made it through only because of his help.

The men were nice about it. I noticed a change in their attitude. Several who had been down on me came to me after the cease-fire and said, "I know what I said to you in the past was pretty harsh but I want you to realize that I was uptight about it. The jungle was hard on me and now I realize you were sick and couldn't handle it."

The experience in the jungle is very distant in my mind. It's like a dream, one that occurred long ago. I thought I would have nightmares but I haven't. I don't even think about it. I've just written that five years off completely. I feel very lucky to have survived. So many guys were killed or died or were terribly wounded in Viet Nam. And so many POWs came home to crippled or destroyed marriages. There has been one big change in my life. I appreciate people and things more. And I'm not scared to face the future.

I've also learned some important lessons about government. When I returned I was given several pamphlets published by the U.S. State Department. Reading them and remembering what the Vietnamese had told me and what I knew from my own experience, I discovered that the truth lay somewhere in the middle. Everyone thinks his government is 100-per-cent red, white, and blue. But there are two sides to every story, no matter whether it be communist or democratic. I learned not to believe everything I read simply because it had the U.S. government seal on it. In a government you're dealing with people. Everybody makes mistakes. Patriotism isn't blind faith. Patriotism is loving your country and doing what's right based on reason and logic.

I've tried to explain these things to my father. I haven't been too successful. His biggest worry was that I had been brainwashed. A month after I came home he was still concerned about it. What it has come down to is that we don't talk about the war any more.

Guy. I filed a formal statement that collaboration with the enemy existed in the camps. I received word from Washington that the Pentagon wanted a complete report. On April 2 I sat down with some legal people and a secretary and composed a nineteen-page report. I charged the PCs with aiding and abetting the enemy, accepting gratuities, and taking part in a conspiracy against the U.S. government. I told how the PCs had made model airplanes of F-105s and B-52s for the North Vietnamese to use for target practice. The planes had a two-foot wingspan and were hung in trees. We lost the majority of our planes in North Viet Nam to small-arms fire.

My report was sent to Washington. I got a telephone call from the secretary—from the air force. I'm not going to mention the fellow's name. He had read my intelligence debriefing and he wanted me to make a statement to the press about it. He gave me the name of Fred Hoffman of the Associated Press in Washington and told me to call him. If Hoffman wouldn't listen to my story about the collaboration, I was to call Sen. Barry Goldwater and tell him about it. This was on a Thursday. I thought about it and said to myself, "No, this is not the way to do it. I'll wait for justice to run its course."

On Friday the officer phoned again, and once more on Sunday. The message was the same: "Call the AP." So I sat down and gave an interview which practically wiped Watergate off the front page of the *New York Times.*

I thought I was doing it with the sanction of the air force. I thought they wanted me to go ahead and get it out in the open. After the story hit the *Washington Post* I got another call from the officer. He said, "Okay, you've done your job. Don't say anything else."

By this time cameramen from CBS, NBC, and ABC were converging on my home in Tucson, Arizona. I called back and said, "My God, what do you mean don't say anything else? That's impossible."

I went into seclusion shortly after I gave interviews to the networks. I didn't believe the PCs should be tried by the press, and I certainly didn't want any publicity myself. I wanted the thing to go through the regular chain of command. An investigation should be conducted; and if there wasn't sufficient evidence, the matter should be dropped.

I traveled to Washington on two occasions and got a lawyer, a full colonel who was an assistant to the Staff Judge Advocate. I was walking the corridors of the Pentagon, beating on the doors, asking that a complete investigation be conducted. The U.S. Army didn't want to press charges against the PCs. But I had the support of the air force, I think, in the office of the chief of staff. I know so. They couldn't publicly come out in support of me, and I understood this. They didn't want to take sides because the full scope of the evidence wasn't known.

I thought my actions might possibly hurt my career. I knew there would be a lot of publicity and I would probably be made the scapegoat. I decided to go ahead. We got out the Uniform Code of Military Justice and looked to see which articles were appropriate for this case. I laid down three conditions before we started. First, I said I would not press charges unless there was sufficient evidence for conviction. Second, I would not press charges if such action would discredit the U.S. Air Force or any of the sister services. And third, I would do nothing to hurt the United States of America.

I set those three conditions and then gave the army, air force, and the marines a rundown on what my charges would be. They were supposed to conduct their own separate investigations by interviewing prisoners who had been at the Plantation Gardens. All the information was supposed to be channeled back to me, at which time I would make the final decision as to whether I would formally press charges.

In late May I went to the president's dinner for the POWs at the White House. I thought it was great. I didn't get to enjoy the dancing because I had to leave at midnight. A meeting was scheduled at 7:00 the next morning at the Pentagon to decide my question.

McMillan. A group of us got together at a Washington hotel and partied for several days before the White House banquet. One dude had a big bag of pot. I bet he had ten-thousand-dollars worth of stuff on him. He went to the White House high. There were about twelve in my group and people at the banquet kept staring at us. We returned to the hotel and partied some more. Everybody had a double room and the guys without wives had invited their girl friends. But the girls refused to sleep with the dudes, so the girls slept together and the dudes slept with dudes. It was like being back in the jungle.

Daly. The eight of us had a hard time getting invitations to the White House banquet. I got one only because I was persistent. I called the Department of Army and they apologized and said there must have been some mistake because I was on the mailing list. When it didn't arrive I called a secretary at the White House. She said I'd be receiving one in a few days. I finally got it three days before I left for Washington. Mike Branch paid his own way to Washington but wasn't allowed to go to the dinner. The newspapers said the next day that he'd received an invitation but he had refused to say whether or not he was coming. I also read that the rest of us received the silent treatment at the dinner. That was a lie. Even Colonel Guy—and I couldn't believe this—acted friendly and came over to shake my hand.

Young. We were shunned a little at the dinner, yeah. It was done by our table positioning. We were shoved in a corner far away from the podium. Colonel Guy saw us. He probably felt that we had no right to be there since we had opposed the war. That was one reason we went, to show that we weren't ashamed.

Guy. At 7:00 the morning after the banquet I was at the Pentagon meeting with the Staff Judge Advocates from the air force, army, navy, and marines. Dr. Roger Shields, chief of POW affairs, and Fred Buzhardt, the Pentagon's general counsel, also took part. I listened as each of the service presented the pros and cons. The marines, air force, and navy, as I understood it, wanted to go ahead. The army's argument was that we should forgive and forget. At 9:30 I said, "Sirs, I've heard enough. Thank you." I walked into the adjoining office and signed the charge sheet.

Young. I learned that Colonel Guy had pressed charges against us when a reporter called me for comment. It wasn't totally unexpected, and we had retained lawyers. We were confident that if the case came to trial it would be thrown out. In fact, we sort of hoped to go to court because we planned to make an issue out of the illegality of the war. And we would show that we weren't the only prisoners protesting in North Viet Nam. One of our attorneys went to Hanoi and brought back photocopies of antiwar letters and appeals that officers and pilots had written and signed, including Colonel Guy. We would have proved it was a selective prosecution. And why were we singled out? Because we came back and stood up for what we did. We didn't claim that we had been forced to sign protest letters as many prisoners did. What does "forced" mean? A slap in the face? A beating?

Guy. The last week in June my family and I set out to drive from Tucson to my new assignment at Homestead Air Force Base, which is just south of Miami. We had a four-car convoy. The second day out of Tucson my sons honked their horns to stop me. They yelled, "Did you hear about Kavanaugh?" I turned on the radio. It was on every news broadcast. Marine Sgt. Abel L. Kavanaugh, age twenty-four, had committed suicide at his home in Denver. So he was dead. I was sorry for his family. But otherwise his death didn't bother me a bit. I thought he must have had a guilt complex about what he'd done in Hanoi. Why else would he kill himself? I continued my drive to Homestead.

Young. I had flown into Denver that morning and was going to see Larry later in the day. I knew he was getting ready to return the next day to Camp Pendleton, the marine base in California. I myself was scheduled for a physical examination at the army hospital in Denver. Halfway between the airport and the hospital I was talking to the taxi driver and I mentioned that I was a POW. He said, "Did you hear about that guy Kavanaugh who just killed himself? Yeah, shot himself in the head with a twenty-five-caliber pistol while his wife was combing her hair in the same room."

When I reached the hospital the staff gathered round and encouraged me to do nothing drastic. I kept myself calm. I personally felt that what Larry did, he did for us. He was a nervous person and there had already been one suicide in his family—his brother had killed himself. And I knew Larry didn't want to report back to the marines. He believed they would try to keep him. But what he did was an attempt, I think, to take the pressure from us and put it on the military. He gave his life for us.

Daly. I was told that the day he killed himself Kavanaugh called Riate and Jane Fonda and Cora Weiss and said that he was afraid and didn't want to return to the marines. In North Viet Nam he always believed that if charges were brought against us, even if they weren't true, there would be no way we could escape a prison sentence. He was one of the three men in the Peace Committee who always said they would rather be dead than to go back to jail.

Guy. I was escorted to the VIP quarters at Homestead by the base wing commander. "We know what you have been through," he said. "You don't have to worry about press harassment here. We're a presidential support base and we have the finest security in the world. The gate guards have been ordered to check all incoming cars. Anyone who wants to see Colonel Guy will not be allowed on the base."

I said, "Great!"

We walked outside and an ABC-television camera was staring us in the face. The wing commander went through the roof. I said, "No comment," and walked on. The reporters smeared the wing commander. They said he ordered me not to talk, which was simply not true.

All the publicity I was getting was very bad. The press played up Kavanaugh's funeral and his crying wife and her threat to sue me. The NAACP attacked me because I had pressed charges against Daly and Rayford. The Chicanos came out with a statement against me. It seemed that everything I said was very paraphrased but the PCs were listened to. I knew this was another case of the press, and I feel much like Mr. Nixon does about the press—they're not telling the whole damn story. I can't blame it all on the press, though, because I told my people to say nothing and I made up my mind not to say anything.

Young. The seven of us served as honorary pallbearers. We didn't touch the casket, we followed behind it. The official marine burial detail was sloppy. It was one of the worst military funerals ever. The officer in charge was obnoxious, their uniforms were dirty, the gun salute was ragged, and the bugler played poorly. It was very possible that this was done on purpose.

I thought the press would really cut us up. But it seemed most of the newspapers were in our favor; I saw only one or two derogatory articles. I think the reporters gave a true interpretation of the situation—that Colonel Guy was a flier who had never seen the war on the ground as we had, a career officer who went by the book whereas we were young enlisted men who hadn't been influenced that much by the military and were still able to think for ourselves. We were more representative of the several million Americans who served in Viet Nam than he was.

IMMEDIATE RELEASE   July 3, 1973
Charges Against Former Army POWs Are Dismissed

Secretary of the Army Howard H. Callaway today dismissed charges of misconduct lodged against five Army enlisted men by Colonel Theodore W. Guy, USAF. The Secretary's decision was based upon the recommendation of Army Chief of Staff, General Creighton W. Abrams.

The five men—Staff Sergeants Robert P. Chenoweth, James A. Daly, Jr., King D. Rayford, Jr., John A. Young, and Specialist Four Michael P. Branch—who were part of a group referred to by the other prisoners as the "Peace Committee," allegedly cooperated with the enemy in a variety of propaganda activities and received favorable treatment.

However, after a careful review by the Army General Counsel and the Judge Advocate General, the charges against the five men were dismissed. The dismissals were recommended because of lack of legally sufficient evidence and because of the policy of the Department of Defense against holding trials for alleged propaganda statements.

In announcing his decision, Secretary Callaway said: "We must not overlook the good behavior of these men during the two to three years each spent under brutal prison conditions in South Vietnam, before they were moved to the north—the lack of food and medical care, the sub-primitive living conditions, and the physical torture. They had a very hard time, and they behaved admirably during this period.

The five Army men were notified earlier today of the decision. No administrative board action against the five men is contemplated. They will be eligible for separation from the service when their medical evaluation and administrative processing are completed.

Secretary Callaway noted that these men will not be eligible for re-enlistment under current qualitative standards for the Volunteer Army.

—from a Pentagon news release

Anton. The secretary of the navy also dropped the prosecution of the two marines, Riate and Elbert. Air force Maj. Edward Leonard, who was thrown into solitary in Hanoi for ordering the PCs to stop dealing with the Vietnamese, refiled charges after Guy's were dismissed. But several months later Leonard's charges were dropped by the Pentagon too. So were those brought against two ranking pilot officers, one from the navy and the other from the marines. I didn't follow the controversy closely. I was interested because I considered Daly a friend and didn't want to see anything happen to him after all he'd been through, although I had mixed feelings about some of the rest of them.

If the matter had been fully pursued, it would have gone much further than the PCs. Everybody knew that. I believe that's why the government chose to drop the charges. The vast majority of POWs were guilty of violating the Code of Conduct. The ones who refused to give the North Vietnamese anything but name, rank, and serial number didn't come home.

Young. I've changed none of my opinions since I've been back. I'm a Marxist who believes the people have a right to control things. The working class in America has an artificial wealth. People have a new house and a car and a television set and they don't consider themselves poor, even though nothing is paid for and they're in hock for the rest of their lives. They don't have a thing, really, except credit. But until they realize this there will not be much opportunity for change.

I'm driving a truck now but I hope to go to law school. In a way I don't have much confidence in myself. I know I'm headed for a hard struggle, and I'm wondering if I'll be able to make it through the long years of schooling. My wife is behind me. My home life has changed 100 per cent since I've come home. I'm working to keep my marriage because I love my wife and children very much.

Most Americans don't want to talk about the war. This is wrong. It just gives the people who got us into it a free hand to get us into another. Even in my own home a discussion of politics is out. My mom has a hatred for the Vietnamese. She can't understand it wasn't their fault that I was held for so many years. I believe I have an obligation to speak out. I could never turn my back on America, because it is me. I just feel sorry for Colonel Guy. I'm sorry he had to be so blind as not to see, not to care.

Daly. As for myself, I'm far from being a communist. I still have my religious beliefs, although they have gone through some changes. In any way I can I will continue to work for peace.

Guy. I received countless threatening letters and phone calls. "We're going to blow your head off." "We're going to get your kids when they come out of school." "We're going to catch your wife on the street." I had to change my unlisted telephone number six times; I don't know how they found out the numbers. When I was grand marshal of the Fourth of July parade in Chicago a man ran out of the crowd and called me a killer.

The constant bad publicity and my frequent trips to Washington put an unbearable strain on my marriage. There were already tremendous readjustment problems. The POWs' divorce rate is quite high. You've got to understand that the wives have been running things for so many years and suddenly the husbands come home and they're shoved into the background. It has an emotional effect on the entire family. In 1969 the government went around and told the wives to keep proper financial records because their husbands would naturally want to know what happened to the money.

At night I would sit down and go through her records and I'd say, "I don't really care but could you tell me what you used ten thousand dollars for in August 1969."

All she had to say was, "I was in Mexico and I had a good time," and I would've been satisfied. But she would end up saying, "You're checking on me." This happened not just in my case but to many of the POWs to whom I talked. Well, we weren't checking on them. We just wanted to know what went on in the five years we were gone, and this created a hell of a lot of friction. I think the biggest thing was that they had built us up into something we weren't. We had become myths.

Then came the Kavanaugh thing. She attempted to blame me for it. After she had a few drinks she would say that I killed him. I was very upset. I couldn't talk to her. We argued a lot. I had the support of my boys. My youngest son, Donny, sixteen, did not believe Viet Nam was right. He told me that if he had been drafted he would have gone to jail—but he wouldn't have run away to Canada. And I had to admire him for that. My oldest said he didn't particularly want to go but would have gone if called, and my middle son said the same thing. They saw what was happening and they agreed with me that I had to get a divorce. We ended it after twenty-two years. After the divorce I married Linda, the daughter of a retired air-force general.

I was very disappointed that the charges against the PCs were dropped. I thought we had enough evidence. The army and navy later conceded they had not conducted an investigation. Then one of the PCs, after he was discharged from the army, went on nationwide TV and admitted that the charges were true.

I didn't want to do anything to harm the country. I thought it would be better to get this thing out in the open. There were 108 men at the Plantation and a total of 566 POWs who came home. Of the 566, there were 497 officers and 69 enlisted men. About 97 per cent of them you can be proud of, they're heroes. My concern was not necessarily for the eight men of the Peace Committee. It was their questioning the authority of a camp commander under prisoner-of-war conditions. I was very worried what the communists would do in the next war. I can just see what's going to happen if the holes aren't plugged. The bad must be weeded out of the system. Our society cannot afford the permissiveness this implies.

In retrospect, I believe our being in Viet Nam was the correct policy. We've learned a lot. And in years to come we will look back and realize we were right. I feel very strongly that any part of the world which wants to be free should get our help. To believe otherwise will eventually lead to our own downfall. We must remain strong. One of the things that disturbs me very much is our détente with the communist forces. One only has to look at their development of advanced missiles and other weapons to tell whether they are sincere. After listening to them for five years, I know their tactics. They are going to keep talking while we let our military strength go down. And then they are going to hit us. I'm very afraid of that.

Davis. Who was right and who was wrong? I could see Colonel Guy's point. He wasn't exaggerating. But then again a lot of people did things in North Viet Nam and how do you measure degree? I find the distinction really hard to draw when I consider the circumstances and the people involved. I think everything probably worked out for the best and now should be forgotten. It was such a fucked-up war.

ACKNOWLEDGMENT

I wish to thank the nine prisoners of war who cheerfully took time out from that most important business of re-establishing their lives in order to help make this book possible.

ZBG

Other titles of interest